THE LANGUAGE OF MURDER CASES

THE LANGUAGE OF MURDER CASES

Intentionality, Predisposition, and Voluntariness

Roger W. Shuy

OXFORD
UNIVERSITY PRESS

OXFORD
UNIVERSITY PRESS

Oxford University Press is a department of the University of Oxford.
It furthers the University's objective of excellence in research, scholarship,
and education by publishing worldwide.

Oxford New York
Auckland Cape Town Dar es Salaam Hong Kong Karachi
Kuala Lumpur Madrid Melbourne Mexico City Nairobi
New Delhi Shanghai Taipei Toronto

With offices in
Argentina Austria Brazil Chile Czech Republic France Greece
Guatemala Hungary Italy Japan Poland Portugal Singapore
South Korea Switzerland Thailand Turkey Ukraine Vietnam

Published in the United States of America by
Oxford University Press
198 Madison Avenue, New York, NY 10016

Library of Congress Cataloging-in-Publication Data
Shuy, Roger W.
The language of murder cases : intentionality, predisposition,
and voluntariness / Roger W. Shuy.
pages cm
Includes bibliographical references and index.
ISBN 978-0-19-935483-2 (hardback : alk. paper) 1. Forensic linguistics—United
States. 2. Murder trials—United States. I. Title.
KF8968.54.S483 2014
345.73'02523014—dc23
2013028107

1 3 5 7 9 8 6 4 2
Printed in the United States of America
on acid-free paper

This book is the product of over three decades of my work in many different types of criminal and civil law cases. Until recent years, like most linguistics professors who consult and provide expert witness, I worked alone on scores of cases. A few years ago my increasing age encouraged me to slow down and alter my practice, so I decided to join forces with Professor Robert Leonard of Hofstra University. We now work on law cases together, enabling me to keep on working long after the time when most sensible people would have retired. Of the fifteen murder cases described in this book, I analyzed twelve of them alone, while I joined forces with Rob Leonard in three more recent ones. Although partnerships are not always easy, working with Rob has been a delight and a privilege. For this reason I dedicate this book to him.

CONTENTS

THE LANGUAGE OF MURDER CASES

1

INTRODUCTION

Murther most foul

Macbeth, Act I Scene 5

The earliest records of the use of the Anglo-Saxon word *murder* (with its variants *myrthrian, murthre, murther,* and *morthur*) designated pretty much what the act means today, except for a time during the Middle Ages, when the term also embraced self-murder (suicide), and later when it was used by some to include the slaughter of people during wars.

Of all the crimes people commit, murder no doubt attracts the most attention of the media and entertainment. Television crime shows are mostly about murders and how they are solved, while a multitude of novels also have the act of murder as their centerpiece. Bookstores even have their own section called murder mysteries. Murder also is prominent in the news media, with sex crimes only slightly less common. History is often the story of murder and the Bible reports murder as the first crime ever committed by human beings. Perhaps people are so fascinated with murder because it is the epitome of crime, the worst and most extreme offense thinkable—the ultimate bad act. Or maybe murder is so popular because down deep many of us have had our own murderous thoughts, even though we knew better than to try to act on them.

We have strict laws about murder (described in chapter 2), but they don't seem to stop people from killing each other. When furious or greedy, some people fail to control themselves and carry out irrational, unthinkable acts even when down deep they may know how wrong they are. No matter how retributive our statutes are, they fail to prevent or deter some people from carrying out these irrational, unthinkable acts. Humans are like that and maybe they always will be.

In a previous book, *The Language of Defamation Cases* (2010), I concluded that using language in the courtroom to settle defamation disputes was a distinct improvement over early humankind's violent solution of bashing heads. Even after the courtly rules of dueling were developed to replace the previous, uncontrolled violence with a more orderly way to resolve disputes, civilized life progressed only slightly if at all, because even the newly organized rules of dueling resulted in seriously maiming or taking the life of another human being. But humanity advanced in a more civil way after laws were created to punish defamers with financial penalties rather than with death or serious bodily injury. And that's where we are today in terms of how we deal with defamation.

It seems that those who commit murder often have somewhat similar grievances to those who consider themselves defamed. Murderers either want to get revenge on someone who has cheated or stolen from them, or they are greedy enough to kill other persons who have something that they want so badly that they are willing to kill them to get it. For such people, revenge or greed can become very hard to control. So we still have murder, as stuck in the violent head-bashing stage as it was in humankind's more primitive periods.

It's not difficult to understand why laws against murder preceded the laws against many other types of crime. For example, laws against defamation and perjury are relatively modern, even though these offenses existed long before they were codified as crimes. Not so for murder laws, however, including those recorded since about 1780 B.C.E. in the Code of Hammurabi and later in the Ten Commandments in about 800–500 B.C.E. (Exodus 20:13 and Deuteronomy 5:17).

Today in many criminal trials the search for liability focuses almost as much on the suspect's mental acts of intentionality and predisposition as it does on the physical act done or the harm caused. Courts and the juries are asked to discover the mens rea, guilty mind, as they assess the evidence about what happened and how it was talked about. Unfortunately, efforts to define and discover the mental state of a guilty mind have not always been successful. Courts and juries have to rely heavily on evidence of suspects' intentionality and predisposition before and during the crime and their voluntariness during interviews by the police. They have to assess indications of mental states that are assumed to reflect the emotions, morals, or cognitive capacities of an allegedly bad person. Truth about the existence and extent of these mental states, however, is difficult for even the most accomplished analysts to determine, and when trials reach the deliberation stage, jurors are expected to follow judges' instructions in order to determine guilt or innocence. They are also instructed to exercise a degree of objectivity that enables them to deal with any *reasonable doubts* they might have about the evidence presented to them.

Modern-day experts in psychology, criminal justice, sociology, and other fields do their best to understand why people commit murder. Law enforcement officers do their best to learn how murders are carried out and who committed them. The courts do their best to bring offenders to trial and mete out the punishment that they consider justified and appropriate. So where does linguistics fit into this? A book about language and murder can be expected to discuss the ways that linguistic analysis can be useful in criminal cases of this type, and that is what this book tries to do.

It all begins with existing murder laws that have not succeeded in defining *intention* and *premeditation* with specificity or clarity. Instead, statutory definitions serve as templates or prototypes for law enforcement officers, prosecutors, judges, and juries to use as they try to interpret any available manifestations of such mental states. Because it is impossible for any science to probe accurately into human minds, including the minds of accused murderers, the best and perhaps only way to asses mental states commonly mentioned such as *intentionality, premeditation, malice aforethought, wanton disregard, heat of passion,* and even the *knowledge* held by suspects or defendants, is through their language. Over the years the mantra, "language is a window to the mind," has been a popular theme in the field of the psychology of language, from the early publications of George Miller and Jerome Bruner to the more current work of Steven Pinker. This theme is nowhere more present than in determining the guilt or innocence of suspects accused of murder.

Throughout this book readers can note that the vaguely worded statutes and legal precedents set the table for the discovery of instantiated definitions that can be used to assess and measure statutory meaning. Without actual instances found in the language used by suspects, witnesses, and those who question them, it is very difficult to determine effectively what is meant by a guilty mind.

On the surface it may seem strange that linguistics has anything to do with murder cases, but, as I hope to show in this book, sometimes it does. Over the past four decades I've been hired as an expert linguist to analyze the language evidence in dozens of murder cases, as have other linguists. In one sense, this book is about the way linguists use the tools of their profession to analyze the language evidence in murder and solicitation to murder cases. In another important sense, it is a book about how the legal terminology of *intentions, predisposition,* and *voluntariness* related to fifteen representative murder cases. Most murder cases involve language evidence, whether in the form of notes or diaries written by the suspects, interviews carried out by the police, legal depositions and hearings, or conversations secretly recorded by undercover agents. Analysts examine such language evidence for clues to the killer's mental states, including their intentions and predisposition that precede the act of committing the crime, as well as the voluntariness of the suspects' talk after they are in custody. And when a murder case comes to trial, it is up to triers of the fact to wrestle with the matter of reasonable doubt.

When linguists are asked to analyze the language evidence in murder cases, their first job is to determine whether the written records of transcripts of interviews, testimony, and other electronically recorded information are accurate representations of the spoken language. A second task is to try to determine whether the important legal terms, *intentionality, premeditation,* and *voluntariness* are actually revealed in the language evidence or whether law enforcement and prosecution have merely inferred that the suspects acted intentionally and were predisposed to do so. The linguist's third job is to examine police interviews and undercover tape recordings for clues that the suspects offered their information voluntarily or whether law enforcement has unduly influenced or even coerced the suspects into agreeing to commit the crime in the future or admitting that they committed one in the past. Although the important legal concept of *reasonable doubt* is the task for juries alone to determine, presentation of the linguist's analysis of the language evidence, including what it can show about the mental states of *intentionality, predisposition,* and *voluntariness,* can play an important role in a jury's decision about how they can deal with the equally abstract concept of *reasonable doubt.*

This book describes fifteen murder cases in which language evidence relating to these four legal terms is relevant. Although many murder cases contain convincing evidence of the suspect's guilt, the cases described here are ones in which the prosecution depended heavily on the language evidence related to intentions, predisposition, and voluntariness, much of which was either ambiguous or vague or sometimes even not present at all.

The primary goal of this book is to demonstrate the ways linguistic theory, research, and knowledge can be helpful in the investigations and courtroom phases of murder cases. It is not intended to be an introduction to linguistics or a primer on murder law, and it is beyond the book's scope to deal with the psychological, sociological, or medical aspects of murder, even though certain language clues occasionally can offer support to experts who specialize in these areas. Here I discuss fifteen very different murder cases that demonstrate how linguistic analysis can contribute to understanding what the evidence tells us, in particular about how the language used by participants either enlightens or contradicts the governing legal terms, *intentionality, premeditation,* and *voluntariness,* and eventually about the jury's task of determining the meaning of *reasonable doubt.*

It is rare when the record of a murder is preserved electronically as it takes place in real time, such as the way videotape captured the murder of Lee Harvey Oswald, the major suspect in the assassination of President John F. Kennedy. Oswald's murder was caught on videotape while law officers were escorting him into court. Such cases have little need for linguistic analysis, because the recorded actions in these videotaped events spoke very clearly for themselves. But video cameras can't be everywhere all the time and video can't always tell us what we need to know about how and why a person did something. In the vast majority of murder cases in which linguistic analysis is used, the language evidence exists mostly in the way the entire murder event was talked about after it happened, usually in police stations and courtrooms. In such speech events, language can provide useful clues to the killer's intentions and predispositions as well as their voluntariness as they talk about what they did.

Because the focus of this book is on the relationship of the legal terms, *intentionality, predisposition,* and *voluntariness* to the language evidence in murder cases, it seems useful to show how these legal terms apply in three different types of cases. In the first type, described in chapter 4, the suspect's intentionality is very clear. This chapter describes cases in which law enforcement agencies have obtained written or spoken language evidence such as murder threats without any clear idea about who produced them. The linguist's primary task here is to discover clues that might help identify the threatener from the language they use in their messages. The second type, discussed in chapter 5, involves cases in which law enforcement officers have gathered language evidence from potential murder suspects by secretly tape-recording conversations with them. Here intentionality, predisposition, and voluntariness are critical to determine. The third type, discussed in chapters 7 through 10, involves murder cases in which law enforcement gathers language evidence from known suspects and witnesses during police interviews and legal proceedings. In these cases, voluntariness is a critical issue, although intentionality and predisposition can also be important.

Chapter 2 provides a brief description of murder laws, foreshadowing and laying the groundwork for the following fifteen case analysis chapters that instance the ways and degrees to which intentionality, predisposition, and voluntariness were or were not manifested through the language used by all parties during murder investigations, depositions, hearings, and trials, as well as how these legal terms can be understood by suspects, law enforcement, and lawyers, judges, and juries. These legal terms guide and influence the ways that murder events are considered and treated by law enforcement and the courts, and especially by juries when they wrestle with the equally vague issue of *reasonable doubt.* It is virtually impossible for statutes and dictionaries to clearly define mental states such as intentionality, predisposition, and voluntariness, but linguistic analysis can demonstrate how these legal terms are given definitional substance through the language used by the participants as they communicate with each other.

Chapter 3 demonstrates the ways linguistic analysis deals with the entire communicative context of the language evidence in murder cases. It shows that the crucial text is not limited to individual components or fragments of language, often called "smoking guns." The communicative context is the entire murder event. Murder events are one of the many identifiable human events such as airplane trips, business discussions, or, relevant to this book, events that culminate in murder. These and other events are composed of internal language structures called speech events. For example, an airline trip event contains separate and individual speech events with passengers, with ticket agents, with airport safety inspectors, with seatmates, with flight attendants, and with others. It is clear to most travelers that some things are appropriate, relevant, and acceptable to say during speech events with ticket agents that are less relevant and acceptable to say to airport safety inspectors. In the same way trial events have their own relevant and acceptable things that can be said at specific times and with specific participants. They also contain various sequentially required speech events such as the opening statement speech event, the testimony speech event, the cross-examination speech event, and the closing statement speech event, among others.

A murder event includes the component sequential phases of contemplating the murder, building up resolve, planning, carrying it out, and subsequent police and courtroom interactions. If any language evidence exists and can be discovered during these sequential phases of the murder event, it can provide evidence of the perpetrator's intentionality and predisposition. Unfortunately, discovery of such evidence during the phases prior to an actual murder is very rare. A major exception to this is when undercover agents tape-record suspects who are thought to be planning to solicit murder before it takes place. In the context of a murder case, various speech events such as diaries, reports of witnesses, police interviews, and even suspects' confessions must be analyzed within the totality of the entire body of language evidence associated with the crime. As will be shown, what is often considered solid "smoking gun" evidence can turn out to be less than convincing when viewed within the contextual evidence of the entire murder event.

After determining whether or not the government's language evidence is accurately recorded and reported, the linguist's next step is to identify the speech events that took place during the time when the crime occurred or is alleged to have occurred. These individual speech events are nested within larger events, in this case the murder event. As will be seen, the murder event often contains internal speech events such as the police interview speech event, the diary speech event, the undercover-recorded conversation speech event, the trial testimony speech event, the Miranda warning speech event, and others. Each of these speech events has its own sequential and structural requirements in order to be judged felicitous, and each plays a role in determining the appropriate understanding of an entire murder event.

Chapter 3 describes the murder event, in which various speech events are component parts. Speech event analysis is very important, because as Gumperz (1990, 9) points out, speech events are recurring occasions that have "tacitly understood rules of preference, unspoken conventions as to what counts as valid and what information may or may not be introduced." A speech event predicts the parameters of what all of the participants, witnesses, suspects, prosecutors, and even judges, can say. The ways that participants talk during such speech events also reflects the power asymmetry that lurks behind its surface under the appearance of investigative and judicial equality. The nature of asymmetrical speech events also dictates how the participants are even allowed to talk with each other. What is and what is not permitted to be said can have deep consequences in determining the significance of the entire language evidence. Most important, however, is how and whether all of the phases of the individual speech events are felicitously accomplished and completed. This will be one of the focuses discussed in chapter 5, which presents three solicitation to murder cases in which linguistic analysis of the suspects' intentions and predispositions played a decisive role.

Other linguistic tools used in murder cases include agenda analysis, which is revealed by the topics participants introduce and their responses to the topics introduced by others, language evidence of the participants' schemas, the felicity of the speech acts used (such as agreeing, denying, threatening, requesting, apologizing, and hypothesizing), the conversational strategies used by police and prosecutors, the grammatical and semantic resolution of ambiguous of words and phrases, the phonetic analysis of disputed spoken passages, and the relevance of nonverbal communication.

As noted above, there are three types of murder cases: (1) where a perpetrator is unknown, (2) where a perpetrator is suspected, and (3) where a perpetrator is in custody. Linguistic analysis in such cases varies, depending on what law enforcement knows about the suspects.

1. CASES IN WHICH THE PERPETRATOR IS UNKNOWN

For the first type of evidence, law enforcement has no idea who might have threatened or perhaps even committed a murder. But when writers or speakers produce threat messages, linguists sometimes can provide law enforcement with linguistic profiles of the unknown producers of those messages, based on the sociolinguistic clues that the suspects' language provides about their age, race, gender, ethnicity, geographical background, social status, education level, religious orientation, occupation, and other characteristics.

Linguistic profiling is an investigative procedure that does not claim to be able to identify murder suspects positively. Rather, it can offer useful clues about certain characteristics of the currently unknown speaker or writer. Such analysis can be used to help police narrow down their suspect lists, and sometimes the police can even confront suspects with a linguistic profile as a strategy for encouraging them to confess.

Chapter 4 describes and illustrates the way linguistic profiling assisted law enforcement in the well-known Unabomber case and how it actually helped identify the person who sent bomb threats to a women's medical clinic in Gary, Indiana. The sole purpose of such analysis is to discover any possible language clues that might help law enforcement eventually identify the senders of such messages, whose intentions and predispositions are normally volunteered very clearly in their own words.

Linguistic profiling is included in this book because it provides clear and indisputable examples of the existence, meaning, and relevance of the three critically important but vaguely defined legal terms, *intentionality, predisposition*, and *voluntariness*. The writers of such threat messages boldly reveal and help define all three of these terms in the language of their threat messages.

2. CASES IN WHICH A PERPETRATOR IS SUSPECTED OF SOLICITING MURDER

The second type of evidence discussed in this book consists of language collected during undercover operations in which law enforcement had been tipped off that certain suspects were considering or planning murder. Either cooperating witnesses or undercover agents then secretly recorded their conversations with suspects for later use against them. Chapter 5 describes three such cases. In one case, the suspects' intentions and predispositions were misunderstood by the prosecution, and in two other cases the suspects changed their intentions during undercover conversations with the help of very persuasive and perhaps coercive cooperating witnesses, leaving open the opportunity to debate the significance of their initial predispositions to not commit the crime.

3. CASES IN WHICH THE ALLEGED PERPETRATOR IS IN CUSTODY

The third type of evidence consists of the written or spoken language of persons who are strongly suspected of murder and who are already in custody or are about to be arrested. Such language evidence sometimes exists in the form of available diaries or letters, but it is found far more commonly in the interviews of suspects and witnesses conducted by law enforcement officers and attorneys. Here questions about the mental states of intention and predisposition are seen in relationship to the voluntariness of the suspects' confessions.

Chapter 6 describes the development of the concept of voluntariness in law up to and including the Miranda warning and its attendant problems. Because voluntariness is a developing legal concept with changing implications and applications for suspects who are mentally incapacitated, are impaired by alcohol or drugs, are juveniles, or are emotionally distraught, it is treated separately from the murder laws described in chapter 2. The analysis in chapter 7 focuses on the voluntariness of three suspects who had diminished mentally capacity. Chapter 8 deals with three suspects who were intoxicated either at the time of the murders or during the police interviews. Chapter 9 describes two juvenile suspects who became easy targets for their police interrogators. Chapter 10 deals with two murder cases in which the suspects were handicapped by being emotionally distraught during the period they were interviewed by the police.

The book concludes in chapter 11 with a focus on ways that the equally vague legal term, *reasonable doubt,* related to the fifteen murder cases described here, along with a summary of these cases and the linguistic tools that were used in each case.

This book was written in order to help linguists, lawyers, and other interested readers understand the use of language evidence in murder cases. Writing for simultaneously different audiences always bears risks, for it is inevitable that the book will contain some information that the separate audiences already may know and don't feel they need to read again. For example, in chapter 2, concerning murder laws and terminology, readers who are law specialists may find information that is already quite familiar to them. I suggest that such readers skim through this chapter and move on to the next ones. Likewise, chapter 3, concerning the linguistic tools used to analyze murder evidence, may be familiar to linguist readers who already know these tools. To them I also suggest skimming through this chapter and then seeing how they were used in the case studies that follow. In contrast, readers who specialize in neither law nor language may find the information in chapters 2 and 3 helpful in order to better understand the murder cases that frame the focus of this book.

I by no means suggest that all murder suspects are innocent of the crimes that they are accused of committing. The cases described in this book may be somewhat unusual because they exist at a point that Solan (2010, 49) calls "the margins of law," where the clarity of intentionality, predisposition, and voluntariness can be debated. Many or even most suspects may be guilty of something, but they are not always guilty of everything for which they are charged and therefore may not deserve the severity of all charges. It is well known that prosecutors tend to bring as many charges against suspects as they can think up, possibly hoping that all, most, or at least some of them will stick. In such cases, it is possible to infer that winning is more important than truth or justice.

Because the primary goal of this book is to demonstrate how linguistic theory, research, and knowledge can be helpful in the investigations and courtroom phases of murder cases, it is not intended to be an introduction to linguistics or a primer on murder law, and it is beyond the book's scope to deal with the psychological, sociological, or medical aspects of murder, even though certain language clues occasionally can offer support to experts who specialize in these areas. Here I discuss murder cases that demonstrate how linguistic analysis can contribute to understanding what the evidence tells us, in particular about how the language used by participants either enlightens or contradicts the governing legal terms, *intentionality, premeditation,* and *voluntariness,* and eventually about the jury's task of determining the meaning of *reasonable doubt.*

Despite the abundance of language evidence that is present in most murder cases, the importance of linguistic analysis is often overlooked. One reason for this is that the intricacies of language, including the larger speech event, are not generally known or appreciated by those who are not trained in linguistics. Even more telling is that most people use their own language so well that they don't realize what it is that they don't know about the way it works. Unfortunately, it is also true that linguists still have not made their field well enough known and available for lawyers, juries, and judges to use the benefits of such help.

Readers probably will notice that the perspective taken in this book tilts heavily toward the defense, primarily because these cases can be considered ripe for such analysis. There is only one reason for this—the prosecutors did not seek linguistic assistance. At any rate, linguistic analysis is in no way related to whether the linguist works with the defense or the prosecution. Such analysis can be as helpful to the prosecution as it is to the defense. For example, as I pointed out in two cases in my 2011 book, *The Language of Perjury Cases,* linguistic analysis can help prosecutors identify disputable points and even weaknesses in their own cases so that they can be prepared for these before the trial even starts. Sometimes linguistic assistance can even assure prosecutors that the language evidence will support their positions. It is rare, however, that prosecutors take advantage of this.

Gathering the language evidence, called intelligence gathering, is done by law enforcement, not by the linguists who analyze it. Linguists can neither add to it nor subtract from it, but they can certainly analyze the intelligence gathered by law enforcement officers and point out if and where interrogations go beyond propriety or make unwarranted inferences, especially relating to the voluntariness of what the suspects say.

The prosecutor is charged with making an intelligence analysis before the linguist even sees the data, and sometimes that analysis is flawed. The major conflicts between the prosecution and the defense often reside in the differences between the prosecutors' intelligence analysis and the analysis made by linguistic experts. Such cases are the focus this book.

Although the subject of false confession is very important, it is not my focus here, even though in three of the cases described in this book the suspects confessed to crimes they likely did not commit. Readers interested in false confessions are encouraged to consult Richard Leo's excellent book, *Police Interrogations and American Justice* (2008).

Readers familiar with my past work may notice that it has been my practice to not provide the outcomes of the cases I describe. Advocacy is the sole job of the attorneys and because linguists are not advocates, the success or failure of cases in relation to the use of linguistic analysis was not the point I wanted or needed to make. Linguistic experts should never be advocates and winning or losing the case depends on many things besides linguistic help. Experts should be only impartial consultants. Nevertheless, for this book I have found it difficult to exclude mention of the court decisions. As will be seen, some defendants were found guilty, some were acquitted, some had their charges reduced, and one conviction is now on appeal and is yet to be decided.

Finally, I should point out that I consulted with attorneys on all of the cases described in this book, and in three of these cases Robert Leonard and I consulted together. One of us testified at the hearings or trials in nine of the fifteen cases, and we consulted and provided expert reports in the other six cases in which the lawyers did not call us to testify. We were paid for our analyses in all of the cases except the Unabomber case described in chapter 4 and the Kevin Rogers case described in chapter 9. In both of these my services were pro bono.

2

MURDER LAWS AND TERMINOLOGY

Before examining the language evidence in the various types of murder cases noted above, it is useful and necessary to understand the variations in murder laws and their governing terminology, especially the legal terms *intentionality, predisposition,* and *voluntariness.* These terms and their underlying meanings are important legal bases for indictments, prosecution, and the disposition of such cases. Commonly, the statutes contain many vague legal terms, especially these three important ones.

Because vagueness is ubiquitous in law, the courts try to resolve the meaning of complex borderline cases by using the strategies of interpretation and construction. Interpretation is the effort to determine the semantic meaning of a legal text, which can work when the text is ambiguous but is not conclusive when the text is vague. Construction is the effort to resolve vague concepts and texts when interpretation fails. To accomplish this, what is needed is evidence that leads to a decision about what that vagueness can really mean. As will be demonstrated, these vague legal terms can be given clearer understanding by examining the actual language used by suspects, witnesses, law enforcement, lawyers, and the courts.

THE CHARGES OF MURDER

Contrary to what some people may think, exactly what constitutes the crime and punishment for murder has been debated for a long time, resulting in complexities about the ways that charges of murder are brought into compliance with federal and state laws and the Model Penal Code. Prosecutors in the United States are said to use four standards to determine whether they will charge a suspect with murder: (1) was a crime committed? (2) do I know who did it? (3) am I sure that I can prove it beyond a reasonable doubt? and (4) is my charging the suspect with murder the right thing to do?

The prosecution usually finds the first standard the easiest to address. The second and third standards depend on effective intelligence gathering by the police and equally effective intelligence analysis done by the prosecutor. When jurors finally have to deal with the important issue of reasonable doubt, they can find this concept difficult, because it often depends on whether the language evidence actually demonstrates that the suspect committed the crime, whether it was committed intentionally and with premeditation, and whether the suspect voluntarily provided inculpatory information, especially a confession, to the police. It is also important for jurors to consider any contextual evidence concerning the mental and physical states of suspects, such as whether or not they are mentally impaired, are under the influence of alcohol or drugs, are juveniles, or are emotionally distraught during their police interviews.

The prosecution and the courts tend to make use of one or more of the following legal bases: common law, the Model Penal Code, and statutory law.

COMMON LAW

Common law is the oldest Western model and it is still prevalent in many jurisdictions, especially in continental Europe. It is judge-made law as opposed to a legislatively crafted statutory law. It is juxtaposed to civil law and is based on the legal codes ultimately derived from Roman law. Since common law was created in England and exported to all of its colonies, its influence exists in the United States, Canada, Australia, India, the former British colonies in Africa, and other places. It is also a basis of law in Europe outside the United Kingdom and in non-British areas such as China, Japan, Russia, and Latin America.

In the United States, common law is still very important in areas such as tort law, contract law, and property law. In contrast, statutory law is applied in most criminal cases. Unless a jurisdiction has a statute criminalizing something, a person cannot be prosecuted. In the United States, the policy behind this is that it's considered fundamentally unfair to convict persons for behavior for which they do not have a fair notice that is provided by statutes that try to describe any types of behavior that can lead to criminal charges. Even though criminal law is statutory, judges can still play an important interpretive role, because the courts develop doctrines and principles through judicial opinions that can have legal force in later cases. Despite the fact that many people do not have easy access to such statutes or that they may not understand the statutes even when they do have access to them, the statutory law system has much to recommend it.

THE MODEL PENAL CODE

In the early 1960s the American Law Institute tried to rationalize and synthesize what was thought to be the best of criminal law, in the hope that this Code would be adopted across the country as a way of standardizing criminal law. This project's goal was much broader than criminal law, but it was successful only in some areas, such as the Uniform Commercial Code, which has been adopted by almost all states. In contrast, the effort to develop a Model Penal Code project was notably unsuccessful in its Uniform Computer Transactions Act, which was adopted by none. The Model Penal Code was somewhat successful in getting states to adopt much of the terminology that was in use during the 1960s and 1970s, but none of the states adopted it wholesale. Since The Model Penal Code was a product of its time, it no longer matches well with current policy attitudes about criminal responsibility. Today, many professors of criminal law call the Model Penal Code "the law of nowhere," despite the fact that it is said to be useful for teaching law students, who will ultimately practice law in a multiplicity of jurisdictions.

STATUTORY LAW

Because of the general suspicion about common law's treatment of crimes and because of the limited influence of the Model Penal Code, the fair notice requirement of criminal law in the United States has become a localized statutory matter. U.S. federal courts are not general common law courts, whereas state courts tend to follow common law unless their statutes either codify or supersede common law principles. This leads to considerable tension about how common law powers affect the treatment of statutes. Using, understanding, and interpreting language is central to law and, as Conley and O'Barr observe, "The details of legal discourse matter because language is the essential mechanism through which the power of the law is realized, exercised, and occasionally challenged and subverted" (1998, 129).

Federal jurisdiction over homicide is limited to certain specialized crimes such as murder committed in the District of Columbia, on a military base, or at a federally insured bank, or the murder of a government official. Most states have general laws regarding homicide, graded in severity with intentional premeditated homicide at the high end, then intentional but unpremeditated homicide, then reckless homicide, then negligent homicide. In most cases, both reckless and negligent homicide are called manslaughter. High profile murder cases usually relate to collateral special homicide statutes, including homicide by drug overdose, which applies to a dealer who provides the drugs, to vehicular homicide by drunk drivers, to homicide relating to child abuse, and to others. In such cases, the facts may fit manslaughter, but public outrage about the crime can demand a more serious penalty. State murder laws apply when the crime is committed within a given state, and there are many variations in murder statutes among the individual states.

Statutes operate as definitions that can be analyzed in terms of conditions that are individually necessary and together sufficient enough to establish that a crime has been committed. Statutes tell us the circumstances in which they apply. They try to embrace the universe of all possible meanings, which later can be determined by the context in which the statutory words apply (Solan 2010, 18–19). Problems arise, however, over how to apply these statutes, especially when inferences have to be made about the defendant's state of mind and about the definitions of key statutory terms. Ensuing trials then become battles over the meaning of legal terms such as *intentionality, mental state, predisposition, voluntariness, willfully, knowingly* and what constitutes *reasonable doubt* (Solan 2010, 26–45).

Concerning such terms, Goodrich (1987, 56–57) observes, "There is a 'paradigm' meaning which clearly states the scope and conditions of rule application. There is only a slight doubt remaining, that appertaining to the infrequent occasion of 'hard' cases concerning 'grey areas' or penumbral, as yet uncertain, context of rule application." However accurate this observation may be about the clarity of the "slight doubt remaining" about the hard cases for legal interpretation, the defendant's mental state remains difficult to determine. Searle (1969, 14) observes, "We all know in one important sense what 'cause,' 'intend,' and 'mean' mean, but it is not easy to *state* exactly what they mean."

Even when it seems clear to everyone what a statutory term means, it often remains unclear whether the case facts fit the definition and whether the right inferences are drawn from the evidence. Because pragmatic inferences are not always clear, the defendant's mental state is difficult to determine. When the words of the statute fall short or exceed the precise intention, judges are required to interpret them based on probable or rational conjectures. The judge presents this interpretive activity as the process of discerning the intention (Hutton 2009, 147).

The drafters of statutes try hard to use legal terms that best capture the common and recurring scenarios and situations that underlie those statutes. The biggest problem occurs when the situations they attempt to describe vary from prototypical cases. This means that it is very difficult to write a statute that is not subject to debate at the margins (Solan 2010, 48).

Linguists who specialize in semantics discover the meanings of words by examining the semantic features that are the properties of that word, contrasting them with the semantic features of other words. The meaning of a word is then represented as a set of features. This approach to meaning works well for concrete objects, but not so well for abstract concepts such as mental states. Abstract words such as *intentionality, predisposition,* and *voluntariness* convey a prototype meaning in which the semantic categories have blurry edges that permit various degrees of inclusion. As Coleman and Kay (1981, 26–27) put it, "A semantic prototype associates a word or phrase with a pre-linguistic, cognitive schema or image; and speakers are equipped with an ability to judge the degree to which an object matches this prototype schema or image." A similar idea was expressed by the eighteenth-century philosopher Immanuel Kant: "Concepts without percepts are empty, and percepts without concepts are blind." This judgment concerning the degree of match then becomes the task of triers of the fact as they determine whether or not the evidence leads to *reasonable doubt*. As the cases described in this book will demonstrate, the statute attempts to indicate the concept as well as it can, leaving the percept, the understanding of that concept, to be obtained by use of the senses that try to provide the concept's ultimate definition. The following chapter attempts to explain how linguistic analysis of the language evidence can lead to such understandings of that language evidence.

It can be useful here to outline the statutes and definitions of homicide. The following summarized statutes and definitions concerning murder, solicitation to murder, and attempted murder emphasize terms that are often repeated in state statutes and the Model Penal Code, where *intention, premeditation, voluntariness,* and other terms for mental states are defined vaguely and indirectly, if they can be said to be defined at all.

THE U.S. FEDERAL STATUTE ON HOMICIDE

The federal statute 18 U.S.C. §1111 includes *malice aforethought, premeditated, maliciously,* and *intent* along with a number of other terms that require understanding even though they are not clearly or specifically defined within the attempted definitions (emphasis added):

> (a) Murder is the unlawful killing of a human being with **malice aforethought.** Every murder perpetrated by poison, lying in wait, or any other kind of **willful, deliberate, malicious,** and **premeditated** killing; or committed in the perpetration of, or attempt to perpetrate, any arson, escape, murder, kidnapping, treason, espionage, sabotage, aggravated sexual abuse or sexual abuse, burglary, or robbery; or perpetrated from a **premeditated design** unlawfully and **maliciously** to effect the death of any human being other than him who is killed, is murder in the first degree.

The federal statute that defines murder in the context of the military, 10 U.S.C. §918, uses similar terms:

> Any person subject to this chapter who, without justification or excuse, unlawfully kills a human being, when he—
>
> (1) has a **premeditated** design to kill;
> (2) **intends** to kill or inflict great bodily harm;
> (3) is engaged in an act which is inherently dangerous to another and evinces a **wanton disregard** of human life; or
> (4) is engaged in the perpetration or attempted perpetration of burglary, sodomy, rape, rape of a child, aggravated sexual assault, aggravated sexual abuse of a child, aggravated sexual contact with a child, robbery, or aggravated arson;
>
> is guilty of murder and shall suffer such punishment as a court- martial may direct, except that if found guilty under clause (1) or
>
> he shall suffer death or imprisonment for life as a court-martial may direct.

In addition to the legal standards provided by common law, the Model Penal Code, and statutory law, there are subcategories of murder that have their own additional specifications. These include solicitation to murder, attempted murder, the degrees of murder, and entrapment.

SOLICITATION TO MURDER

Crimes of solicitation occur when one person advises, counsels, urges, persuades, or incites another person to commit a crime with the intent that the person so solicited will actually carry it out. Solicitation is an inchoate crime, meaning that the advising, counseling, urging, persuading, or inciting is accomplished by the act of asking, regardless of whether or not a crime was ever committed.

Solicitation to murder has its own federal and state statutes that are given separately from other murder statutes. The key terminology that frames the linguistic analyses of the murder cases described in this book are emphasized below:

The federal statute, 18 U.S.C. §373 reads:

> (a) Whoever, with **intent** that another person engage in conduct constituting a felony that has as an element the use, attempted use, or threatened use of physical force against property or against the person of another in violation of the laws of the United States, and under circumstances strongly corroborative of that **intent,** solicits, commands, induces, or otherwise endeavors to persuade such other person to engage in such conduct, shall be imprisoned not more than one-half the maximum term of imprisonment or (notwithstanding section

> 3571) fined not more than one-half of the maximum fine prescribed for the punishment of the crime solicited, or both; or if the crime solicited is punishable by life imprisonment or death, shall be imprisoned for not more than twenty years.

ATTEMPTED MURDER

Attempted murder, like solicitation to murder, is an inchoate offense that is distinct from the crime being attempted. It is an uncompleted, interrupted, or botched action of an actor who intentionally, deliberately, or recklessly tries to kill another human being. The Model Penal Code §5.01 describes attempted murder as an attempt that includes any act representing a substantial step toward commission of a crime, such as enticing, lying in wait for, following the intended victim, or unlawfully entering a building where a crime is expected to be committed. In the indictments given by some states, the charge of attempted murder indicates that the defendant intentionally took at least one direct but ineffective step toward killing another person. Taking a direct step means that the defendant did more than merely plan or prepare to commit murder or arrange for another person to commit it. A direct step puts a plan in motion that reveals a definite and unambiguous intent to kill. The wording of an Illinois model indictment for charges of attempted murder says (key words relating to mental states emphasized):

> The attempted murder was done **willfully** and with **deliberation** and **premeditation** if the defendant acted with that state of mind. A decision to kill made rashly, impulsively, or without careful consideration of the choice and its consequences is not deliberate and premeditated. On the other hand, a cold, calculated decision to kill can be reached quickly. The test is

the extent of the reflection, not the length of time. In order for a person to be guilty of attempted murder, that person should have **deliberately, intentionally** or **recklessly** with extreme disregard for human life, attempted to kill someone. There should be some substantial step towards committing the crime.

DEGREES OF MURDER

Statutes that define different degrees of murder rely on many of the same terms emphasized above. Common law includes no degrees of murder, and simply treats murder as a capital offence. Nor does it recognize the category of negligent homicide included in the Model Penal Code (MPC §210.0(1)), which describes the degrees of murder as follows:

[1] *Deliberate and Premeditated.* Typically, a murder involving the specific intent to kill is first-degree murder in jurisdictions that grade the offense by degrees if the homicide was also "deliberate" and "premeditated."

[2] *Willful, Deliberate, Premeditated.* Nearly all states that grade murder by degrees provide that a "willful, deliberate, premeditated" killing is murder in the first degree.

[3] *Intent to Inflict Grievous Bodily Injury.* Malice aforethought is implied if a person intends to cause grievous bodily injury to another, but death results. In states that grade murder by degree, this form of malice nearly always constitutes second-degree murder.

[4] *Extreme Recklessness.* ("Depraved Heart" Murder)—Malice aforethought is implied if a person's conduct manifests an

extreme indifference to the value of human life. In states that separate murder into degrees, this type of murder almost always constitutes second-degree murder.

Over time, descriptions of various types of unlawful killings have been developed, leading to the creation of the concept of manslaughter, which includes three generally recognized types:

1. *intentional* killing committed in "sudden heat of passion" as the result of "adequate provocation" (voluntary manslaughter).
2. *unintentional* killing resulting from the commission of a lawful act done in an unlawful manner (involuntary manslaughter). This is akin to criminally negligent homicide.
3. *unintentional* killing that occurs during the commission or attempted commission of an unlawful act (involuntary manslaughter). This type of manslaughter is sometimes called "unlawful-act manslaughter," or if the killing occurred during the commission of a nonfelony, "misdemeanor-manslaughter."

Further refinements include the phrase *heat of passion*, which specifies requirements for an adequate provocation that occurs at the time of the killing. Since such provocation has to be "adequate," the *reasonable person* doctrine applies, which relates to whether or not the killers had the chance to cool their passion. Considerable controversy also exists about the nature of the stimulus that created the killer's heat of passion. Attempting to narrow this down, the Model Penal Code holds that insults, for example, do not apply to the provocation of heat of passion.

Common law makes no distinction between involuntary manslaughter and manslaughter based on criminal negligence, but the

Model Penal Code distinguishes them, calling involuntary manslaughter a lesser offense.

In addition, statutory law includes important provisions concerning killers who suffer *extreme mental or emotional disturbance* that can provide a reasonable explanation or excuse for committing the crime. Interpretations of this provision are debated in court, as chapter 7 in this book illustrates.

ENTRAPMENT

In statutes related to murder and other criminal cases, entrapment is said to occur when (1) the defendant is not ready and willing (predisposed) to commit the crime; (2) when creation of the crime comes not from the defendant but rather from the government agents who investigate the crime; and (3) when those agents persuade, induce, or coerce the defendant to commit a crime that they otherwise would be unlikely to commit. If there is reasonable doubt in the mind of a reasonable person about these qualifications, the entrapment defense can sometimes apply. The burden of proof is usually on the defense to prove entrapment by clear and convincing evidence or by a preponderance of the evidence.

Here we see the important but vague legal terminology at its best. Being "ready and willing" means that the defendant intends and is predisposed to commit the crime. But when the idea of creating the crime comes from the government agent rather than from the defendant, the defendant cannot be shown to have had the necessary predisposition. If the language evidence is clear that the government agent persuaded, induced, or coerced the defendant to commit the crime, prosecutions can be severely hampered. But disputes sometimes exist about whether the agents merely offered the target what appeared to be the opportunity to commit the crime or whether they coerced them into committing it.

MURDER INDICTMENTS

Murder indictments also use some of these vague legal terms, usually beginning with the date, place, and defendant's name, followed by words to this effect: "... committed the offense of FIRST DEGREE MURDER in that the said defendant, without lawful justification and with the intent to kill," followed by the names of the victims and the relevant statutes. Some indictments in solicitation to murder cases include "premeditated intent," as Count 1 in one of the solicitation to murder cases discussed in chapter 5 reads (emphasis added):

> That the defendant MICHAEL EMERIC MOCKOVAC in King County, Washington, during a period of time intervening between August 3, 2009 through November 12, 2009, with **intent** to promote and facilitate the commission of the crime of Murder in the First Degree of Dr. Joseph King, to-wit: with **premeditated intent** to cause the death of Dr. Joseph King, did offer to give or gave money or other thing of value to another to engage in specific conduct which would constitute such crime or would establish complicity of such other person in its commission or attempted commission had such a crime been attempted or committed; Contrary to RCW 9A.28.030(1)(a), and against the peace and dignity of the State of Washington.

The task of the prosecution is to demonstrate intentionality and predisposition and the task of the defense is to show that these legal terms are not demonstrable from whatever evidence is available.

THE DIFFICULTY IN DEFINING LEGAL TERMS

It would be prudent for linguists who are asked to consult on murder cases to become familiar with the legal lexicon outlined above. Since laws themselves are written as definitions (Solan 2010, 93) and since legal terms make for an interesting linguistic study in themselves, what stands out to linguists who consult with attorneys in murder cases is the vagueness of many of these legal definitions. Even though mental states like "intention" are innately difficult to define, laypersons such as jurors might feel the need for something a bit more precise than they can find in the statutes. Legal scholars apparently have the same problem. For example, Glanville Williams, in his *Textbook of U.S. Criminal Law* (1978, 51), threw up his hands at trying to define "intention" and observed:

> The general legal opinion is that intention cannot be satisfactorily defined and does not need a definition, since everyone knows what it means. This is generally true. Trouble has been caused in the past because when judges have offered to give definitions or tests of intention for the benefit of the jury, they have used wide language going beyond the ordinary meaning of the word.

A few years earlier the courts had despaired in much the same way over terms such as "hard core pornography" and "obscenity." Supreme Court Justice Potter Stewart vented his frustration about attempts to define "obscenity" by coming up with his famous Casablanca Test ("I know it when I see it"), which echoed lines from the movie by the same name:

> I shall not today attempt further to define the kinds of material I understand to be embraced... but I know it when I see it. (*Jacobellis v. Ohio*, 387 U.S. 184, 197 1964)

This apparent semantic surrender, however, did not prevent the court from continuing to try to define the meaning of obscenity. In 1973 in *Miller v. California* (413 U.S. 15, 24–25), Justice Warren Burger wrote the majority opinion that defined obscenity as contingent on whether the average person applying contemporary community standards would find that the work, taken as a whole, appeals to the prurient interest; whether it describes in a patently offensive way any sexual conduct specifically defined by the applicable state law; and whether it, when taken as a whole, lacks serious literary, artistic, political, or scientific value. Many complained that this attempted definition also seemed vague and difficult to apply, after which the court listed some specific acts as examples, including offensive representations or descriptions of ultimate normal or perverted sexual acts that involved masturbation, excretory functions, and lewd exhibition of the genitals.

Somewhat later, because this additional definition of obscenity still didn't seem to satisfy, some of the court's terms purportedly were further clarified, including "average person," which was then defined as both sensitive and insensitive adults but did not include children. The meanings of "indecent materials," "patently offensive," "prurient," and "social, artistic, or scientific value" continue to be debated by judges, lawyers, and the general public. The Supreme Court finally quit trying and subsequently passed the burden of defining such terms along to the state courts, which seemed to be a handy solution to a knotty semantic problem. We are left with a situation in which some definitions are clearer than others; some are ambiguous, allowing for more than one interpretation; and some are vague, making it difficult to determine how to interpret them.

No matter how vague many legal terms may be, the situation is not likely to change. One reason for this is that the statutes can only provide prototypes from which the language in evidence conveys the meaning. Another reason stems from the nature of language itself. Words are leaky vessels for pinpointing meaning. Once we think we have a word pinned down, it suddenly and unexpectedly acquires some surprisingly new meaning. In 2011, for example, the word *occupy* suddenly began to represent public objections made by huge numbers of Americans to the excesses of Wall Street, the sinking economy, and resulting job losses. They were angry enough to set up makeshift tents in public spaces all over the country as a means of national protest during which the movement's name, Occupy Wall Street, took on still another recognized meaning that went far beyond the conventional meanings of the word *occupy*.

The writers of statutes cannot possibly be expected to think up all of the current and potential future contexts and uses of such words as *intention* and *premeditation*, to say nothing about the meanings of *voluntary, knowingly, malice aforethought*, and *reasonable doubt*. Some courts recognize two ways to find the meaning of a statute: (1) the definitional approach that analyzes the semantics of words and expressions in the statute, and (2) the ordinary meaning approach, which tries to determine what the ordinary reader might understand by the words (Solan 2010, 93). Courtroom battles are often fought over these competing approaches to meaning. In contrast, when the language appears to be so plain that it admits of no other meaning, things might be expected to go more smoothly. Unfortunately, that does not always happen.

Especially troubling is the fact that many of the efforts to define these important legal terms do so by using defining words that are equally unclear. For example, *malice aforethought* is defined by words such as *willful, deliberate, malicious, and premeditated* and left at that. Likewise, *manslaughter* is defined as killing without *malice, in the heat of passion*, in an *involuntary* manner, even though these purported defining terms are themselves undefined. The Model

Penal Code's definition of the degrees of homicide includes manslaughter, which it defines with terms such as *deliberate, premeditated, willful, intent,* and *extreme recklessness,* ending the issue as though the meanings of these terms were somehow clear to all.

These terms also appear in federal statutes that distinguish murder from manslaughter, which is described as the unlawful killing of a human being without *malice*. It is of two kinds: *voluntary* (stemming from a sudden quarrel or *heat of passion*) and *involuntary*. Again we see our old friends, *malice, voluntary,* and *heat of passion,* with little guidance about precisely what they can or must mean to the prosecution of an individual case. Reprising the thoughts of Professor Williams about *intentionality* and those of Justice Stewart about *obscenity,* we are left with the feeling that these terms are implicitly defined and that everyone knows what they mean. They may be sufficient for the statutory purpose of prosecution, but when it comes time to analyze the language evidence in specific cases, they must acquire considerably more focus and attention.

MURDER TERMINOLOGY IN LAW DICTIONARIES

Since the above noted terms are admittedly necessary in the context of law, linguistic experts and others might expect to find helpful definitions in specialized law dictionaries, such as *Black's Law Dictionary* (eighth edition, 2004) and Bryan Garner's *A Dictionary of Legal Usage* (1995), especially about the ways they define killers' mental states before the crime was committed and how they define these states while the murder case is discussed at trial, in police interviews, and in undercover recordings. But the following is what we find.

TERMS RELATED TO MURDER *BEFORE* THE MURDER TOOK PLACE

Intent: Black's defines intent as the state of mind accompanying an act, especially a forbidden act. It distinguishes between motive (the inducement to commit the crime) and intent, which is the mental resolution or determination to carry it out. When the intent to commit an illegal act exists, the motive becomes immaterial. Garner contrasts the nonlegal use of intent (the desire that a consequence will follow from one's conduct) with the legal usage, which refers to the way persons contemplate how the consequences of their acts will necessarily or probably follow from that act, whether or not these consequences are desired for their own sake. He points out that legal scholars agree that intention cannot be satisfactorily defined and, since everyone knows what the word means, it does not even need to be defined.

Premeditation: Black's defines a premeditated crime as one carried out with willful deliberation and planning. It was consciously constructed beforehand. This concept is important for determining the type of homicide as well as for the sentencing and punishment that follows. Garner adds that because premeditation invariably precedes a bad act of some kind, the word has taken on strongly negative connotations. Premeditation is a term sometimes considered when a claim of entrapment is raised.

Malice aforethought: Black's says this is the requisite mental state for common law murder, encompassing any one of the following: the *intent* to kill, the *intent* to inflict grievous bodily harm, *extremely reckless indifference* to the value of human life, and the intent to commit a dangerous felony. *Malice aforethought* is premeditated malice, preconceived malice, or *malice prepense* (sixteenth-century French for *aforethought*). It means that a design was conceived before the fatal act. Today, the major requirement is that the intention not be an afterthought. Garner is a bit more helpful for laypersons, as he contrasts the different meaning of *malice* in law (the intentionally unlawful action) from the meaning used by the general public (a wicked state of mind).

Deliberate (adjective): *Black's* says this word means *intentional, premeditated,* fully considered, unimpulsive, slow in deciding. Garner says the same.

From both of these law dictionary resources we learn that in law *malice aforethought* simply means that one person murdered another person *intentionally*. A precise definition of *intention* along with the ways an intention might be discovered and proved, however, is not and probably cannot be specified. Similar to the statutes, these law dictionaries sometimes define terms circularly, using other undefined terms as synonyms, without defining what either term includes or how their meanings can be discovered and proved.

TERMS RELATED TO THE ACT *WHILE* THE MURDER TOOK PLACE

Terms relating to the murder while it was taking place are important for applying penalties to the crime. Law dictionaries offer the following:

Wanton (disregard for life): Black's defines wanton acts as unreasonable or maliciously risked harm carried out while the perpetrator is utterly indifferent to the consequences. In criminal law, *wanton* usually connotes malice, while *reckless* does not. *Black's* cites Perkins and Boyce *Criminal Law* (1982, 879--80):

> Wanton differs from reckless both as to the actual state of mind and as to the degree of culpability. One who is acting recklessly is fully aware of the unreasonable risk he is creating, but may

be trying and hoping to avoid any harm. One acting wantonly may be creating no greater risk or harm, but he is not trying to avoid it and is indifferent whether harm results or not. Wanton conduct has properly been characterized as "vicious" and rates extreme in the degree of culpability. The two are not mutually exclusive. Wanton conduct is reckless plus, so to speak. Garner gives the essentially same definition.

Heat of passion: Black's Law Dictionary says that heat of passion includes rage, terror, or furious hatred suddenly aroused by some immediate provocation. The cause of such heat of passion usually derives from something another person said or did. In common law, heat of passion could serve as a mitigating circumstance that would reduce a murder charge to manslaughter. *Black's* adds "To constitute heat of passion included in this requirement it is not necessary for the passion to be so extreme that the slayer does not know what he is doing at the time; but it must be so extreme for the moment that his action is being directed by passion rather than by reason." Garner's law dictionary does not include a definition for *heat of passion*.

Recklessness: Black's defines recklessness as rash heedlessness, an unjustifiable risk to harm others with indifference to that risk. It is more than negligence, a deviation from what a reasonable person would do. Garner says that *recklessness* (also called *advertent negligence*) has several gradations of meaning, but it primarily refers to an act in which the actor does not desire the consequence but foresees the possibility and takes the risk anyway. Disputes in court exist over whether or not the actor actually recognized the danger. Murder resulting from a reckless act (lacking consciousness of the danger) could be considered manslaughter.

Knowledge: Black's says that knowing something is having or showing awareness or understanding; being well-informed, deliberate, conscious. The Model Penal Code distinguishes between the mental states of one's objectives and the mental state of one's knowledge at §202(2)(a) & (b). Garner defines knowledge as the required awareness of a fact or condition, contrasting with *notice,* which requires merely a reason to know about a fact of condition. Knowledge is subsumed within *notice,* because actual awareness is well above the threshold requirement of a reason for a person to be aware. Garner adds that voluntariness generally refers to the cause, while unintentional refers to the effect.

TERMS USED IN THE JUDGES' INSTRUCTIONS TO JURIES *AT THE ENDS OF TRIALS*

Near the end of a murder trial the judge usually instructs the jury members to use their own perceptions about whether or not the prosecution has proved its case. The phrases *reasonable doubt* and *presumption of innocence* are commonly used.

Reasonable doubt: Black's says the concept of reasonable doubt, which is commonly used in jury instructions, is a doubt that prevents one from being firmly convinced of a defendant's guilt, or the belief that there is a real possibility that a defendant is not guilty as charged (MPC §1.12). Jurors are instructed to begin with the presumption that the defendant is innocent and to preserve this assumption throughout the trial. Garner does not include a separate entry for reasonable doubt, but in his entry under *burden of proof,* he explains that in criminal cases jurors should consider reasonable doubt, which is equivalent to balance of probability in civil cases.

Presumption [of innocence]: Black's defines "presumption" as "A legal inference or assumption that a fact exists, based on known or proven existence of some other fact or group of facts." Garner says much the same thing: "A presumption of fact is simply an argument; it is an inference that may be drawn from the establishment of a basic fact."

Preponderance of the evidence: Black's says these words mean "the greater weight of the evidence... that has the most convincing force; superior evidentiary weight that, though not sufficient to free the mind wholly from all reasonable doubt, is still sufficient to incline a fair and impartial mind to one side of the issue rather than the other." Both *Black's* and Garner point out that this expression is the traditional measure of persuasion used in civil cases rather than in murder cases.

STANDARD DESK DICTIONARY DEFINITIONS

In fairness to law dictionaries, standard desk dictionaries do no better at providing totally helpful definitions for the above cited terms. For example, *Merriam-Webster's New Collegiate Dictionary* defines *malice* as "desire to cause pain, injury or distress to another; *intent* to commit an unlawful act or cause harm without legal justification or excuse." The same dictionary defines *intent* as "the act or fact of intending; the design or purpose to commit a wrongful or criminal act; the state of mind with which an act is done." Note the circularity that this dictionary uses when it tells us that "intent" is the act of "intending." Sidney Landau's authoritative book on lexicography, *Dictionaries: The Art and Craft of Lexicography* (2001, 157) condemns circular definitions, noting that they are of little value: "Circularity does not just make things difficult—it makes them impossible." However, abstract terms such as *malice* and *intent* admittedly are among the most difficult to define.

It should be noted that vaguely worded legal terms are not limited to statutes relating to murder. For example, 18 U.S.C. §875(c) prohibits transmitting in interstate or foreign commerce any communication containing any threat to injure the person of another. At the time of this writing, the current status of the meaning of the "true threat" doctrine (the expression of intent to engage in violence or bodily harm) was being debated before Sixth Circuit Court (*United States v. Franklin Delano Jeffries II*, No. 11-5722). The issue is whether reasonable persons would construe that threat writers intended their threats to be taken seriously when the communicators of such threats actually did not intend to be threatening. The courts often rely on dictionary definitions, all of which include the word *intended*, in their definitions of *threat* or *threaten*. This would indicate that any communicated threat would have to be intentional. Missing here, however, is the last part of the well-known sender/message/receiver communication triad. Dictionaries do not define *threat* in a way that allows for a reasonable sender's intention of its meaning or the receiver's perception of how the threat was intended. Dictionaries can't be expected to define messages in ways that senders of those messages intended them or in the way receivers of those messages understood them. This may be adequate reason for the courts to not rely so heavily on dictionary definitions of certain difficult words.

By their own admission, dictionaries are always a step or two behind actual language practice and, like the drafters of statutes, lexicographers find it impossible to think of all the possible meanings that a word might have. The drafters who came up with the statutory restrictions about "using a firearm in committing a drug offense" probably never dreamed that one day someone would be caught trading an unloaded gun for narcotics. Was this actually *using* a firearm to commit a drug offense? If not, what does *using* mean? The courts argued over this definition and finally decided that *using a firearm* included trading an unloaded gun for cocaine, even though lexicographers had never managed to think of an occasion in which *using* could be expressed in such a context.

Some lawyers and judges often speak and act as though language has a discoverable plain meaning in which the language admits of no more than one meaning and this meaning is easily accessible to competent native speakers. As they do this, they appear to be unaware of the ways that language vagueness is addressed in other nonlegal contexts studied by specialists in linguistics, who use the discourse clues of context, nonverbal signals, response uptake, pragmatic meaning, speech acts, and many other linguistic devices that can demonstrate either understanding or lack of understanding of the disputed words.

Linguists who specialize in semantics discover meanings of words by examining the semantic features that are the properties of that word, contrasting this with the semantic features of other words. The meaning of a word is represented as a set of features. This approach to meaning works well for concrete objects but not so well for abstract concepts, such as mental states. Abstract words such as the mental states of *intentionality, predisposition,* and *voluntariness* convey a prototype meaning in which the semantic categories have blurry edges that permit various degrees of inclusion. As Coleman and Kay (1981, 26–27) put it, "a semantic prototype associates a word or phrase with a prelinguistic, cognitive schema or image; and speakers are equipped with an ability to judge the degree to which an object matches this prototype schema or image." Judgments about the degree of match is the task of triers of the fact as they determine whether or not the evidence leads to *reasonable doubt.* As noted earlier, a similar idea was expressed by the eighteenth-century philosopher Immanuel Kant: "Concepts without percepts are empty, and percepts without concepts are blind." As the cases described in this book will demonstrate, a statute attempts to indicate the concept as well as it can, and the percept, the understanding of that concept, is obtained by use of the senses that provide the concept's ultimate definition. The following chapter attempts to explain how linguistic analysis of the language evidence can lead to such understandings of that language evidence.

Because this book is not intended to be a legal treatise, I have only sketchily described some of the legal language used in murder cases in order to highlight the issues that relate to the ways linguists might understand and make use of the language evidence in them. From reviewing the laws, it would appear that it is possible to find mutual understandability of terms indicating the suspect's state of mind such as *intentionality, predisposition,* and *reasonable doubt.* Although they are not the focus of this book, the defining characteristics of other abstract mental states such as *wanton disregard, heat of passion, voluntary, extreme mental,* or *emotional disturbance* also might be expected to be understandable. If such mutual understanding were the case, however, we might expect to find few disputes about the meanings of these prototypical terms in specific murder cases.

However, such disputes abound, which suggests that even though prototype legal terms like these may be very useful for the courts, they still lack the necessary clarity and understanding required of jurors to make prudent decisions in murder cases. The best way to do this is to examine the actual language evidence, because language is virtually the only window to such mental states.

Because legal theory is most concerned with the ordinary types of intentions, it is understandably difficult to define terms relating to mental states, such as *intentionality* and its kin. Statutes are prototypical. Like dictionaries, murder laws cannot be expected to define and contextualize intentions in all of the specific descriptive situations that arise in potential, individual murder cases. On the other hand, the analysis of language evidence can provide very useful clues about what the suspects' intentions were. In addition, suspects may have the intention of offending or even hurting their victims without having the intention of killing them. Legal rules applied to fact situations are often opaque, and truth can vary, depending on whether or how the subsequent act is described and discussed.

The following chapter describes the linguistic tools that can be used when dealing with the vague legal terms in murder cases—*intentionality, predisposition,* and *voluntariness.* The legal strategy of interpretation cannot work, for it is limited to ambiguous expressions. Construction, the legal strategy for resolving vagueness, allows a line to be drawn that can convert vagueness into specificity. One place to discover that specificity is in the language evidence of murder cases, the only window to the mind of the speakers that can enlighten the vagueness of these three critical legal terms.

3

ANALYZING MURDER LAW TERMINOLOGY AND EVIDENCE

Linguists focus on the entire body of language evidence available, from large chunks to small. Very important are the largest chunks, speech events, for they prescribe what and how talk is allowable and predictable (Gumperz 1990, 9; Shuy 2011, 22). Nested within speech events are other levels of language, such as the speakers' schemas and agendas, identified by the topics introduced and the responses given to those topics (Shuy 2011, 24–25). Speakers' agendas provide important clues to their intentions and they provide evidence of their schemas during the speech events in which they find themselves. Throughout individual speech events, the participants also employ speech acts, such as offering, agreeing, denying, requesting information or clarification, and others (Searle 1969). Language also provides indications about whether the participants are either cooperative or uncooperative as they employ various language strategies to influence their listeners (Shuy 2005, 15–29). Finally, semantic, syntactic, and phonetic analysis of the even smaller but still very important bits of language can help resolve ambiguities in the participant's speech or writing.

SPEECH EVENTS

The place to start an analysis is by first identifying the speech event, because it strongly influences understandings of the rest of the language contained within it. The notion of speech events appears to have begun with Dell Hymes's (1972) proposed reaction to Noam Chomsky's (1965) proclamation that the proper role of linguistics is to find the internalized rules of language and not the language performance that descriptive linguists had held. Opposed to Chomsky's notions of language competence found in the mind, Hymes argued that communicative competence is found in the way speakers and writers use their language in a variety of real-life contexts.

Central to communicative competence is the speech event (Hymes 1972). Speech events are identifiable human activities in which speech plays a central role in defining what that speech event is. In fact, such events cannot take place effectively without the language that defines them (Van Dijk 1985, 201). Hymes's insights about the context, culture, and history of speech events has had a profound effect on analysts of spoken and written discourse as well as on studies of the ethnography of communication (Bauman & Sherzer 1974; Duranti 1997).

Following Hymes's model, Gumperz (1990, 9) pointed out that speech events are recurring occasions that have "tacitly understood rules of preference, unspoken conventions as to what counts as valid and what information may or may not be introduced." This means that in order to appreciate the work done by the smaller language units of sounds, morphemes, words, and sentences, we have to see how these fit into the larger patterned language structures, beginning with the speech event in which the language takes place. The speech event influences not only the parameters of what can be said by the participants (what counts as valid, in Gumperz's definition) but also the orderly sequence in which things can be said within that speech event. In many speech events there is also an element of asymmetrical power that predicts these parameters. Commonly, one participant enjoys a superordinate position (doctor, judge, therapist, boss, buyer, teacher), while the other participant holds a more subordinate role (patient, suspect, witness, client, worker, seller, student). An individual's contributions during such speech events are influenced by this asymmetrical power relationship. The conversational power of police interviewers over suspects and the conversational power of lawyers over witnesses in the courtroom provide two important examples of the asymmetry of language power in the legal context.

SCHEMAS

Clues to participants' schemas flow naturally from the speech event (Shuy 2005, 205–206). Accurately or not, speakers relate their previous and current knowledge, attitudes, beliefs, and values to the new information they receive (Bartlett 1932). During this process, both suspects and law enforcement officers sometimes process new information inaccurately. Evidence of the participants' schemas will be seen in most of the cases described in this book, but the solicitation to murder case of Davis in chapter 5 provides an excellent example. From the very beginning of the recorded conversations in this undercover investigation, Davis's language reveals that his schema was that he was in a speech event in which the undercover agent was reporting progress of his covert investigation into Davis's wife's romantic relationship with another man, while the agent's schema was that the speech event was about soliciting her murder. Davis's continuing schema was apparently unclear to the agent and to the prosecutor who indicted him for soliciting his wife's murder.

AGENDAS

Although linguistic efforts to determine intentionality provide nothing equivalent to DNA, the agendas of speakers, as revealed by the topics they introduce, are the strongest clues available about such intentions. Speakers' intentions are made even clearer when they recycle that same topic over and over again (Shuy 2005; 2011). Almost equally strong clues to intentions come from the responses speakers make to the topics introduced by other speakers. In most human interactions, people introduce and respond to what is on their minds, the best window available to their intentionality. An exception to this occurs during many police interview speech events that consist entirely of questions by one person with answers by the other, in which case suspects get no opportunity to introduce their own topics. This can be seen in the police interviews of two juvenile suspects, Carter and Rogers, described in chapter 9.

SPEECH ACTS

People get things accomplished with their language, largely through speech acts such as requesting, agreeing, denying, confirming, conjecturing, apologizing, offering, promising, warning, advising, admitting, threatening, regretting, praising, complaining, giving opinions, congratulating, and many others. Each of these speech acts has its own felicity conditions in order to count as clear and effective speech acts (Searle 1969). In undercover recorded conversations in solicitation to murder cases and in law enforcement interviews in all types of cases, it is essential for analysts to determine the felicity of offers, agreements, and denials, as the cases in chapters 5 though 10 illustrate.

CONVERSATIONAL STRATEGIES

Law enforcement officers often have a difficult time eliciting admissions of suspects' intentions or predispositions to commit murder and their admissions that they actually committed the crime. In such cases the police sometimes employ certain conversational strategies that they believe can help lead to the desired admissions of guilt more quickly. People commonly use conversational strategies to negotiate the discourse into the directions they want conversations to go (Hansell and Ajirotutu 1992, 85–94). My book *Creating Language Crimes* (2005) describes and illustrates twelve such strategies used by the police or undercover operatives in a number of criminal cases. Such strategies include being ambiguous, blocking the target's words, manipulating the tape recording, interrupting the target at crucial points, speaking on behalf of the target, using the hit-and-run strategy, camouflaging the illegality of the venture, inaccurately representing what the target said, and others (Shuy 2005, 15–29). The use of some of these strategies is illustrated in all but one of the cases in this book.

SMALLER LANGUAGE UNITS

By "smaller," I refer to the comparatively smaller size of critically important sentences, phrases, and words in relationship to the larger language units of the entire speech event, the cumulative evidence of participants' schemas, the ongoing topics and responses that comprise the speakers' agendas, the sometimes important critical speech acts, and the occurrence of certain conversational strategies. On the surface, the smaller isolated sentences, phrases, words, and speech sounds may sometimes be thought to be the most critical passages that occur. These are identified as the locus of the alleged smoking guns, which naturally can be important but often are less powerful when contextualized within the larger language units noted above. Sometimes the lexicon is ambiguous, sometimes the syntactic referencing goes unnoticed, and sometimes the actual speech sounds are misheard and transcribed inaccurately, as several cases in this book illustrate.

This is not to say that these smaller language units, the words, phrases, sentences, and speech sounds are unimportant, for suspects often verbally express their guilt (or what may appear to be their guilt) very clearly in such contextually isolated expressions. Even when they do so, however, it is important to pay close attention to what was said prior to that point, for this is where analysis of the speech event, schemas, agendas, speech acts, and conversational strategies can help illuminate those isolated, decontextualized words or sentences, whether they are produced by suspects, law enforcement officers, or prosecutors.

SEQUENCE OF THE USE OF THESE LINGUISTIC TOOLS

The language evidence in most law cases, including murder cases, is most effectively analyzed in more or less the above noted sequence, starting with identifying the speech event that prescribes and predicts the participants' schemas and agendas. Speakers' schemas and agendas are supported through their use of speech acts, which in turn give evidence of their cooperativeness, clarity, ambiguity, and the meaning of what they say or write. That is, the larger language units provide contextual meaning to the increasingly smaller language units. Case examples in this book illustrate how these linguistic tools were used, and the final chapter provides a summary of where and how they were analyzed in each case.

THE IMPORTANCE OF STARTING WITH THE SPEECH EVENT

Often in criminal cases, including murder cases, the intelligence gathering carried out by law enforcement officers and the intelligence analysis made by prosecutors tend to focus primarily on the smaller levels of language that are isolated and decontextualized individual words and sentences within the entire body of language evidence. Such decontextualization often fails to show how the isolated expressions comport with the speech events, agendas, schemas, and conversational strategies of the writers or speakers. Such failure can lead to serious misunderstandings of the language evidence and, in some cases can lead to convictions that might not have happened if a more holistic linguistic analysis had been provided.

Even though the speech event is so central to language analysis, it has not been recognized commonly in the analysis of murder cases. Because of this lack of recognition, the remainder of this chapter identifies the structures of various types of speech events that are found in the following murder and solicitation to murder cases. In many of them, the police and prosecutors focused only on the isolated words and sentences in the suspects' confessions without attending to the contextual crucial language in which they exist. In other cases, the police inferred that a suspect had confessed, in spite of the actual language evidence that indicated otherwise.

It is important to distinguish between a life event and the various speech events that can occur within that life event. Life events contain language processes occurring within them. Events take place in real time, sometimes in just an instant (a chance "hello" on the street), and sometimes over longer intervals of time (a dinner party or a concert). Within life events such as attending a concert, various speech events can take place. These speech events might include individual conversations with fellow attendees, verbal interactions with ushers, or discussions during intermissions. The life event is the concert; the speech events are structured units of language that occur within that life event. For the purpose of this book, the life event is the murder event that includes all the relevant speech events that precede, follow, or take place during the murder.

As the murder event is described, it is important to note how the important legal concepts and terms, *intentionality, predisposition,* and *voluntariness* are found and interpreted within it. The first step in dealing with these legal terms is to recognize the holistic nature of the entire murder event. Admittedly difficult to define terms like the above can achieve a more definitive meaning when they are instanced within the contextualized sequence of the various stages of the entire murder event. This sequence begins when potential murderers first feel seriously offended or when they slaver over something they greedily desire. Next, they think about how they can seek revenge or obtain the desired item. Then, they strengthen their murderous thoughts by deciding to take action. Next, they plan how to do it. Then they carry out the murder. Finally, they are caught and interviewed about what has happened. This murder event sequence relates directly to law enforcement's need to discover not only the suspects' methods, means, and opportunities but also their intentions and predisposition. This sequential structure of a murder event commonly takes the following shape.

Phase 1: The language used in thinking about murder

As noted in chapter 2, whether or not the crime was premeditated is important, because evidence of premeditation brings more severe penalties than unpremeditated murder. People who carefully (or carelessly) leave discoverable evidence of their thoughts about murder can be judged to be worse criminals than those who carry out the crime at the spur of the moment without malice aforethought.

It is natural to infer that when people kill other people, they probably thought about committing the criminal act before they carried it out. However accurate this inference may be, premeditation can be extremely difficult to prove, and nobody needs proof more than law enforcement, prosecutors, the courts, and jurors. Since nobody is able to get into the minds of criminals, any useful evidence of the killers' mental states of *premeditation* has to be determined by retrievable language evidence that reveals the murderers' purported mental states that led them to commit the crimes. If any language evidence exists during this phase, it is usually the best indicator of such premeditation. This is most commonly found in perpetrators' notes, messages, or diaries, or from witnesses who report that the killers shared their thoughts with them. Murderers also may describe their premeditation in later confession statements, but more often than not these inner thoughts reside only in the minds of the murderers themselves. Unless there is specific language evidence to guide them, linguists are no more gifted at probing into the minds of murders than are psychologists, police, prosecutors, judges, or juries. When the government can produce witnesses who claim to have heard or seen evidence of the perpetrator's premeditation, the police interviews with them are usually preserved as electronic recordings and written transcripts. Since such evidence is in the form of language, it can be linguistically analyzed.

Phase 2: The language used in building resolve and intent

Mental states such as the intention to murder can lead to a suspect's resolution to act on that intention. In law this is called *guilty mind*—something that is obviously very difficult to discover and prove. Without clear evidence, law enforcement often has to infer a guilty mind from the circumstances relating to the murder context. Although some inferences can be more useful than others, at best they are estimates or guesses, hardly the basis of strong certainty. Since it is virtually impossible for inferences to meet the proof standard of "clear and convincing evidence," they tend to fall into the proof standard of "beyond a reasonable doubt," which sometimes can be less that convincing.

In the investigation of auto accidents, it is common and natural for police to infer clues to intentions. Such clues can be based on the physical evidence, such as tire tracks and skid marks. In murder cases, the police may make similar inferences. Clues of this type can be based on evidence such as the direction of snipers' bullet trajectories. In robberies, inferences can be based on such things as fingerprint residue left at a crime scene. Often inferences or clues such as these are questioned and debated at trial, especially when they are based on actions that cannot be fully confirmed or shown to match the assertions upon which they are based. In contrast, noninferential clues to intentions can be found in the recorded spoken or written language used by participants in conversations, police interviews, trial testimony, and other relevant contexts in which language evidence exists. Unlike inferences based on purportedly reliable physical circumstances of a crime, language can provide somewhat clearer clues to human intentions. Therefore, linguists use analyzable language evidence in their search for clues to the mental states of speakers or writers.

Language clues are comparable to the pots and shards collected by archeologists as they try to reconstruct facts about our historical past. These pots and shards do not tell the whole story of course, but they can provide important clues about it. Similarly, when people talk or write, they leak evidence of their mental states in the topics they introduce, in their responses to the topics brought up by others, in their attention and uptake in conversations, in their use of speech acts, in what they don't say, and in other ways that can provide clues to their underlying intentions. Again, it should be emphasized that such analysis does not and cannot actually delve deeply into any speaker's mind, but what people say or write offers useful indicators concerning what they are thinking about, contemplating, planning, and, yes, even intending. Chapter 5 describes crimes of soliciting murder in which recorded undercover conversations frequently reveal clues to suspects' intentions and predispositions.

Phase 3: The language used in planning murder

The third phase also occurs before the murder is carried out. It is difficult to find evidence of premeditation about whether or how murderers planned the crime unless the language evidence noted above is present (the notes, diaries, conversations with associates). When there is no available language evidence of this type, the killer's planning phase must be inferred from the information gathered after the crime has been committed. The most useful evidence derives from undercover tape recordings of government agents with people suspected of trying to kill someone. When such undercover recordings exist, it is important to discover whether the suspects themselves introduced and planned the murder or whether undercover agents generated such planning. It is equally important to discover whether any speech acts of agreement to commit the murder actually occurred and whether the participants in the solicitation to murder speech event ever reached an agreement about the act. It is also often the linguist's task to determine from the recorded language evidence the degree to which suspects may have been pressured, guided, coerced, or otherwise influenced by the undercover agent in such conversations. Chapter 5 discusses such cases.

Phase 4: The language used in carrying out the murder

Most commonly the linguistic work in murder cases takes place after the victim has been killed and a suspected perpetrator is in police custody or is about to be placed into custody. At that time the linguist's role is to analyze what was said not only by suspects and witnesses but also by the police officers who interviewed them. These interviews are speech events of two types—the police interview speech event and the witness interview speech event—both of which have their own structure and dynamics. Examples of these are discussed in chapters 7 through 10.

In rare cases, such as when a 911 call is being made while a murder event is taking place, experts in voice identification can analyze any audible voices on a telephone after either the victim or the witness has dialed 911 for help and lets the phone dangle while the murder is in progress.

SPEECH EVENTS WITHIN A MURDER EVENT

As noted earlier, the murder event contains various speech events that occur within any of the four phases mentioned above. If language evidence exists in those phases, it's possible that the legal concepts of intentionality, predisposition, and voluntariness can be clarified. Linguistic analysis can also be helpful for any specific and unambiguous language evidence available in the speech events of notes, messages, diaries, or recorded conversations of the suspect with associates or accomplices, or in undercover tape recordings of a suspected killer. Each of these speech events can contain language that manifests linguistic rules of specificity and clarity relating to the speaker's or writer's intention and predisposition. A friendly conversation with an associate, for example, could contain a confession speech event in which intention and predisposition was made either felicitously or not. Notes and message speech events can have the same specificity or vagueness.

The most common role of linguistic analysis, however, takes place after the murder has been committed, the stage in which the language used by all parties yields the greatest possibility for linguistic analysis. This opportunity often occurs in the police interview speech event with suspects and witnesses, in any available undercover conversations, and in the language used by all relevant participants during the speech events of courtroom hearings and trials. The larger the body of language evidence, the more help linguistic analysis can be.

Although the field of law considers murder and other crimes primarily as illegal acts, it is a natural for ethnographers and linguists to view them as types of sequentially structured language events in which the controlling legal terms may be more clearly exemplified and instanced through the language evidence than they can be defined by vaguely worded statutes or dictionaries. For example, the business transaction speech event contains a structure of required sequences that cannot be violated. I cite this example in *The Language of Bribery Cases* (2013), where the five sequential phases of business transaction speech event are as follows:

The structure of a business transaction speech event

Phase	*buyer*	*both*	*seller*
		1. Problem	
	states problem and need; asks about control; requests help		indicates interest; offers conditions; demonstrates ability and control
		2. Proposed negotiation	
	suggests dimension of offer; outlines conditions		considers dimensions; may demand further conditions
		3. Offer	
	makes offer		negotiates offer; agrees or disagrees
		4. Completion	
	finishes transaction	"It's a deal" shake hands; sign contract; or reject deal	finishes transaction
		5. Optional extension	
	offers other	future deals and relationships	agrees or disagrees about future deals and relationships

Various speech acts are nested within this speech event. The required phases of the business transaction speech event are usually accomplished through the use of speech acts such as reporting, requesting, offering, agreeing, disagreeing, accepting, rejecting, predicting, and others, all of which have required felicity conditions (Searle 1969). In addition, the same speech acts can vary in significance based on the sequential phase of the speech event in which they occur. For example, the speech act of the agreement offer in phase three conveys very different significance from the agreement to make future deals in phase five. That is, the significance of the same speech act can vary according to the phase of the speech event in which it takes place. Relevant to a murder confession speech event, the significance of a suspect's admission about committing a robbery is not a significant admission that he committed a murder that took place during that robbery.

Linguists have described and analyzed many speech events, even in the legal context, including bribery (Shuy 1993; 2013), political lobbying (Shuy 2013), tax consultation (Shuy 2013), car sales (Shuy 1998), courtroom testimony (Shuy 2010), defamation (Shuy 2010), and perjury (Shuy 2011). The available language evidence in many murder events can vary, however, because the early predisposition stages of this crime are seldom recorded and made available for linguistic analysis. Even the self-report evidence given by suspects during their interviews with police officers can be misleading, because the police interviewers' main task of eliciting a confession can contaminate such evidence. This effort can lead them to exert various types of influences on the suspect, including misleading or even coercing them.

The following describes the structures of the undercover solicitation to murder speech event, the police interview speech event, and the courtroom speech event.

THE UNDERCOVER SOLICITATION TO MURDER SPEECH EVENT

When law enforcement has a strong suspicion that a person is planning to hire a hit man to kill someone, the common strategy is to carry out an undercover taped sting operation. For various reasons some alleged suspects try to find someone, usually a professional assassin, who could be hired to do the murder for them. The major goal of law enforcement in such operations is to establish the suspect's intentionality and predisposition and, more importantly, to prevent the murder from taking place.

Because the hit man and the target are engaging in a type of business transaction, the language evidence in such cases commonly takes the form of a business conversation speech event (as described above). One major difference from a legitimate business transaction, of course, is that the topic is murder rather than commerce. Another difference is that in the murder speech event, the person who makes the recording is the only participant who knows that it is being taped. This is important because targets can be less aware of how important it is to listen very carefully and say what they have to say very clearly. It is dangerous for them to let ambiguities go by without clarifying them.

Otherwise, the conversation in the undercover murder speech event patterns after the structure of the business transaction speech event. It begins with a clearly stated problem, after which there is a proposed negotiation about how to deal with that problem, followed by an offer and finally a completion that usually, but not always, is an agreement. In a solicitation to murder speech event, unless the target has a number of murders in mind, the optional extension phase of a business transaction speech event is unlikely to be relevant. Like the business transaction speech event, the murder speech event can fail at any of these stages. Such failure can come when both participants don't recognize and understand the problem in the same way, when the offer is not clearly understood by both participants, when the participants have different schemas about the event, and when the concluding speech act of agreement, if present, is not understood and agreed upon by both participants. These are speech event issues for which linguistic analysis can play a crucial role, especially regarding intentionality and predisposition.

It would seem logical that anyone who is in the business of trying to hire a hit man would have the predisposition and intention to have the target killed. In some cases, however, the tape-recorded evidence of suspects' intentionality and predisposition is not always as clear as the prosecution may believe. In each of the three cases described in chapter 5, the defendants most certainly had serious complaints about their alleged victims, but the language evidence in these cases shows that the degree to which they wanted to take their complaints was significantly created, planned, and encouraged by the agents tape-recording them. In one case, the agent was so vague and secretive about hiring a hit man that the language used by his target demonstrated that he didn't even understand what the agent was talking about. In a second solicitation to murder case, the undercover police officer began his vague offer to help the target with a problem that was not clearly specified. In a third case, the speech event began initially as a friendly conversation in which the cooperating witness consoled the target about his financial management problems with his business partner. Eventually the agent created and orchestrated most of the murder plan and vigorously coerced the defendant into agreeing to have it done. A fourth solicitation to murder case is not discussed until chapter 7 because its focus is on the voluntariness of a mentally incapacitated target. In all four solicitation to murder cases, initial identification of the speech event was critical because doing this clearly identified the sources of the targets' intentionality, predisposition, and voluntariness.

THE POLICE INTERVIEW SPEECH EVENT (WITH SUSPECTS AND WITNESSES)

Even when there are compelling eyewitness reports and other similar evidence, the police interview is a form of intelligence gathering that is extremely important for eliciting a confession. When suspects do not confess, their contradictory statements can often support a prosecution. I do not make light of how difficult it can be for police officers to conduct interviews with their suspects. Suspects often lie to avoid their guilt, ramble irrelevantly, or feign ignorance about what happened. On the other hand, police interviewers are frequently impatient, and from the beginning of the interview they predictably hold a schema of the suspect's guilt. Such a schema can be expected because, as Goodwin (1996) points out, most people, including law enforcement officers, have a "professional vision" that causes them to categorize information in ways that comport with that of their professions and occupations. Schemas are not bad in themselves, but they have to be recognized and accounted for when the police try to obtain new information.

Police interview speech events have a predictable structure, along with rules that prohibit police officers from spoon-feeding inculpatory details to suspects. Interviewers are required to follow authorized Miranda procedures, are prohibited from offering certain types of promises, and are required to avoid using coercive behavioral or language techniques. Police interviews have a preferred, although seldom followed, sequence in which interviewers are urged to proceed through four sequential steps as they try to discover the relevant facts. Gudjonsson (1992) provides a fully elaborated description of the structure of proper police interviews. What follows here is a more simplified version of the process that Gudjonsson provides.

Step 1 is to let suspects have the opportunity to tell their own versions of what happened while the interviewer listens but does not interrupt, threaten, or accuse. At this point the interviewers' task is to absorb these versions and mentally compare them with what is perceived to be the known facts. However, if suspects admit crimes or otherwise incriminate themselves during step 1, the interviewer's work obviously is done and the interview can end. But if this doesn't happen, interviewers are encouraged to move to the second step.

The interviewer's task in step 2 is to clarify the suspects' narratives and try to get them to correct or amplify what they've already said, especially when contradictions have become apparent. Interviewers are urged to probe in order to learn more about what the suspects have claimed up to this point. They are to seek this amplification or clarification by using *wh-* questions (who, what, where, when, how) but still without seriously challenging what the suspects have said previously. At this point, interviewers are mentally building their reasons for challenging the suspects when they move to step 3, but they are not yet ready to do so. If suspects have still not exposed their guilt, the interviewer is urged to move to the third step.

If suspects have contradicted themselves about the known facts, step 3 is the point at which the interview can turn into an interrogation. Now suspects are no longer simply the providers of their own stories. The inconsistencies in their accounts, along with what the interviewers believe they know to be the facts of the case, are now the critical issues for interviewers to pursue. If the evidence gathered so far is reasonably convincing about the suspects' potential guilt, interrogators can now challenge them about the truth of what they've said, warn them about the consequences of lying, and even accuse them of committing the crime. By step 3, most of the fact-finding part of the interview is over. If there is sufficient reason to believe that the suspects are guilty, interrogators can progress to the fourth step.

In step 4, after the investigators have pointed out the suspects' inconsistencies or outright lies, interrogators attempt to elicit a confession or admission about the suspects' involvement in the crime. This is the time to learn the suspects' intentionality and predisposition, but the issue of voluntariness of their answers during this step can become a subject of debate at trial. Even after the interviewer has elicited a confession, some suspects will continue to deny their guilt. At this point, the police interview is turned over to the prosecutor, whose job it is to do an intelligence analysis that will determine whether or not to indict.

The speech event structure with witnesses is similar to that of suspects, except that steps 3 and 4 are omitted unless the police have come to believe that the witnesses are being untruthful, in which case the police can probe for inconsistencies and presumed inaccuracies in much the same way they do with suspects in step 3.

Police interviews with both suspects and witnesses are normally memorialized in electronic recordings, in written transcripts, in summary reports constructed by the interviewers, or in various combinations of these. Since the police interview speech event consists of interactive language, it is subject to linguistic discourse analysis. Such analysis relates directly to the legal terms such as *intentionality, predisposition,* and *voluntariness.* The tools that linguists use to analyze the language evidence found in police interviews can either support or question the definition and relevance of these legal terms. By showing how the specific language used either instances their relevance or fails to do so, the linguistic analysis can help to move the vagueness of the legal lexicon into explicit reality, based on what was said and how it was said.

THE COURTROOM TESTIMONY SPEECH EVENT

Linguists have the opportunity not only to analyze any language used during the intelligence gathering done by law enforcement but also to analyze the intelligence analysis carried out by prosecutors' indictments and reports in which they decide whether or not the intelligence gathered by law enforcement is sufficient to prosecute the crime.

When the case reaches the stage of hearings and trials, prosecutors then use their intelligence analysis of the interrogation speech events in a different speech event—the courtroom testimony speech event. The structure of the courtroom testimony speech event is well known and understood by lawyers and judges, but it is very new and unfamiliar to most suspects and witnesses. Even though it can also seem annoyingly slow and tedious to the juries who hear it, this structure has important advantages for the trial process, for it makes it orderly and efficient for the court's purposes. Here, lawyers are in total control, subject to occasional comments, advice, and admonition by judges. Lawyers ask witnesses all the questions and witnesses are supposed to answer them relevantly unless they don't understand, in which case they are allowed to request clarification. Otherwise, the testimony speech event is very different from the police interview speech event, where interviewees are supposed to be encouraged to first tell their own stories in their own ways. During the courtroom speech event, witnesses are somewhat advantaged by having their lawyers present, but sometimes even this advantage does not help them much, because opposing lawyers can hamper the witness's lawyer's efforts to help them. In short, witnesses in the courtroom speech event are at the disadvantage of engaging a language event that is very unfamiliar to them, because it flies in the face of the normal everyday verbal interaction that is so common and familiar.

At this point in the legal process, the linguist's focus turns to the language used by defendants and witnesses under oath as well as to the language of the prosecutors. In addition to discovering and analyzing the defendants' and witnesses' misunderstandings of the language used in this speech event and any misuse of it by the lawyers, the linguist's tools and procedures include analysis of the topics and responses, speech acts, conversational strategies, pragmatic meaning, and ambiguities related to semantics, syntax, and phonetics used by all parties.

Any assessment or analysis of this courtroom interaction must begin with the fact that this is a courtroom testimony speech event, for it, like all types of speech events, prescribes what is relevant to be said at what time and in what sequence. Once the structure and sequence of this speech event are recognized, other linguistic analyses can follow, including whether there is language evidence supporting the defendant's intention, premeditation, and voluntariness. Since these important but vague terms are difficult for the law to define, the logical place to find solid footing is in the actual language used by witnesses, police, prosecutor, and the suspects themselves. The question is whether there is language evidence to support the charge that the defendants had the intention and premeditation to voluntarily carry out the murder. Another question is whether the witnesses' answers were voluntary. If the defendants' language evidence demonstrates as much, the vague terms of the law can find definition. If such language evidence does not show this, the prosecution has to develop the criminal charges out of inferences made by the police and prosecutor. When criminal charges are based on inferences, considerable room is left for juries to have reasonable doubt.

SOME PROBLEMS CONCERNING INTELLIGENCE GATHERING AND INTELLIGENCE ANALYSIS

When law enforcement officers gather intelligence and prosecutors analyze it to determine whether it is sufficient to prosecute, sometimes serious problems occur, including selecting and using only part of the language evidence; inaccurately representing the language evidence; presenting conflicting language evidence; overlooking the importance of linguistic analysis of the language evidence; and failing to recognize the coerciveness of police interactions with civilians.

1. Selecting and using only part of the language evidence

The linguist deals with the entire body of language evidence, not just the small parts of it that police interviewers consider smoking gun evidence. One question is whether the intelligence gatherers had preserved the entire evidence or just parts of it. Whereas some law enforcement agencies preserve and present the entirety of their interviews with suspects, others choose to record and preserve only those portions of the interviews in which the suspect purportedly confessed to the crime. Although linguists cannot supply evidence that hasn't been preserved, they can call attention to the parts of interviews that reveal the existence of potentially important missing language evidence. Clues to such missing evidence are sometimes found in the participants' references to something that had been said earlier but not kept as a record during these speech events. The importance of missing language evidence is seen in some of the cases described in chapters 5, 7, 8, 9, and 10.

Whereas the courts require *all* of the intelligence evidence collected by law enforcement to be turned over to the defense at a reasonable period before trial, the intelligence gathering done by the police sometimes follows a different standard in which only selected parts of the interactions with suspects are recorded and preserved. Even though undercover tape recordings gathered during an investigation must include *everything* collected, whether or not the prosecution considers it to be germane to the case, this requirement can be made meaningless if the police decide to record only parts of their intelligence-gathering operation. Such practice leaves the door open for the defense to bolster its case by using analyses of any linguistic traces or grammatical references to non-provided evidence.

Similarly, prosecutors cannot pick and choose from the existing recorded evidence only that which supports their charges against a defendant. Some prosecutors can skirt this requirement by selecting only that which they consider the "relevant" parts of the recorded conversations and, more commonly, they can isolate and use at trial only parts of the tape-recorded transcripts that they prepare for the jury to see and to use at trial. When this happens, alert defense attorneys can argue strongly and justifiably that the prosecution is responsible for the entirety of the tapes and transcripts, not just the parts they feel are "relevant." At such times the defense can reveal the evidence that the prosecution provided in discovery but omitted at trial. If such omissions are significant for the defense, the result can be embarrassing to the prosecution.

2. Inaccurately representing the language evidence

Although tape recordings are the actual evidence in trials, the government commonly prepares transcripts of the recorded language to make it easier for juries to follow. These transcripts are sometimes inaccurate in parts and linguists well trained in phonetics and sociolinguistics can often identify and correct the errors in the government-produced transcripts. The tapes cannot be altered, of course, but when the prosecution's transcripts do not accurately reflect the tape-recorded language, this enables defense attorneys, with the help of linguists, to argue for introducing their own defense transcripts. At trial, arguments often take place about whether transcripts prepared by the government or those of the defense can be used as aides for juries. When judges see and understand that the prosecution and defense transcripts are significantly different in crucial passages, they may neutrally conclude that each side can use its own transcript versions. In spite of the differences, however, some judges will allow only the prosecution's transcript and in rare cases when the tape recordings are very scratchy or unclear, judges may rule that no transcripts will be used as aides to the jury, as is seen in a case described in chapter 10.

3. Presenting conflicting language evidence

Linguists also employ the standard scientific method of comparing and contrasting different versions of the same event. For example, the linguist carefully compares the accuracy of recorded interviews with the accuracy of police reports or summaries of that same event. When an officer reports or testifies that the defendant said one thing, but the tape or government transcript indicates something different from what is in that testimony, the officer's words can be impeached.

When law enforcement officers are called as witnesses at trial, the structure of this courtroom testimony speech event is in the hands of the lawyers who question them. After establishing the officer's credentials, it is common for the prosecutor to guide them through their written reports representing the results of their interviews with witnesses and suspects. Although it can be expected that the substance of the officers' answers will match the substance of their interviews with and reports about the defendant, sometimes it doesn't, as when the officers infer something suspects said that differs from what the tape recording indicates that they actually said. Careful comparison of the two is often one of the linguist's tasks.

4. Overlooking the importance of linguistic analysis of the language evidence

Despite the abundance of language evidence that is present in most murder cases, both the defense and prosecution sometimes overlook the important potential of using a linguistic analysis. One reason for this is that the intricacies of language are not generally known or appreciated by those who are not trained in linguistics. Even more telling is that most people, especially lawyers and judges, have learned to use and understand language so well that they don't realize what it is that they don't know about the way it works. At the same time, however, it must be admitted that linguists have not made their field available enough for lawyers, juries, and judges to reap the benefits of their help. According to law professor Janet Ainsworth (2008, 1), courts in the Anglo-American legal system have generally failed to incorporate insights from pragmatics and sociolinguistics into their judicial decision making, preferring instead to impose normative judgments about how language *should* be used and interpreted by speakers and hearers. Problems occur when the courts adopt a literal, uncontextualized view of meaning that overlooks the ways that conversational implicatures and social and situational context affect the interpretation of utterances, including interpretation of the legal terms relating to mental states of all the participants, especially by law enforcement officers and the courts.

5. Failing to recognize coerciveness of police interactions with civilians

Solan and Tiersma (2005, 71) argue that police–citizen encounters are inherently coercive—a view that has significant implications for how we can understand the language produced within these encounters, including evidence of a speaker's intentionality, predisposition, and voluntariness. For example, while law enforcement officers produce utterances in their interviews with suspects and witnesses that on the surface may look like polite requests, the power asymmetry that exists between police officers and citizens can cause citizens to misinterpret such utterances as commands. This can be particularly problematic when the goal of police interviews includes determining the intentions of suspects as well as admissions of their guilt.

Linguists analyze the language evidence found in undercover tape-recorded conversations, police interrogations of suspects, and the statements and interviews of witnesses in the effort to clarify, support or reject semantic interpretations such as intention, premeditation, and voluntariness. Since most murder cases in which linguists are called to consult involve these vaguely defined legal terms, it is important to try to determine how they can or cannot be instanced in specific individual language contexts. As noted earlier, the laws and codes necessarily provide only vague prototypical definitional outlines, often trying to define with synonyms that are similarly vague or undefined. Therefore, when linguists are asked to consult with attorneys in murder cases, discovering instances in the language evidence that relate to these terms of law can become a rich source of analysis.

Using actual murder cases, the following chapters provide linguistically grounded, critical examinations that highlight the ways the necessarily vague statutory terms of *intentionality, predisposition, voluntariness,* and *reasonable doubt* can be given flesh by language evidence in murder and solicitation to murder cases.

4

LINGUISTIC PROFILING WHEN THERE IS NO KNOWN MURDER SUSPECT

As noted earlier, this book addresses three types of murder cases, the first of which involves the receipt of anonymous threat messages when law enforcement has no knowledge about who the senders might be. In such cases, law enforcement has little to go on outside of whatever clues they can get from the anonymous written or spoken language. In messages like these, the language used by the writers virtually always makes their intentions and predisposition very clear, and it's usually very obvious that the writers sent their murder threats voluntarily. Two linguistic profiling cases are described here first, because they serve as models and touchstones for how the offenders have made the critical legal terms of intentionality, predisposition, and voluntariness indisputably clear. This clarity contrasts with the relative lack of such clarity found in the other murder cases discussed in the rest of the book.

We don't know when linguistic profiling was first practiced, but its history goes back at least as far as the Old Testament of the Bible, where Judges 12 describes the aftermath of a battle in which the Gileadites had soundly defeated and killed 42,000 Ephraimites, after which they occupied and controlled the shore of the Jordon River. After the battle ended, some of the surviving Ephraimite soldiers disguised themselves as civilians and requested permission from the victorious Gileadite soldiers to let them cross the river. Suspecting that these purported civilians were really some of the surviving Ephraimite soldiers, the Gileadites devised a linguistic profile test, asking them to pronounce the word *shibboleth*. The /sh/ word initial voiceless fricative was not in the Ephraimites' language, and therefore they pronounced the word with an /s/ sound instead. The linguistic test worked, and the Gileadite soldiers slew them on the spot.

Another historically recorded case of linguistic profiling is reported to have taken place during the Revolt of the Sicilian Vespers that broke out in Palermo on Easter in 1282. The records are not totally clear and they may be less than totally factual, but it is reported that the Sicilians rebelled against the army of the French king, Charles of Anjou, who had been ruling the kingdom of Sicily for sixteen years. While Sicilians were celebrating on the night of the Vespers, some French officials joined them. A few of the Frenchmen then made sexual advances to local Sicilian women, after which the Sicilians grew angry and began to riot. Thousands of French inhabitants were slaughtered as the local Sicilians broke into French homes, businesses, and even the Franciscan and Dominican convents. In order to distinguish the local Sicilians from the unwelcome French invaders, it is said that the rebels required them to pronounce the word *ciciri* (garbanzo beans). The Sicilians then slaughtered some three thousand French men and women who couldn't pronounce the initial "c" with the proper Sicilian /ch/ sound, and after a few weeks King Charles lost control of the country (Runciman 1958, 212).

Today, linguistic profiling is based on more linguistics features than the fricative /sh/ used by the Gileadites in the word *shibboleth* and the affricate /ch/ used by the Sicilians in the word *ciciri*. Linguistic profilers now rely on research from dialect geography, lexicography, sociolinguistics, historical linguistics, and psycholinguistics, all of which use the linguistic tools of phonology, grammar, semantics, and pragmatics. Although few linguists specialize in all of these areas, an expert will know a lot about some of them and is well enough trained in the others to be able to provide helpful information to law enforcement agencies. For the past few decades, linguistic profiling has become a useful way to help law enforcement narrow down lists of suspects and, in some cases, even use it to confront suspects with these linguistic profiles as a way of convincing them to admit their crimes.

Linguistic profiling differs from behavioral profiling. It is believed that the idea of behavioral profiling originated in the Behavioral Science Laboratory of the Federal Bureau of Investigation, where specialists in psychology and criminology worked together to assess the behavioral characteristics of as yet unidentified criminals. Necessarily, the profilers base their conclusions on research information and theories of cognitive psychology, on their personal experience with previous crimes, and on their subjective interpretations based on whatever facts about a crime are available, including the type of crime and whatever physical evidence exists. Turvey (1999) warns that it is an artful process that can produce confirmation bias, because it begins by searching for proof to confirm a theory, rather than by beginning with evidence data. Even though behavioral profilers begin with little or no evidence data, their technique is believed to be valuable in some investigations and it has achieved considerable status in the area of criminology.

When individuals or organizations receive hate mail or threat messages, the FBI and nongovernment forensic psychologists may be asked to provide their behavioral profiling services. Until recent years, however, behavioral profiling had not taken full advantage of the analysis and assistance that linguistic profiling can provide.

To do linguistic profiling effectively, it helps greatly if the linguist's training and competence includes a strong background in language variation and change. In fact, the linguistic profiler would do well to have specialized in sociolinguistics, because it is the variability of language that offers many clues to the possible identity of an anonymous writer or speaker. Other types of language clues also may be evident, relating to such things as the person's political beliefs, social standing, economic status, ethnicity, and attitudes. The sole focus of linguistic profiling is to point out sociolinguistic features about suspects that their own language use suggests.

The important legal concepts of intentionality and predisposition are virtually always apparent in such threat messages, for otherwise the writers would have had no purpose for sending them. The transparency of intention and predisposition in such cases serves as a touchstone upon which the issues of intentionality and predisposition are less than clear in the thirteen murder cases described in chapters 5 through 10.

The first linguistic profiling case described here occurred in one of the most notorious murder events of the 1990s, the case of the Unabomber, a man that the FBI ultimately identified as Ted Kaczynski.

THE UNABOMBER CASE

Between 1978 and 1995, sixteen mailed packages containing homemade bombs killed three people and seriously injured twenty-three more. Until 1986 the bombs sent in intricately whittled wooden boxes had been mailed or planted in various locations in the country. Two were sent to professors in Illinois, two to professors in California, one to Yale, one to a professor in Tennessee, one to a professor at MIT, two to airline executives, and one to a California computer store. During the following seven years, no more bombs were sent. But the bombings resumed in 1993 with bombs mailed to a California geneticist, a New Jersey advertising executive, and a California lumber lobbyist. Most of the bomb packages contained short notes or letters, parts or all of which survived the explosion in one shape or another.

In the fall of 1994, FBI Special Agent Sharon Smith took my graduate seminar in linguistics and law at Georgetown University while she was working on her PhD in psychology. At that point I had been consulting with security officers of various corporations about various threat messages, and it occurred to Agent Smith that her FBI colleagues on the Unabomber Task Force might benefit from an analysis I called linguistic profiling. At that time, the FBI already had an ongoing program using psychologically based criminal profiling. This program compared the behavioral characteristics of current crime settings and types with past crimes of a similar nature in the effort to determine specific behavioral characteristics that might help them discover or narrow down lists of suspects. As mentioned above, the major difference between a psychological criminal profile and a linguistic profile is that the former makes predictions based on comparisons of the apparent behavioral characteristics of the unknown perpetrator of the current crime with the known behavioral characteristics of past similar crimes. In contrast, the findings of linguistic profiling are based entirely on existing and known spoken or written language evidence. Rather than relying on inferences about the suspect by comparing the bombings with past similar crimes, the Unabomber case provided some written texts that provided a considerable amount of physical language evidence—the messages he sent with the bombs, the letters he wrote to magazines and newspapers, and ultimately his long manifesto.

A linguistic profile does not claim to identify specific authors. Instead, it describes how the suspect's language matches social, economic, education level, and other information that previous sociolinguistic research has identified to be characteristic of specific societal groups. Its purpose is to help law enforcement narrow down its list of existing suspects or to suggest directions for locating new ones (Campbell and DeNevi 2004).

In May1995, before the Unabomber had sent his manifesto to the newspapers, Special Agent Smith approached me about the possibility of providing the FBI with a linguistic profile of the bomb messages and letters written by the then unknown Unabomber. After I agreed to do this, a group of agents met with me at my home in Washington, DC to explain the case and leave with me the brief notes the Unabomber had sent with his bombs along with some letters the Unabomber had written to several magazines and newspapers as he tried to convince them to publish his still unfinished manifesto.

On June 28, 1995, about six weeks after my first meeting with the FBI agents, both the *Washington Post* and the *New York Times* received a fifty-six-page typewritten manuscript in the mail, demanding that unless they published it, the author would "start building our next bomb." Evidence of his intentionality and predisposition could not be clearer. The writer called for a worldwide revolution against the effects of modern society's "industrial–technological system." Immediately, both newspapers turned over this manifesto to the FBI. Earlier, this anonymous author had also written similar letters to *Penthouse* magazine and *Scientific American*, saying that he intended to plant only one more bomb if they would publish his paper in serial form or as a book. At around the same time, the *San Francisco Chronicle* received an anonymous letter in which the author threatened to blow up an airliner at the Los Angeles airport. These notes, letters, and now the manifesto combined to constitute the language evidence available for producing a linguistic profile of the suspect.

Shortly after the FBI Task Force received the manifesto, they also sent it to a large number of college professors who specialized in the history of science, hoping that the language used in the manifesto would jog their minds to recall a particular student who might have written it. Searching for a former student who may have written term papers about these ideas was probably not the most efficient way to identify the criminal, and it turned out that the professors' responses were deemed to be not very helpful. On the other hand, the manifesto now provided a much larger language corpus to supplement the previous corpus of a few letters sent to magazines and the fragments of handwritten notes sent with the bombs.

Many sociolinguistic clues for identifying characteristics of the writer were evident in these writings. For example, the author wrote about going out in the "sierra" (not used as a proper noun) after a hard day's work, little realizing that such an innocuous expression could help the FBI identify Northern California as one location in his past life. On the other hand, the fact that his writings did not include other common western terms, such as "ranch," "fork" (for a branch of a stream), "gulch," "range," or "mesa," led to the suspicion that his western use of "sierra" was not native to him. His use of the Northern dialect variant, "rearing children," as opposed to the Midland dialect's "raising children" offered one of the clues that he had possibly grown up in the Northern dialect area ranging from New England to the Upper Midwest.

Another clue to the Unabomber's background location was found in some of his spellings of common words that matched those being used by the *Chicago Tribune* during the 1940s and 1950s. During this period the *Tribune*'s editor was spearheading a movement toward what he considered more standardized spellings of English, including changes in the spelling of base forms of words ending with doubled consonants, such as "willfully" changed to "wilfully," and the change in other words such as "clue" to "clew."

I was aware of this because I lived in the Chicago area in the 1950s. It is possible, if not likely, that a literate Chicago area schoolboy might well have adopted some of the *Tribune*'s spellings as his own, which is one of the reasons why my linguistic profile hypothesized that the Unabomber grew up in the Chicago area, a hypothesis that was eventually shown to be accurate.

These unconventional spellings also suggested a clue to the writer's age. If the Unabomber had grown up during the period of the *Tribune*'s spelling reforms, he would have to have been around fifty years old at the time his bombs were sent, which was verified after Ted Kaczynski was captured. Other clues about his age came from terms Kaczynski used that date a writer as having grown up in the 1960s, such as the expression "Holy Robots," borrowed from Batman's assistant, Robin, in the popular 1960s *Batman* television program. Other 1960s fad terms found in the Unabomber's writings included "playing footsy," and "working stiff."

The Unabomber's gender references indicated that he was either ignorant of or isolated from the inclusive gender reference practices that were beginning to be expected during the time of his writing. He used "he" and "him" where other writers were avoiding the masculine pronoun in references to both sexes. His sociological terms also gave clues to his age, such as his frequent use of "other directed" and his many references to individual "drives," which suggested his acquaintance with the sociology of the sixties, possibly that of David Riesman.

The Unabomber's lexicon also gave clues to his religious background, as he commonly used expressions such as "unclean thoughts," "time of troubles," "the human soul," "cradle to grave," "impersonal demon," "sin" (many times) and "God's will." He also told a parable of a weak neighbor and a strong neighbor, using language that is very similar to biblical style: "If he lets the strong man survive and only forces him to give the land back, he is a fool, because when the strong man gets it he will take again all the land for himself." His possibly Catholic background came through in his lament that modern society postpones having children, consistent with the church's ban on birth control. He argued in favor of spanking children and, in references to the sex drive, frequently mentions "sublimation" as the answer.

These language clues provided a stark contrast with the FBI's ongoing behavioral profiles. In 1980 after the first bombs were placed and exploded, the FBI's behavioral profiler opined that the murderer was eighteen to twenty-two years old, with some undergraduate education, possibly a frustrated, withdrawn college student with low self- worth, who may like to torture animals and set fires. In 1985, the FBI profile added ten or so years to the bomber's age and opined that he may be an unmarried loner working as a technician and living near the crime scenes. The FBI's revised profile in 1986 said he was probably a male in his late thirties or early forties, with two to four years of college, who changed technical jobs frequently, had a rich fantasy life, and was excessively neat and clean.

By 1993, the Unabomber had begun to write letters to magazines and newspapers under the pseudonym of Freedom Club (FC), offering them first rights to publish his still uncompleted manifesto (which he referred to as a book or a serialized essay). These letters contained language that suggested a much more educated bomber than the FBI originally thought. Now another revised FBI profile said he was a loner who was highly intelligent, technically competent, and a voracious reader in the areas of science, history, psychology, and the social sciences. It is difficult to know what this profile meant when it added that he had high self-esteem but low self-concept.

In 1995, at about the time the FBI had received my linguistic profile, the previous versions of the FBI behavioral profile continued to evolve. More in keeping with my linguistic profile, the FBI now suggested his age as between forty and fifty, but it held fast to his education being that of a high school graduate with some college and trade school training. My linguistic profile may have convinced them about the bomber's place of origin, however, for that version of the FBI's profile said the Unabomber lived, worked, attended school, or made extensive visits to the Chicago area. The profile continued, however, that he was a loner with low self-esteem but at the same time had a strong sense of superiority and had spent some time on a college campus.

The letters the Unabomber sent to magazines suggested that he was a well-educated person (a fact that became more apparent after the *New York Times* and *Washington Post* later published his manifesto). In those letters he used a learned vocabulary, including words such as "surrogate," "oversocialization," and "tautology," along with complex grammar (including the subjunctive), and most of the times wrote in a rather lucid style. Whatever one might think of his radical ideas, his sequential organization of these ideas was usually logical, and he gave evidence of having read enough into such fields as history, archaeology, and sociology to feel that he had the right to discount the contributions that scholars in these fields had made about the "well-being of the human race." On the other hand, the references he cited usually were not up-to-date, his uses of punctuation and spelling would not be acceptable in the humanities or social sciences, and he shifted back and forth from the scholarly to the casual styles in a less-than-expected scholarly fashion. He was clearly a well-educated man whose writing would need a considerable amount of editorial help if it would ever become publishable. It was clear that his writing style would not pass muster in the humanities or social sciences but might with some help get by in a hard science. This suggested that his academic background was likely in the hard sciences (it turned out to be mathematics).

He took a dim view of college professors, calling them "university intellectuals" and noting in one letter, "people with advanced degrees aren't as smart as they think they are." It was apparent that if Kaczynski was himself a college professor, he certainly did not think much of his peers and he had no empathy for the profession. The fact that his manifesto contained references to books and articles without indicating dates or publishers suggested that he was no longer associated with the university life and that he had little access to academic libraries. In truth, there were no such libraries in or near where he then lived in the very rural area of Lincoln, Montana.

The Unabomber's writing, therefore, provided some reasonably useful clues about his education, age, occupation, religion, and geographical background, along with a broad sense of his personal life. As it turns out, he had indeed been a college professor at one time, was Catholic, grew up in Chicago, was about fifty years old, once lived in Northern California, and because he eventually chose to live in rural Montana, he no longer had access to his much needed up-to-date academic library resources.

Linguistic profiling is a humble task that makes no claim to be able to provide exact identification of suspects. It simply can't do this, and my linguistic profile of the Unabomber was no exception. It had absolutely nothing to do with Ted Kaczynski's ultimate capture. The credit for this, of course, goes to his brother David and David's wife, who noticed that the topics and ideas in the manifesto were similar to those in the letters that Ted had written to them, after which David heroically identified his brother and pointed out exactly where he was currently living in Montana. Not many murder cases have the advantage of a close relative available to compare the topics and ideas of two sets of written texts in this way. FBI agent James Fitzgerald confirmed this during the subsequent legal process. Whether or not the information produced by David Kaczynski and his wife could be considered a linguistic profile, it certainly did the much needed job.

Even though linguistic profiling turned out to have nothing much to do with Ted Kaczynski's capture, this case still illustrates one way that it's possible for linguistic profiling to assist law enforcement. Here, the task was to compare the note fragments, letters to the media, and manifesto in order to try to discover clues that might help the FBI seek a single anonymous writer among 300 million potential American suspects.

The more common use of linguistic profiling occurs when several suspected authors of messages are already on the radar screen of law enforcement. Comparison of such evidence documents can be a useful way to determine which of the suspects is the more feasible one to pursue. In this sense, linguistic profiling is not the same as conventional authorship analysis, which attempts to identify authors of anonymous documents. The current conventional approaches to authorship identification are (1) stylistic comparisons of known and unknown writers that focus on language features such as lexicon, morphology, usage, and punctuation (McMenamin 1993; 2002), and (2) statistically oriented approaches that focus primarily on syntax (Chaski 2001). Since the Unabomber case had language evidence from only one unknown writer, conventional authorship analysis comparisons were neither relevant nor useful. The only product possible was a linguistic profile, which by definition could not identify a single, specific murderer but rather could discover clues about the general characteristics of such a writer so that law enforcement might be better informed about what type of person to look for.

Aftermath

Thanks to his brother, the FBI located Ted Kaczynski at his Lincoln, Montana cabin and arrested him immediately. Ted was later tried for murder, found guilty, and sentenced to life in prison. I include this case here because his writings clearly indicated his intentionality and predisposition to kill people, and there was no question that he wrote these things voluntarily.

As an ironic side note, a month or so after I submitted my linguistic profile to the FBI, I retired from teaching at Georgetown University and moved to Missoula, Montana, only about sixty miles from where Ted Kaczynski had been living in a simple cabin in the woods. It may have looked like I had some idea of where he was. As a matter of full disclosure, I most certainly did not.

GARY, INDIANA WOMEN'S MEDICAL CLINIC

In some cases in which there is language evidence to compare threat messages with the writings of possible suspects, linguistic profiles can also offer a range of possible clues, including the writer's ethnicity. A murder threat that took place in Gary, Indiana provides an example of how such clues to ethnicity played a significant role in helping to resolve the case. It began when over a period of three weeks, an anonymous writer had sent three carefully typewritten bomb threat messages to the director of a women's medical health clinic.

Women's medical clinics that perform abortions sometimes become targets of fierce opposition, but this clinic did not do abortions, removing this as the threat writer's possible motive. Baffled by the case, the Gary police called in the FBI to help them, after which the special agent in charge asked me for whatever assistance I could provide. Since there were no comparison documents to analyze, the conventional authorship analysis approach was not relevant. Instead, this case called for a linguistic profile of the apparently lone threat writer.

As I examined the three long and rambling threat messages, the language used in them made it clear that the writer provided an undeniable intention and predisposition to kill everyone in the building when it was to be bombed. Further examination made it evident that the writer was well educated and used English in a way that was mostly consistent with that of a native speaker of American English but was also inconsistent in other small ways. For one thing, the writer used the adjective "proper" in expressions such as "she did not give a *proper* exam" and "she was not given *proper* care." Since this adjective is used in this context far more by British speakers than by Americans, its presence here suggested that the author had a British English background, as opposed to that of most American English speakers. Also consistent with a writer of British background was the spelling of the noun "device" as "devise."

In addition, the bomb threat letters contained syntax that used subject-object-verb sequences several times, as in "she will finally the seriousness of the problem recognize," where the expected English syntactic pattern of subject-verb-object would have been "she will finally recognize the seriousness of the problem." The bomb threat messages also contained more repetition for emphasis than would be used by most American writers, and the messages often deleted articles that both American and British speakers would use habitually, as in the writer's missing "the" in "you know time is soon" and the missing article "a" in "you can be transferred to better position" and "I will not give warning."

In addition, the writer sometimes omitted prepositions and pronouns where English syntax expects them, as in "if I address it [to] her," and "you should change [your] place of employment." These linguistic features all suggested a writer who could have been educated in a former British colony, such as Pakistan, where the remnants of Hindi–Urdu subject-object-verb syntax, article deletion, and pronoun deletion might remain along with telltale elements of British English.

Although research on gender differences is fairly recent and is by no means complete, some findings are believed to characterize female language, such as frequent tentativeness and hedging; indirectness; the use of politeness markers and formal reference terms such as "Ms." and "Mr."; frequent use of "so" intensifiers with emotional import such as "I'm so happy"; certain adverbs such as "surely"; certain characteristically female adjectives such as "lovely," "charming," and "delightful"; and a tendency to miniaturize, as in "our nice little home," "her little black dress," or "the child's tiny hands." In addition, female writers are said to focus more on the feelings of the people being mentioned, while males are purported to be less concerned about recipients' feelings.

This bomb threat writer used many tentative and hedged expressions such as "it seems like," "she seemed confused," and "I suppose I should have." The writer even justified writing the letters by explaining that this was done "on the advice" of others, a justification that more assertive male threat givers might not be as likely to believe necessary. The writer also relied heavily on expressions of feeling, such as "I felt completed," "I deeply regret," "my hopes were crushed," and "I was so upset." The writer politely thanked the reader for taking the time to read the letter and apologized for being a bother while also saying "please" many times and, very oddly for a bomb threat letter, explaining that he or she had no desire to hurt anyone. Also evident was the "so" emotional intensifier in expressions such as, "I was so upset" and "there is so much danger in your clinic" and empathetic expressions such as, "you are surely in harm's way" and "how sad for you." Since it is difficult to imagine that most male threat writers would use such language, I hypothesized that the author appeared to be female.

The FBI had already interviewed all ten of the employees at that clinic, thinking perhaps that the threats may have been the result of some internal conflict, but their interviews yielded nothing suspicious. Because at this point the FBI had no identifiable suspects in the case and they had no comparison documents, I suggested that they start by going back to the ten employees and asking them and the director to write narratives telling everything they did, saw, felt, and thought from the time they got up in the morning until they went to bed on the day that the most recent bomb threat appeared. In contrast with the FBI's previous interviews, I was more interested in how the employees said things than in the content of what they might say. I wanted to look for linguistic clues that might match those of the language of the writer of the bomb threats. Thus, the original linguistic profile was transformed into a type of authorship identification analysis.

One of these writing samples produced by this exercise stood out strongly with language features that were very similar to those found in the bomb threats. Although the FBI knew the identities of each of the writers, I had asked to be intentionally blinded to this information. The FBI agents were surprised (but no more than I) when my analysis demonstrated a very good match between the language of the threat messages and the writing sample composed by the female director of the clinic, the very person who originally reported this matter to the police. She had grown up in Pakistan, where she spoke both Urdu and English and went to British schools, leaving the abovementioned clear ethnic traces of this in her three threat messages. What had started out to be a task of linguistic profiling ended up fulfilling the task of authorship identification.

Not being linguists, the law enforcement agencies did not notice the Hindi–Urdu, British English, and female style clues in the three bomb threat letters, nor did they associate them with the language of the clinic director. Linguists trained in ethnic variability can do this. There could be no question about the intentionality and predisposition of the writer, who obviously also wrote these threats voluntarily.

Aftermath

When I submitted my analysis, the FBI agents were baffled about any motive that the director, a physician, might have had to send these bomb threat messages to herself. When the supervising agent showed the clinic director how my linguistic profile matched her own writing sample, she confessed immediately and also revealed her motive for writing those threats. She tearfully explained that her husband had been studying medicine at a California medical school, where recently he had failed his exams. She admitted that she wanted to move back to California to help her husband study to retake the exams and finish his medical training. Apparently she could think of no other excuse to do this than to invent a bomb threat scenario that she felt would be an adequate explanation for her to close the clinic and move back home with her husband. The empathetic expressions to the alleged victims of the bombing were clearly uncharacteristic of conventional threat messages. The FBI concluded that the director had no real intention to kill anyone and since no physical harm occurred, no criminal charges were brought against her.

In most linguistic profiling cases, there is usually no question about the intention, predisposition, or voluntariness of the sender of the anonymous messages. On its surface, the language of the threat messages in the Gary clinic bomb threats appeared to provide clear evidence of the suspect's purported intentionality and predisposition to kill people. Although this is true of virtually all threat messages, in this case the investigators subsequently concluded that although the director wrote the threats voluntarily, she did not actually have the intention or predisposition to kill anyone.

The language evidence can be very different in solicitation to murder cases, when the targets still are only suspects and the government's task is to determine intentionality and predisposition that is elicited voluntarily. Even when murder suspects are in custody where the primary task is to elicit a confession, it is the language used by the suspects, police interviewers, and lawyers that frames the issues of intentionality, predisposition, and voluntariness.

The rest of this book describes thirteen murder cases in which law enforcement provided known suspects and defendants for whose cases the legal terms intentionality, predisposition, and voluntariness were not nearly as clearly represented as they are in most threat message cases.

5

INTENTIONALITY AND PREDISPOSITION IN MURDER CASES

Clear intentionality, predisposition, and voluntariness of the writers of most anonymous threat messages can serve as touchstones or comparisons for solicitation to murder cases in which intentionality and predisposition are less apparent to law enforcement and sometimes can only be inferred. As noted in chapter 3, it is rare that any evidence about intention exists during the four phases of thinking about, building resolve, planning, and carrying out a murder. The situation is a bit different in solicitation to murder cases, however, especially when conversations between suspects and undercover agents either demonstrate or fail to demonstrate the suspect's intent and predisposition. Because recorded language evidence exists in such conversations, the door is open for linguistic analysis about the accuracy of the government's charges, especially when the prosecution infers predisposition and intent that is not indicated in the actual language evidence. There are several ways that the prosecution can mistakenly infer the intentions and predispositions of suspects, as the three solicitation to murder cases described in this chapter illustrate.

Since Husserl (1963), philosophers of language have agreed that for an utterance to have meaning, we must assume a context that includes the writer's or speaker's intention. Tyler (1978) observed, "When intentions are unclearly revealed, we *assume* a context which included the author's intention" (385). To discover whether or not such assumptions are accurate, I suggest that it is best for the analysis to be accountable for the entire context, beginning by identifying the speech event, then noting the schemas and agendas, then the speech acts and conversational strategies, and finally the smaller units of language, where linguistic analysis can help resolve grammatical, semantic, pragmatic, and phonetic ambiguities. Knowing what is meant by intentions, predisposition, and voluntariness involves all levels of language, not just the alleged smoking guns found in contextually isolated words and phrases.

Levinson (1992, 15–16) argues that intentions are closely linked to effective communication: "Communication involves the notion of intention and agency, and only those inferences that are openly intended to be conveyed can be properly said to have been communicated." He goes on to say that understanding intention is satisfied only when the sender's communicative intention becomes mutual knowledge to both the sender and the receiver.

In murder cases, mutual knowledge of the intentions of suspects and the law enforcement representatives with whom they talk is not always easy for the participants to discover or for later listeners to understand. For one thing, as Solan observes, people are more likely to attribute bad intentions to those people whose actions appear to lead to bad results than to people whose actions appear to lead to good results. He adds that our bias toward blame derives from our tendency to expect the good. When bad acts happen, it is easy for us to use our sense of morality to infer that people suspected of being bad actors automatically are guilty (Solan 2009, 517–518). It's even easier for law enforcement and the courts to do this, for their professional vision leads them naturally in that direction.

As noted in chapter 3, the terms that figure strongly in murder law, *intention* and *predisposition,* refer to mental states that typically have to be inferred, which makes their exact meaning extremely difficult to identify unless there is convincing, illustrative, and definitive evidence of this intended meaning found in actual language contexts. The most convincing indication of intent, of course, occurs when a person says explicitly and performatively, "I intended to do X." But performative statements like this are not frequent in murder cases—or anywhere else in life.

When criminals do something illegal, it's easy to think that they genuinely intend to do what they do. Often this is true, but occasionally they do it without really intending to. We recognize this concept more easily in some acts than in others. For example, in most fatal automobile accidents we tend to assume that the person guilty of causing the accident may have been reckless or negligent but did not necessarily cause the accident with intentionality and predisposition. In contrast, most murder cases include the assumptions of intentionality and predisposition that are just the opposite and often quite rightly so. The fact that statutes specify different degrees of murder, including manslaughter and reckless homicide, is a recognition that an intention to kill is not always present in persons who cause a victim's death.

Closely related to *intention* and *predisposition* are the inferences and interpretations that law enforcement officers, prosecutors, and judges need to make about the mental states of *malice aforethought, heat of passion,* and *recklessness.* As important as these mental states are, they relate primarily to the degrees of murder, which is not the focus of this book.

It is not surprising that statutes and dictionaries have difficulty trying to define mental states such as intention and predisposition. Philosophers of language have argued about intentionality for decades. John Searle's book *Intentionality* (1983) summarizes philosophical thought about intentionality and then provides the author's own analysis of the relationship between language and intentions, beginning with the fact that the social phenomenon of language derives from the intentionality of the mind.

Searle postulates that not all mental states and events involve intentionality. For example, "beliefs, fears, hopes, and desires are intentional, but there are forms of nervousness, elation, and undirected anxiety that are not intentional" (Searle 1983, 1). The latter are states that do not intend anything, whereas mental states are intentional performances (Searle 1983, 27). As will be seen in chapter 10, it is not uncommon for law enforcement officers to misunderstand nervousness and anxiety as evidence of guilt.

Except for unintentional actions, as when orthodox Muslims or Jews accidentally eat pork thinking it is chicken, there normally are no actions without corresponding intentions (Searle 1983, 82). The problem is that many actions people perform are done spontaneously, without forming any prior intention or predisposition to carry them out. Similarly, people can have a prior intention or predisposition to do something without ever acting on it. Even intentional acts, such as hitting a person who has grievously offended you, can be accomplished without prior intention or premeditation to perform such acts.

Knowledge aforethought is an equally relevant expression of the suspect's mental state. People can know that something will be the consequence of their action even when that consequence is not their intention. As an illustration of this, Searle cites the case of dentists who know (have knowledge aforethought) that when they drill their patients' teeth, this act will cause the patients pain, even though it is not the dentists' intentions to cause that pain (Searle 1983, 103).

The thesis of this book comports with Searle's observation that the intention of an action is identified by the intentional content (result) of that action, especially as it is revealed by its best indicator, language. Searle, a language philosopher, was referring to language when he said that identification of an intention can be satisfied "if the action represented by the content of the intention is actually performed" (Searle 1983, 79). It is also consistent with linguists who view the meanings of abstract words as semantic prototypes with blurry edges as well as with Kant's view that concepts without percepts are empty.

Tiersma (1986, 222–232) discusses *intention* from the perspective of speech act theory, noting that courtroom debates are often about a speaker's intention but without any language evidence of that intention. Following Austin (1979) Tiersma argues that intentions are mental states in which an explicit expression of that intention matters most (similar to Searle's "intentional content" and Kant's "percept"). Tiersma also points out that unless there is such explicit language available that can illuminate speakers' intentions, we are left without conclusive evidence of what the speakers' intentions really were. He argues that intentions are mental states including the predisposition to carry out a future act such as murder, but even speakers' mental states about carrying out a future act do not reveal their actual intentions to carry it out. Instead, we need to know a speaker's illocutionary intent, which means that the speaker's utterances are intended to produce on hearers the illocutionary effect of what such speakers are saying. This understanding of the speakers' illocutionary effects requires the existence of actual language expressions of speakers' mental states rather than reliance on inferences made by law enforcement, prosecutors, juries, or anyone else. When language evidence does exist, this is an area in which linguistic analysis can be most helpful. Without such language evidence, jurors have to rely on inferences and apply the "reasonable man" principle to come to their conclusions about guilt or innocence.

This chapter describes three solicitation to murder cases that center on controversies about the suspects' predisposition and intentionality. In each case there was considerable language evidence to enlighten those issues.

THE STATE OF TEXAS V. T. CULLEN DAVIS

When people commit murder without leaving notes, diaries, or conversations with associates, law enforcement usually has to infer the suspects' intention and premeditation based on assumptions about the means, method, and opportunity of carrying out the murder. However, proving intention and predisposition in solicitation to murder cases can get sticky when the suspects believe they were in a speech event that differs from the one understood by the undercover agent and the prosecution.

One noteworthy example of this was the solicitation to murder case of a millionaire owner of an oil equipment company in Fort Worth, Texas, T. Cullen Davis. In *Creating Language Crimes* (2005) I detailed the cooperating witness's use of various conversational strategies that cleverly made his undercover-recorded conversation look like a speech event in which Davis had recruited him to find a hit man to kill his wife. However, linguistic analysis of the language evidence in this purported solicitation to murder case demonstrated that the cooperating witness tried to manipulate the conversation to make it look as though Davis wanted to have a hit man kill several people. Careful dissection of the recorded conversation further revealed that Davis had a very different intention and predisposition from soliciting murder. Discovering this was not a matter of getting into Davis's mind, for there is no way that linguists or anyone else can do this. Nor was it based merely on inferences. Instead, it was a matter of carefully analyzing the government's own evidence—the recorded language that was used by both men.

The police had a very logical reason to infer that Davis was predisposed to want his wife killed. Davis's marriage to Priscilla had fallen on rocky times and eventually they separated, with Davis moving out of their home that everyone in Fort Worth, Texas still refers to as "the mansion." Shortly after Davis and Pricilla separated, a masked man broke into the house one night, shooting and killing both Pricilla's new live-in boyfriend and her daughter by a previous relationship, at the same time superficially wounding Priscilla in the process. Even though she could never positively identify the shooter's masked face, Pricilla subsequently testified that she knew this person was Davis. A couple of her friends who allegedly were somewhere near the vicinity of the mansion claimed that they saw a masked man leave the scene and they corroborated Priscilla's identification, even though their ability to identify Davis was equally handicapped by the ski mask covering the man's face. A year later, based on this less than convincing eyewitness testimony and with the prosecutor's inference about Davis's predisposition and intention, Davis was tried for murder but was quickly acquitted by the jury. Premeditation and intention could not be proved, and it turned out to be a bad day for the prosecutor, who had political aspirations that could be enhanced greatly if he got a conviction of this rather famous Texan.

Not surprisingly, soon after the murder trial ended, Davis filed for divorce. As the divorce process moved slowly along, rumors spread that Priscilla was being intimate with the judge who presided over their divorce proceedings. Now law enforcement had a new logical reason to infer that Davis might want his wife dead, and so the prosecutor made that inference. But things didn't go quite the way the prosecution expected.

Meanwhile, in an effort to get the goods on Priscilla's liaisons with the judge, Davis asked a midlevel employee in his company to spy on their activities and report back to him what he found. For reasons that were never made clear, that employee went straight to the police and told them that Davis had asked him to find a hit man to kill Priscilla, the judge, and the corroborating witnesses at his previous murder trial. The police then wired the employee up with a body microphone and sent him off to talk with Davis and capture tape-recorded language evidence of this alleged solicitation to murder.

That tape became the major evidence used at Davis's subsequent trial for soliciting murder. The smoking gun evidence was part of a conversation between Davis and his employee, which was made in Davis's car in a Fort Worth parking lot. And even before the trial began, the prosecution leaked portions of a transcript of that conversation to the press. The following alleged smoking gun passage appeared in the local newspapers:

EMPLOYEE: I got Judge Eidson dead for you.
DAVIS: Good.
EMPLOYEE: I'll get the rest of them for you. You want a bunch of people dead, right?
DAVIS: Alright, but—

Interestingly, the newspapers chose not to include the exchange that immediately followed the above point at which Davis was interrupted:

EMPLOYEE: Help me too.
DAVIS: I got to have an alibi ready for Art when the subject comes up. So give me some advance warning.
EMPLOYEE: I will. I gotta go.
[End of conversation]

Lawyers for the defense sensed that something was wrong with the prosecution's interpretation of this passage and called me to analyze the tape to try to determine whether or not this exchange allegedly about soliciting murder was what the prosecution believed it was.

The first step in any such analysis begins with the speech event itself. The question was whether this really was a solicitation to murder speech event in which the employee was reporting the status of his progress in getting a hit man to kill the judge or whether it was something else. Often linguistic expert witnesses are not given all of the information that supports the defense case. This can be good, because it helps prevent the expert from being tempted to become an advocate. In this case the defense lawyers withheld from me the information that Davis previously had asked his employee to spy on Priscilla and the judge. In fact, I didn't learn about this until after the trial was over.

Even without this knowledge, however, I noticed that the conversation had some unusual characteristics that didn't seem to fit a solicitation to murder speech event. For one thing, the intonation and pace of Davis's allegedly critical responses, "good" and "alright," cited in the passage above were not enthusiastic responses to his employee's statements about getting people dead. In addition, Davis's timing was slightly off, and when I listened to the whole taped conversation, I noted that this segment actually was part of a longer topic about a man named Art, which on the surface at least seemed to be unconnected to Davis's soliciting the murder of Priscilla and the judge.

It was only after I testified at trial that I learned that Art was the employee's immediate boss in Davis's company and that Art had complained to his own boss, Davis, that this employee was taking too much time off work. Absent this knowledge, it made no sense that Davis would need to provide an alibi for the employee's missing work time, since finding hit men can be done during off-work hours. In contrast, spying on Davis's wife and the judge would be more time consuming and would therefore be more consistent with Art's complaint to Davis about the employee missing so much work. But since I wasn't told about this matter of spying on the judge and Priscilla, I soldiered on with my analysis without knowing who Art was or what role he played in all this.

Correcting the transcript and topic analysis

As always, an early linguistic task is to determine the accuracy of the government's transcript. The conversation was fast paced and full of interruptions and overlaps, and the recording quality did not make it easy to hear. I listened to it many times with better equipment and listening skills than those of the government and I was able to correct the prosecution's transcript in many places, including the crucial passage that was leaked to the press. Next, knowing that isolated "smoking gun" passages extracted from the entire conversation can be misleading, I did a topic analysis of the entire tape, after which it became clear that the passage cited by the press occurred as a small portion of an ongoing topic about Art, which topic the employee had himself introduced. After the employee brought up the topic of Art, Davis responded:

> DAVIS: I told him that, uh, to treat you like any other employee and so don't give me too much pressure in that regard. I can't say you're gonna be gone a day or two every week or so.

It is important to report that the government also was videotaping this conversation from a van parked across from Davis's car. The year was 1978, and the recording equipment used by the police was still rather primitive. The audio track on the video recording was weak and very hard to hear, but after listening to it numerous times, enough of it was audible for me to correlate its timing with the somewhat clearer recording made simultaneously by the body mike that the FBI had hidden under the employee's shirt.

Nothing remotely incriminating had been said up to that point in the conversation, at which time Davis suddenly got out of his car and walked back to the trunk, muttering that he needed to get his sunglasses. The video showed that the employee took advantage of Davis's distance from his concealed body mike, lowered his voice considerably, and began a monologue that Davis would not likely be able to hear. Meanwhile, just as the employee began to talk, Davis got out of the front seat of the car, still continuing to talk a bit louder to the employee about Art, their ongoing topic. Since there is considerable overlapping speech in this brief exchange (noted by the brackets below), I presented a transcript of it to the jury in two columns:

Davis	Employee
Davis is out of the car and walking toward the trunk	
	Well look, this fuckin' murder business—
You better—	
	—is a tough son of a bitch
alright	
	Now you got me into this
[give me,]	[into this goddamn deal.]
[give me]	[Right?]
good (inaudible)	
	I'll get the rest of them dead for you. You want a bunch of people dead, right?

Alright, but I	
[uh, you know,]	[di- di-]
	Help me too
[inaudible]	[okay?]
I got to have an alibi	
Ready for Art when the—	
	Okay?
—when the subject comes	
[up]	[alright.]
Davis returns to the front door of the car	
So give me some advance notice	
	I will. I gotta go.
The employee then exits the car and the conversation ends	

When I testified at trial, I asked the jury to read down Davis's side of the exchange and see for themselves that he continued on the topic of their ongoing conversation about Art. Then I had them read down the employee's side of the chart showing that he was talking about murder, a very different topic from Davis's. Thus, here we had two simultaneous and very different conversational topics. It was only by chance that Davis's crucial words "good" and "right" appeared at places where the government inferred that these words were responses to the employee's statements. The employee thought he got what he needed, so he then used the hit-and-run conversational strategy "I gotta go" before anything else could be said that might clarify things.

Linguistic analysis demonstrated that Davis's actual intention and predisposition could be discovered in the government's own taped evidence.

Unfortunately for the prosecution, the conversation on the tape didn't comport with their transcript of it. The topics a speaker introduces and responds to in a conversation are the best available clues to that speaker's agenda, in this case revealing strong clues about what was going on in Davis's mind. In fact, the two men were in two different speech events at the same time, which showed that Davis's intention and predisposition related to the benign topic of the employee's task of spying on Priscilla and the judge, rather than the inculpatory topic about soliciting their murder.

Aftermath

This case was a classic example of the prosecutor's inferring the wrong predisposition and intention of Davis, based on his failure to recognize the trickery in the confidential informant's effort to produce a speech event that Davis did not recognize. Subsequently the jury acquitted Davis of all charges. The prosecutor, who had hoped that winning this case might propel him into the opportunity to be elected Texas attorney general, was devastated by the results. After the trial ended, the newspapers reported that the prosecutor began to see Priscilla on a romantic basis. A few months later, the press reported that while he was taking her to a Thanksgiving Day dinner, he accidentally shot himself in the foot with a gun that he carried in his car.

THE CROWN V. MOHAMMED ARSHAD

The prosecution's inferences concerning Davis's anger and frustration with his wife for having romantic associations with their divorce court judge was, in many ways, similar to the inferences the prosecutor made about the anger and frustration of a Pakistani father, Mohammed Arshad, who had recently migrated to Dundee, Scotland with his wife and three adult daughters (details of this case can be found in *Creating Language Crimes*, 2005). As a Muslim, Arshad's problem stemmed from his culture and belief that his twenty-four-year-old middle daughter could not get married earlier than her twenty-six-year-old older sister and that the marriages of his daughters must be arranged by their parents in order to ensure they married men who came from an appropriate social strata. In Arshad's culture if a younger daughter should marry before her older sister, the older unmarried daughter was then thought to be doomed to a life of spinsterhood, and it was unthinkable for daughters to marry below their family's caste.

Therefore, Arshad became very angry and frustrated when his youngest daughter violated the required age sequence of marriageable daughters and ran off to marry a man that was not of suitable character and caste. Even more troubling to him was that the new couple had disappeared and would not even telephone him. One day he complained about this to a friend, who offered to find someone who, as he said, "could help you with your problem." Soon after that conversation, a man named Peter called Arshad and explained, "I can help you with your problem." Neither man mentioned the nature of Arshad's "problem" in this call, but the prosecution inferred that the "problem" was his new son-in-law and that Arshad intended for him to be killed. Then, not realizing that Peter was an undercover policeman pretending to be a hit man, Arshad agreed to meet with him.

In this case the entire evidence for solicitation to murder was derived from two following tape-recorded meetings of Arshad and Peter, in which the policeman kindled Arshad's anger at his daughter's new husband to the extent that Arshad's intention might seem to be consonant with hiring someone to murder the husband. But was that his actual intention? The tape-recorded evidence revealed that Arshad was not specific or even decisive when he said he wanted "something to be done" that could bring his daughter home to him and have her marriage annulled. Policeman Peter's language suggested that he inferred that Arshad was talking about murdering the husband. Arshad's language indicated that he thought the topic was about Peter doing some private investigating that would have less drastic results. The following demonstrates these conflicting versions of Arshad's intent and predisposition.

Since this conversation follows the business transaction speech event with its five phases described earlier, it can be analyzed in this way.

Problem phase

> Arshad: My daughter has been seeing someone without my knowledge and they went and got married...This guy is not letting her speak to me...I get threatened by it...I want to have him not out of the picture, still in the picture, but not in a moveable way...I want him removed so nobody knows where he is.

Here Arshad clearly outlined his problem and indicated a desired result that fell short of soliciting murder. His expressions "not out of the picture" and "still in the picture but not in a moveable way" were confusingly vague, and his "I want him removed so nobody knows where he is" was a less than specific indication of intent to have him murdered.

Proposed negotiation phase

In what can be considered the negotiation phase, the men discussed the issue further, while Arshad's anger and frustration increased to the point that he said: "I want him removed so nobody knows where he is...he's got to be removed from this earth." Then, after more encouragement from Peter, Arshad blurted out: "But the body has to be seen by the parents or whoever but he does not exist any longer."

Ambiguity of verb references

Arshad's use of "the body" obviously suggested murder to the policeman, but they had still not reached the offer stage of this speech event, so Peter then probed for it by picking up on Arshad's use of "the body" and starting the negotiation with an action falling short of murder: "Okay, what sort of injury are you thinking to his family?" Rather than answering this question, Arshad then repeated his frustration in detail, adding that he thought his daughter was "very frightened." Perhaps realizing that he had still not received the answer he needed, the policeman continued: "What do you want to happen to him then?" Arshad replied, "He has got to go." The policeman asked if this meant "you want him to die?" but Arshad's answer only repeated the same unspecific phrase, "He's got to go."

Ambiguity of noun references

Since they were now at an impasse and the offer phase of this speech event was still unclear about what "he's got to go" meant, Peter switched the topic to methodology, asking, "How do you want this done?" Arshad was silent for thirteen seconds, after which Peter asked, "What have you thought?" An answer to this question might certainly be expected to show Arshad's intention and predisposition. But again Arshad did not tell him anything specific, so the policeman recycled Arshad's earlier use of the word "body" and explained that if the new husband simply "disappeared from this earth," Arshad's daughter would have to keep on waiting for him to return and therefore she would be unlikely to come back home to her family. Since Arshad apparently had not thought this through, Peter used the conversational strategy of scripting him to understand that it would work out better if her husband's body was found.

Meanwhile, Arshad became even more emotionally agitated and explained that he had himself once thought of buying a gun with a silencer, although he didn't say what he planned to do with that gun. Because the conversation had still not yielded the quid pro quo offer that the policeman was looking for, he switched his topic back to the idea that Arshad began with—the need to locate his daughter. Without being explicit, Peter now volunteered to be the private investigator who would locate the couple, asking, "Is that why you're talking to me? I think you leave that to me."

Ambiguity of pronoun references

Still not explicitly referring to murder, Peter asked Arshad, "Are you sure you want *this* done?" Arshad answered, "I am two hundred percent sure," which grammatically referred to their ongoing topic of searching for and locating Arshad's daughter. Either missing or ignoring this grammatical reference, the policeman associated Arshad's response to his "this" to killing the husband. He then moved immediately to the topic of what "it" would cost to do such a "big thing," which added a second vague reference, "big thing," to his preceding ambiguous "it." Arshad responded that his friend had told him "it" would cost about 500 pounds. Note that this amount is consistent with the cost of an investigation done by a private detective but inconsistent with the ongoing rate of a hit man.

Now that Peter inferred that they were both talking about a hit, he warned that they didn't want to "attract the attention of the police" about "this" and "the deal." Continuing vaguely, Peter added, "We have to find them and we have to do that side of it and then we have to carry it out." Perhaps in Peter's mind, he had now clarified that "that side of it" referred to locating Arshad's daughter, while "to carry it out" referred to killing the husband. The legal question here was what Arshad understood based on Peter's vagueness. Intentions are useless diagnostics unless the meaning is clear to both parties.

Completion phase

Since the policeman apparently thought that Arshad had made his offer to carry out the hit, he then recycled the topic of the price, now suggesting 5,000 pounds. Recalling that his friend had told him "it" would cost about 500 pounds, Arshad quickly rejected Peter's suggestion, saying, "Thanks for your time anyway." Peter gradually reduced his price to 3,000 pounds and requested 200 pounds in advance.

Although Arshad clearly agreed with 200 pounds and although his agreement presumably satisfied the completion phase of this speech event, an important question remained about exactly what the job was he had just agreed with. The prosecution believed that he had agreed to have his daughter's husband murdered. The defense believed that he had agreed to have Peter carry out an investigation that would locate his daughter and bring her home to him.

Analysis of the language evidence in this case centered directly on the legal terms *intention* and *predisposition*. The prosecution believed these terms related to soliciting murder and the defense believed they related to locating the missing couple. In terms of the structure of a murder speech event, however, its vagueness made it neither complete nor satisfactory evidence of soliciting murder. If the prosecutor had done a satisfactory intelligence analysis of the actual language used by both parties, it's at least possible that he would not have indicted Arshad.

Aftermath

I was prepared to testify about these things at Arshad's trial, but two days before it was to start, I was hospitalized and had surgery.

Arshad's lawyer pleaded for a postponement, but the judge denied it. Apparently the defense attorney was unable to communicate my analysis during the trial. The Dundee jury subsequently found Arshad guilty of soliciting murder.

THE STATE OF WASHINGTON V. MICHAEL MOCKOVAC

The solicitation to murder statute relates to someone who has the intention and predisposition to commit murder. The circumstances strongly corroborate that intention and predisposition if that suspect solicits, commands, induces, or otherwise endeavors to persuade another person to engage in such conduct. These conditions directly related to a 2011 solicitation to murder case of defendant Dr. Michael Mockovac, a prominent eye surgeon whose main office was located in an upscale Seattle, Washington suburb.

The prosecution believed that Mockovac clearly and indisputably asked his friend, the business manager for his company, to locate and hire a hit man to murder the physician who with Mockovac was co-owner of their eye surgery corporation. In fact, the undercover tape recording showed that Mockovac eventually did exactly that. Despite this evidence, Mockovac's defense lawyers believed the tape recordings that provided the major evidence in this case might give them an opportunity to use the entrapment defense, as described in chapter 2. The judge's jury instruction about entrapment in this case was the following:

> Entrapment is a defense to a charge of Solicitation to Commit Murder in the First Degree if the criminal design originated in the mind of law enforcement officials, or any person acting

> under their direction, and the defendant was lured or induced to commit a crime that he had not otherwise intended to commit.
>
> The defense is not established if the law enforcement officials did not more than afford the defendant an opportunity to commit a crime. The use of a reasonable amount of persuasion to overcome reluctance does not constitute entrapment.
>
> The defendant has the burden of proving this defense by a Preponderance of the evidence. Preponderance of the evidence means that you must be persuaded, considering all the evidence in the case, that it is more probably true than not true. If you find that the defendant has established this defense, it will be your duty to return a verdict of not guilty.

The most effective way to demonstrate whether the criminal intention and design in this case originated in the minds of the law enforcement officers is to carefully analyze all of that language evidence, noting especially where that evidence shows that the defendant was lured or coerced into making such an agreement. As in bribery and other areas of criminal law, entrapment depends heavily on determining the suspect's intention and predisposition.

As noted earlier, the structure of the solicitation to murder event has five phases, the first four of which are obligatory—the problem, proposed negotiation, offer, and completion. The optional extension phase is not commonly found in solicitation to murder cases. The following describes the relevant four phases in this case.

The problem phase

Some background first. Mockovac, recently divorced, lonely, and depressed over the recent downward spiral of his eye surgery business, was certain that his co-owner was cheating him financially.

Whether or not his suspicion was accurate, it gradually built up in him such fury and anger that one day he carelessly revealed it to his firm's business manager. After an initial unrecorded conversation with Mockovac, the business manager went straight to the police and told them that Mockovac had asked him to find a hit man to kill the co-owner. Predictably, the police then wired up the informant and sent him out to secretly tape record all further conversations with Mockovac in an attempt to obtain specific information that would demonstrate his desire to have his business partner murdered. This taping went on for three months.

The first few tape-recorded conversations might be considered "warm-ups," as the informant established rapport and support and offered sympathy to Mockovac about his bitter feelings against his co-owner. The informant gleefully joined with Mockovac as they complained about problems caused by the partner's bad management and the company's subsequent business losses, adding that this was negatively affecting his own financial security as well.

Ambiguity of "gone" and "removing him"

Subsequent recorded conversations revealed that Mockovac would love to see his partner "gone." He clearly pointed out that winning his ongoing legal battle with his partner over the control and ownership of this business partnership would be a satisfactory way, as Mockovac put it, "of removing him." To this point, Mockovac's expressions "wanting him gone" and "removing him" referentially can be associated only with wanting his partner out of their unhappy business relationship. In terms of the structure of a murder event, to this point Mockovac had provided no evidence of his intention or a predisposition to murder. Undaunted, the informant doggedly persevered, taping many more conversations in which he fueled Mockovac's anger and resolve with his own statements, such as the following:

- He's draining our company…it's affecting everyone.
- I'm surprised how he gets away with doing business this way.
- He's basically trying to wipe out the office and make it look like it never existed.
- If I were in your shoes, I wouldn't trust this person.
- I cannot imagine being a partner with someone like him.
- I've never met a person more greedy anywhere in the world.
- The whole business is gonna die. We're all gonna be unemployed.

In terms of a murder speech event, however, these tapes still had only accomplished the phase 1 statement of the problem. Mockovac could not disagree with the informant's statements.

The proposal negotiations phase

The informant waited as long as he could for Mockovac to propose that he wanted his co-owner killed, but he couldn't get it. Instead, the proposal came from the informant, who introduced this topic and then recycled in several times. The first mention was this:

- I made some calls [to Los Angeles] about the thing we talked about. I told them that you're interested. So they can do it.

Ambiguous referencing

There is nothing in their recorded conversations to indicate that the informant's reference to "the thing we talked about" was to find a hit man. To this point in the evidence conversations, "the thing we talked about" had been only their agreement about how evil the co-owner was and that the ongoing civil law suit would settle the problem. The informant made this call to Los Angeles on his own initiative. He then continued with a clearer proposal about how to make Mockovac's business partner "go away":

- He's not going to go away, so let's make him go away...the easiest way to do it.
- Street robbery, you know, is the most common way to do it.

The informant carefully built on Mockovac's own term "go away," now suggesting a street robbery as a cover for the implied murder. The significance of this proposal is that it came from the informant rather than from Mockovac, who was the person with the problem that had not been directly or indirectly identified with a solution of murder. The informant then suggested various places where "it" could be done, including Los Angeles, Miami, and Australia, locations in which he claimed to have friends who could do "it." But Mockovac still did not agree to the informant's proposal. Instead, his consistent response was a different proposal that would remedy his problem. He wanted to go ahead with an ongoing lawsuit against his partner before even thinking about anything more drastic, saying:

- First of all, I think there's a chance after the deposition that this whole thing may disappear...to be honest, it's just a financial thing.
- Don't say anything to anyone. I want to have the depositions done.
- We'll see this thing, the, uh, you know, a chance for the thing to fall through.

The informant countered with a warning that might even be considered threatening, "This is serious stuff we're talking about and

I don't want em to wait," to which Mockovac continued his denial, "Let's not make them think that this is absolutely gonna happen."

To this point it is clear that Mockovac had not agreed to the informant's guarded and indirect proposal about his contacts in various cities who could do the job of having his partner "go away" (hinting murder). In fact, Mockovac's intention and predisposition were evidenced when he added the excuse that he wouldn't even be able to come up with money for doing such a thing anyway. But his tagged-on remark left that door open when he said, "I'm going to have to figure out how—." Since the last word in this sentence did not have the falling intonation that indicates completion of his sentence, we can't know what he was going to try to figure out. The informant took advantage of this and quickly said something off topic before Mockovac could complete his thought, at the same time illustrating both the interruption strategy and the hit-and-run strategy.

Realizing that his proposal was still not getting to the point he needed, the informant then tried another approach—an appeal to Mockovac's greed. He introduced the topic of an executive insurance policy that he understood would leave the business to whichever partner survived the death of the other partner, as he said: "And then, once the practice is free, we can talk about, you know, about the insurance policy." This appeal to Mockovac's greed also got nowhere, because Mockovac immediately defused it by pointing out that the informant was wrong about that insurance policy:

> Mockovac: Well, that would be only if, that has to happen because if the business splits, then we each get to keep our own insurance policies.

As their conversations continued over the following two months, the informant continued to offer hints and vague suggestions about hiring a hit man, but these yielded nothing more than Mockovac's continued indecisiveness:

- I don't know what you think, but I don't, I don't know what to do anymore.
- I might be a little paranoid.

Picking up on this, as the informant got more and more specific, now directly urging Mockovac to agree to the killing, Mockovac began to understand more clearly that the informant was talking about a hit, which might be a sure way to settle the problem, but he was still a bit indecisive about it:

> Informant: They want to know if you want to send a message.
> Mockovac: I don't know about that. My inclination is I really don't care. I just want the motherfucker out of my way. I don't feel any personal vengeance. I'm a little uneasy. In fact, to be honest, I go back and forth. Am I really doing the right thing? This is a new world for me, my friend. I know for you it's not, you're used to it. I'm not. I do go back and forth, but here's what I think. The only sure way is this. Every other way is months to years of pain. I have qualms, but at the end of the day I agree that it's like this is the only sure way to go.

The offer phase

In conventional solicitation to murder cases, an offer is conceived and made by the person who wants the killing done. In contrast, here the offer was created and made by the informant. Mockovac's purported agreement to the informant's offer was questionable, as was evident by the informant's response to it. However much Mockovac's statement "this is the only sure way to go" may sound like he was finally in agreement with the informant's offer, even the informant was unclear and requested clarification:

> Informant: But what do you want to do? Do you want to just sort of tell me tomorrow? Sounds like you need to think about it a bit. It's obviously got to be sorted out.

On the following night the two men met at a bar. We cannot know what happened or was said during most of the conversation, because the informant recorded only the part that best served the prosecution's case. He didn't record their whole conversation, but he did capture on tape Mockovac's words:

> Mockovac: It gave me some time to contemplate, like twenty-four hours to think about it. It's absolutely the right thing to do.

This appeared to establish Mockovac's intention and predisposition clearly enough for the prosecutor, even though Mockovac was offering the speech act of his opinion that this was "absolutely the right thing to do," not an explicit "Let's do it" or "I agree to do it." Nevertheless, the prosecution treated this as the speech act of Mockovac's final agreement to do it. The question here is whether opining that something is an absolutely right thing to do is equivalent to agreeing to do it. The police, oblivious to this distinction, arrested him immediately. It also went unnoticed by the prosecutor, who considered it a smoking gun and charged him with soliciting murder.

A nagging question is how far can an informant go in order to induce a suspect to agree to commit a crime? In addition to these inducements noted above, the informant also produced fears of threats from the alleged hit men:

- Next time I talk to them, you know, I want to be ready to pay them the money and execute, because if I do it again [delay] and they're like, "Fuck, this guy is not serious."

- You're not gonna freak out on me like the next day? My ass is on the line too. I'm still fuckin' nervous. If we fuck it up by not giving them money, they're probably not going to kill us but they'll fuckin' make sure we pay them, and probably more than that.

Mockovac's attorneys believed the case looked very bad for him, even though the informant made the offer himself rather than getting Mockovac to make it and even though the murder speech event did not contain the necessary speech act of agreement that is required for the completion phase. To the defense lawyers, Mockovac's only hope appeared to be to claim entrapment, which meant admitting that their client was guilty of the crime of soliciting murder but was induced, coerced, and lured to commit a crime that he initially resisted, did not intend, and was not predisposed to commit.

In summary, it is clear from the government's own evidence that Mockovac's initial intention and predisposition to have his business partner killed was not found in the language evidence. Instead, he wanted to see what would happen in the ongoing lawsuit, about which he was fairly confident. Mockovac reasoned that the lawsuit would make his partner "gone" and be "removed." The informant, not satisfied with Mockovac's scenario, built one of his own, claiming to have thugs who would solve the problem in a more fatal way. Following the very procedures specified in entrapment law, the informant created the idea of the hit and encouraged, induced, and facilitated it by himself. Mockovac was a distracted but compliant dupe, and eventually he was worn down enough to become an easy target for the informant.

Here the government appeared to interpret the legal expressions *intentionality* and *predisposition* to their own advantage. The tape-recorded evidence clearly showed that Mockovac's intentions and predispositions were to settle his problems with his business partner in the courtroom, but not to have him killed, even though he opined that the latter might be the best way. It took considerable effort over some three months of conversations for the informant finally to get what he and the prosecution believed to be Mockovac's agreement to the murder.

Aftermath

Robert Leonard and I were prepared to provide testimony about this at trial, but Mockovac's defense attorneys decided not to call on us. The jury subsequently found Mockovac guilty of solicitation and attempted murder. The judge rejected the defense effort to use an entrapment defense and did not consider the undercover witness's actions to be outrageous. Mockovac was sentenced to 240 months in prison, after which he hired new attorneys, who petitioned for a new trial based on the incompetence of his trial lawyers and on the informant's outrageous conduct.

6

VOLUNTARINESS IN MURDER CASES

Having described murder cases in which law enforcement did not yet know who the perpetrator might be (chapter 4) and cases in which suspects were believed to be planning to solicit murder (chapter 5), I now turn to cases in which suspects were in custody and were being interviewed. In these cases attention is focused on the voluntariness of what suspects said to the police and how the interviewers talked with them. I treat cases involving voluntariness separately here, even though the issue of voluntariness was certainly present along with intentionality and predisposition in the cases described earlier.

Various definitions of voluntariness were given in chapter 2, one of which was from *Black's Law Dictionary*: "Voluntary means something done by design or intention, unconstrained by interference; not impelled by outside influence." From this definition we can understand that voluntariness is a mental state that relates directly to predisposition ("by design") and intentionality. As *Black's Law Dictionary* continues, voluntariness should "not be impelled by outside influence," suggesting that the best evidence of the presence or absence of voluntariness can be found in the actual language used by suspects who are alleged to be speaking voluntarily when interviewed by the police.

There can be no dispute that one primary goal of the police interview speech event is to get suspects to voluntarily admit their crimes. This is complicated by the fact that the police begin with schemas of the suspects' guilt, and in highly stressful situations such as police interrogations, suspects are naturally nervous. As noted in chapter 5, Searle pointed out that even though involuntary nervousness, elation, and undirected anxiety such as grief are not intentional, they easily can lead the interviewer to misinterpret suspects' nervousness and grief as being evasive or dishonest.

As noted in chapter 3, the preferred sequence of the police interview speech event includes four sequential steps, the first two of which are to let the suspects volunteer their own uninterrupted version about what happened and their accompanying intentions. Even when the police try hard to do this, they may not find it easy, particularly with four types of subjects, including those (1) who are mentally impaired or slow, (2) who are under the influence of alcohol or drugs, (3) who are juveniles who find it difficult to understand the questions and tell their own sides of the story, and (4) who are emotionally distraught during their police interviews.

Even when the interviewers have the best of intentions, suspects like these can become defenseless sitting ducks during the speech events of police interviews and court hearings. In fact, this is one of several reasons why defense lawyers try to prevent their clients from testifying at hearings and trials, where the rigid rules of the trial testimony speech event place them at a distinct verbal and cultural disadvantage.

Linguists are not qualified to offer expert opinions about the mental states or capacities of suspects, but an analysis of the language used by suspects can provide evidence to either support or question assessments about mental capacity that are made by expert psychologists and psychiatrists. In the same way, linguists are not qualified to identify the chemical degrees of inebriation, but analysis of the language used by suspects can either challenge or support the physical measures used to determine drunkenness. In contrast, there is an abundance of linguistic research on the language of children that linguists can use to enlighten a jury's understanding of a juvenile's speech during questioning by police, lawyers, social workers, and judges. As will be noted, no laws deal with whether a suspect is or is not emotionally distraught during investigations, but linguists can discover and provide clues found in the language used by suspects when they are so emotionally overcome that it hampers or even alters their responses. In each of these four conditions, linguistic analysis addresses the important issue of whether or not the suspects produced their language evidence voluntarily.

It should be pointed out that similar problems exist when the police and prosecutors interview suspects who are nonnative English speakers. Although this population experiences important difficulties during police interviews, that issue is not the focus of this book. This population has been analyzed and described elsewhere by other linguists (i.e., Berk-Seligson 1990, 2009; Eades 2008, 2010).

It can be helpful here to summarize the historical development of the legal lexicon's term, *voluntariness*. In the eighteenth century, judges in England began to object to the common law's treatment of confessions that were the product of torture, threats, or beneficial promises. These objections evolved to the requirement that all confessions be made voluntarily. By 1897 U.S. courts defined a voluntary confession as one that excluded direct or implied promises or any other improper influences (*Bram v. United States*, 168 U.S. 532, 18 S.Ct. 183). In 1936 the U.S. Supreme Court ruled that involuntary confessions violated the due process clause of the Fourteenth Amendment to the Constitution (*Brown v. Mississippi*, 297 U.S. 278). In that case, three murder suspects were beaten until they confessed and then were threatened that if they changed their story, they would get the same treatment again.

The purpose of excluding involuntary confessions was to deter misconduct by the police, to invalidate unreliable confessions made under duress, and to ensure that any admissions were made freely and rationally. The tricky part of this is that involuntary confessions are allowed to be used if defendants themselves opened the door to such a confession. The ways that police interviewers open this door also can be subject to linguistic analysis. Length and conditions of the interrogation also are important factors in determining voluntariness, along with any evidence of coercion, threats, and force by the interviewers.

In 1944 the meaning of *voluntariness* was expanded from rough physical conduct by the police when the court added that a valid confession required the courts to examine and account for the totality of the circumstances. In *Ashcraft v. Tennessee* (322 U.S. 143, 64 S.Ct. 921) defendant Ashcraft was relentlessly interviewed for thirty-six hours without rest or sleep and, contrary to inferences made by the police interviewers, he still did not confess. The Supreme Court found that even if this defendant had confessed, he was coerced to the extent that a confession could not be deemed voluntary. Up to this time, because the technology of tape-recording interrogations had not yet developed, the major evidence relating to interrogations was the accounts given by the suspect and the police, which were sometimes conflicting. Confirmable language evidence was not yet available. In other cases in the 1950s and 1960s the U.S. Supreme Court ruled that threats and certain promises made by the police also were improper.

In a 1963 case (*Townsend v. Sain*, 372 U.S. 293, 83 S.Ct. 745) an accused murderer who was high on narcotics suffered from withdrawal symptoms while being questioned. The police then brought in a physician who gave him a therapeutic dose of hyoscine and phenobarbital to soothe his stomach pains, after which the suspect admitted the murder and was subsequently convicted. The doctor's report failed to mention that the combination of these two drugs produces the same effect as scopolamine, which was known to be a truth serum. Based on this information, the Supreme Court reversed Townsend's conviction, maintaining that his confession was not the voluntary product of his rational intellect and was therefore coerced.

A landmark Supreme Court decision in 1966 (*Miranda v. Arizona*, 384 U.S.) was directly aimed at voluntariness. This decision mandated that advice about a suspect's constitutional rights was a prerequisite to all police interrogations. Although the U.S. Constitution provides that no persons should be forced to become a witness against themselves, up to that time there was no law requiring police interrogators to advise suspects about their right to counsel before and during the interrogation and their right to remain silent without answering any questions. Suspects were also to be warned that anything they said could be used as evidence against them, and they were required to make a "knowing and intelligent" waiver of these rights before any interrogation could begin. In order to ensure that suspects made this "knowing and intelligent" waiver, the police were to ask them if they understood these rights and if so, if they were willing to talk. Since 1966, the Miranda decision has gone through considerable debate and interpretation about what it means to knowingly and intelligently waive one's rights, what it means to have an attorney present, what it means to remain silent, and what it means to make a knowing waiver. All of these speak to the issue of voluntariness.

Although Miranda attempts to give the surface impression of protecting voluntariness, the results cannot always be considered successful. First of all, the warning is given in the physical context of a police station under conditions that are very unfavorable for the suspects. Ainsworth (2008, 3) points out: "Under the inherently intimidating and coercive atmosphere of incommunicado police interrogation, it is highly questionable that any resulting confession could be considered a product of the unfettered free will of the suspect." It's clear that the police have all the power in such contexts and the suspects have none. Perhaps the physical context of a police station can't be helped, because that's where law enforcement is located. It would seem odd and inefficient to require the Miranda warning to be given in a hotel room or a public park.

The greater problem is the language used by the police in that police station context, for the Miranda warning conveys a mismatch between the language used by law enforcement and language required by the suspects. One issue is the register in which Miranda occurs. Suspects under tension resort to what O'Barr (1982, 65–71) calls the speech register of "powerless language," which is characterized by the use of hedges, hesitation forms, intensifiers, and others, all of which can cast doubts on the suspects' convincingness, truthfulness, competence, intelligence, and trustworthiness. Under such circumstances it is estimated that about 80 percent of suspects waive their rights.

False beliefs about Miranda are also problematic. The research of Rogers, Rogstad, et al. (2010) revealed that 31 percent of the suspects interviewed thought that their silence could be used as incriminating evidence against them at trial. When the researchers compared their findings with college students who had no experience with the legal system, they found an almost identical figure. They took this to indicate that the issue was the subjects' failure to comprehend the Miranda right. They also found that some suspects waive their rights just to get the interrogation over with as quickly as possible. The case of Kevin Rogers in chapter 9 illustrates this false belief. Some suspects believe that even though they admit the crime in their interrogation but refuse to sign a written confession statement, they are off the hook. Others believe the police have to "play fair" during the interrogation and therefore are not allowed to lie about what other purported eyewitnesses have said.

The most problematic issue, however, is what Rogers (2008) calls "meta-ignorance"—not knowing what one doesn't know. Suspects who think they know what Miranda means are not motivated to listen carefully to what is recited to them. Because they hear Miranda warnings frequently on television cop shows and confuse their familiarity with accuracy, Rogers found that 73.8 percent of pretrial detainees thought they had an average or better knowledge of Miranda. When a sample of police chiefs were asked this question, 89.4 percent shared the pretrial detainees' perceptions. Meta-ignorance of the Miranda warning remains undetected once suspects tell the police that they "understand" that warning, making the concept of a "knowing and intelligent" waiver highly suspicious.

In the effort to provide voluntariness, Miranda has set some important required language guidelines or scripts for the police to follow in questioning suspects. Unfortunately, there are no equivalent guidelines or scripts available to help suspects as they try to respond to the rights that are read to them. On this matter, *Davis v. United States* (512 U.S. 452 1994) said the following:

> The suspect must unambiguously request counsel... Although a suspect need not speak with the discrimination of an Oxford don, he must articulate his desire to have counsel present sufficiently clearly that a reasonable police officer in the circumstance would understand the statement to be a request for an attorney.

We know from judicial decisions in recent years that when suspects respond to the warning that tells them they can have a lawyer present and they respond using expressions such as, "Could I call my lawyer?" "Could I get a lawyer?" "Do you mind if I have a lawyer with me?" and "I think I will talk to a lawyer" (note the powerless, polite, and hedged language), the courts have ruled that these responses are not considered invocations of the suspect's rights. As for the Miranda right to remain silent, the courts have ruled that suspects' statements such as "I don't want to talk about it," "I don't have anything to say," and other similar responses are too ambiguous or equivocal to be count as invocations (Ainsworth 2008, 8–9). Apparently only unambiguous, clear, explicit, unequivocal, and performative invocations are acceptable in the judicial system, such as "I hereby declare that I want a lawyer here with me at this time." Sadly, few people talk like this in any context and much less so during high-pressured Miranda warning speech events.

The follow-up question "Do you understand these rights?" also can be relatively meaningless in the Miranda context. Powerless people tend to say "yes" whether or not they understand, because it's too embarrassing to admit ignorance. One can only wonder what the police response would be if they got a response of "no." It might be similar to the response of my son's high school algebra teacher, who, after my son said he didn't understand a problem, asked him, "What is it that you don't understand?" If my son knew what he didn't understand, he obviously wouldn't have needed to tell her that he didn't understand. As a measure of comprehension, the "Do you understand your rights?" question is laughably ineffective and it desperately needs to be rethought. According to Miranda (1966, 475), the heavy burden rests on the government to demonstrate the validity of the purported waiver, which includes understanding what it is. So far at least, this heavy burden has been relatively ignored. As Ainsworth (2008, 19) observes, "These rights are easy to waive but nearly impossible to actually invoke."

Similarly as in the United States, the U.K. police caution has come under considerable criticism because of its ambiguity and confusing nature (Rock 2007, 148–165). There the equivalent version of the U.S. Miranda warning to suspects is called the police caution. Its wording is as follows:

> You do not have to say anything. But it may harm your defense if you do not mention when questioned something which you later rely on in court. Anything you say may be given in evidence.

Things seem to be no better for defendants about the "right to silence" part of the police caution used in Australia's Evidence Act. Recently, the attorney general complained that the older version was easily exploited by the defense because it is very suspicious when a suspect says nothing during the interview and then provides exculpatory information at trial. The older caution reads:

> You are not obliged to say or do anything unless you wish to do so, but whatever you say or do may be used in evidence. Do you understand?

In keeping with the attorney general's complaint, the wording recently has been changed to stress the purported harm that may come to suspects if they remain silent and then introduce the unsaid exculpatory information at trial. It now reads:

> You are not obliged to say or do anything unless you wish to do so. But it may harm your defense if you do not mention when questioned something you later rely on in court. Anything you do or say may be given in evidence. Do you understand?

It has been suggested that this change obviously favors the prosecution.

The U.S. courts are equally vague about what happens when suspects unaffirm their rights by remaining silent for a while then beginning to talk. In *Oregon v. Bradshaw* (462 U.S. 1039, 1983), well into his interrogation the otherwise silent suspect suddenly asked, "What's going to happen to me now?" The police and eventually the court interpreted this as his willingness and desire for a generalized discussion of his case that allowed the police to continue to interrogate him.

A U.S. example of the ongoing debate about the meaning of the right to remain silent surfaced in 2010 in the case of *Berghuis v. Thompkins* (130 S.Ct. 2250) in which the U.S. Supreme Court ruled five to four that persons being interviewed by the police are required to articulate their answers to the Miranda warning and to announce audibly that they want to remain silent. The case originated when Van Chester Thompkins was being questioned about a shooting in which one person was killed. Instead of invoking his Miranda right to remain silent, Thompkins simply remained silent, which seemed to him to be what the Miranda warning allowed him to do. In fact, he remained silent through two hours and forty-five minutes of constant questioning, at which point the detective asked him if he believed in God and prayed, to which Thompkins spoke for the first time, saying, "Yes." The detective then asked him, "Do you pray to God to forgive you for shooting the boy down?" Thompkins again answered, "Yes" but refused to produce a written statement.

After Thompkins was convicted, his subsequent appeal was denied by the Michigan court of appeals. The U.S. court of appeals for the sixth circuit, however, reversed the appellate court's decision and ruled in favor of Thompkins. The case then went to the U.S. Supreme Court, where Justice Kennedy, writing for the majority, opined that Thompkins's mere silence in the face of questioning was not a clear and unambiguous invocation of his right to remain silent.

Thompkins's lawyers argued that his statement should be suppressed because even though he had never adequately or explicitly waived his right to remain silent. In contrast, the Supreme Court argued that his "yes" to the religious questions was not coerced and it established an *implied* waiver of his right to remain silent. In Justice Kennedy's words, "Simply *presuming* an invocation after some initial period of silence...would override the wishes of those suspects who wanted to listen and deliberate further, rather than to end the questioning." In short, this creative ruling was that by being silent during the interrogation, Thompkins did not invoke his right to remain silent, but he waived his right when he said, "yes" to the detective's questions about religion. Justice Kennedy added that the accused are required to talk in order to indicate their unwillingness to talk. On this point the court relied on the 1979 decision in *North Carolina v. Butler* (441 U.S. 369), which ruled that the police may *imply* a waiver of Miranda rights when the suspect remains silent.

Justice Sotomayer wrote the dissenting opinion, saying: (1) that it is counterintuitive for defendants to speak after they are told they have the right to remain silent; (2) that in such cases detectives should presume that the suspects have invoked their rights to silence when they remain silent for almost three hours of questioning; and (3), citing Miranda, "...the fact that an individual eventually made a statement is consistent with the conclusion that the compelling influence of the interrogation finally forced him to do so. It is inconsistent with any notion of a voluntary relinquishment of the privilege."

In this case, five Supreme Court justices agreed that Thompkins's silence *implied* his waiver of rights, supporting this ruling with the Butler case that said essentially the same thing. In their dissenting opinion, four Supreme Court justices agreed that Thompkins's silence during all but the last fifteen seconds of the interrogation *implied* that he had actually invoked his right to remain silent. The nine justices also were split on how to imply meaning about what constitutes being coercive or voluntary. These decisions seem to suggest the need for clarity about what the Miranda warning's "right to remain silent" really means. And how long do suspects have to continue their silence before detectives can infer that this was their real intention? And do the courts understand how psychologically difficult it is for humans to remain silent when barraged with questions? And how can suspects who are unfamiliar with the niceties of the interrogation speech event know that breaking silence on a topic perceived to be unrelated to the interrogation topics constitutes a waiver of their right to remain silent about the substantive topics and questions of the interrogations? Then there is also Justice Sotomayer's interesting question about the logic of a rule specifying that the only way to remain silent is to break that silence by saying they want to remain silent.

This is not to suggest that Thompkins was innocent of this crime, for he did say that he'd pray that God would forgive him for killing the boy, and I understand that there also was other evidence strongly suggesting his guilt. But the court's meandering path about Miranda raises some serious questions about the relationship of language and law.

Although it is always difficult to determine any defendant's state of mind, interrogations that are electronically recorded can reveal linguistic clues to the suspect's voluntariness as well as the ways that police questioning can open the door to defense attorneys' claims about their clients' lack of voluntarily admitting their guilt. The problem of how to prove voluntariness was aided considerably in the 1990s, when several police departments began to tape-record police interviews with suspects. By recording the whole interview from beginning to end, the police found that they could prove that they had not coerced or otherwise tarnished the required legal procedures. But not all law enforcement agencies agreed to follow the practice of tape-recording. Some argued that it was not cost-effective, while others apparently rejected it out of fear that it could be embarrassing to reveal their incompetent or coercive questioning strategies and techniques.

Still other agencies accepted the idea of tape-recording the interviews but limited their taping to the recapped final confession statement, perhaps reasoning that all the jury needed would be this decontextualized part of the entire interview. Such end-loading of the interview then came under severe criticism by defense lawyers, who equated it with giving the jury only a *Reader's Digest* recap of Shakespeare's *Hamlet* in which many important parts of the story were completely omitted.

Sometimes even such recaps, however, can offer internal language evidence showing that previous exchanges between the suspect and the police had taken place before the police taped only the recapped confession. A good example of the way the police used a recapped admission of guilt is the case of *State of Texas v. John Lezell Ballentine,* on which I consulted in 1998. Ballentine eventually confessed to murdering two men by shooting them in the head. From the following excerpts of the recapped tape recording used at trial we can learn that an earlier unrecorded interview had taken place, primarily because the interviewer introduced unrecorded topics that did not appear in the recapped tape, including the following:

- And I'll repeat what we already went over earlier.
- You were telling me about after you were out of the house that night.
- You said that he threatened you.
- Remember telling me something about going to that one guy that lived in that two-story house?
- I thought you told me that you were not a gun person.

The fact that the substance of these briefly mentioned topics was not in the recapped evidence on tape indicates clearly that there was a preceding unrecorded interview in which these topics had been discussed. In this case, the police officer had not made available to the jury any of the previous interview context that might have indicated possible undue persuasion or coercion by the police or even the suspect's denials of guilt. We can't know if such problems existed because the evidence presented was only the bare confession itself, not the process by which the officer elicited it. More important to this case, we can't even know whether Ballentine voluntarily produced that portion of his confession that was recapped.

The police interrogation speech event sometimes bears a striking resemblance to other areas in life in which the focus is on winning. When good sports teams compete against weaker opponents, they relish the thought that they know they can win such games. Police interviewers have a similar advantage because suspects have so few resources to call on while defending themselves. Because many suspects of this type are fairly inarticulate, the temptation for some interviewers is to save time and cut corners by leading the suspects about what they should say. Competent, patient, responsible interviewers avoid this, but not all police interviewers are competent, patient, and responsible. Either deliberately or unintentionally, some apparently are tempted to take advantage of this type of suspect. In short, these suspects become easy prey for interviewers who might be overly eager, clever, self-deluding, or tricky.

The following chapters describe voluntariness in four categories of suspects' police interviews. Chapter 7 deals with a range of uneducated suspects with diminished mental capacity that relates to their voluntariness, beginning with the case of Jerry Townsend, who was without doubt seriously mentally and socially retarded; followed by the case of Benjamin Hauswirth, who was more mentally competent than Townsend but still very slow both mentally and socially; and concluding with the case of Larry Gentry, who was slightly more functionally competent than Hauswirth but who nonetheless had apparent diminished capacity both socially and mentally. The speech events in the cases of Townsend and Gentry were interviews with the police. In the case of Hauswirth, the speech event was an undercover conversation with a policeman.

Chapter 8 describes cases in which the voluntariness of suspects was limited by their impairments by alcohol and drugs. Chapter 9 deals with the voluntariness of juvenile suspects, and chapter 10 with the voluntariness of suspects who were so emotionally distraught that they were less than competent to provide useful information that would enable them to know what was happening to them.

There are legal precedents for the first three of these types of impairment, but the law says little if anything about the emotional stress that can affect the voluntariness of suspects in murder cases. Nevertheless, I include this category because it is possible that even without legal precedent, juries might find this information helpful and important as they decide such cases.

The role of the linguist is to assess the totality of the surrounding language circumstances, including the language evidence relevant to the suspect's age, intelligence, education, and emotional state by closely analyzing the language used during the interviews. Voluntariness is also affected by the interviewer's failure to give a proper Miranda warning, by the nature and length of the questioning and detention, by the denial of food or sleep, or by threatening. In these cases, the law provides the typical prototype definitions for triers of the fact to go on, but it can't supply the defining instances found in the flesh of living language. That's what linguistic analysis can contribute.

7

VOLUNTARINESS OF MENTALLY INCAPACITATED SUSPECTS

This chapter examines a topic that has been much debated in the courts—the voluntariness of suspects who have various degrees of mental incapacitation. In the nineteenth century, the legal test for insanity was the McNaughten Rule, which asserted the presumption of sanity unless the defense could prove that at the time the act was committed the accused persons possessed such defects of reasoning capacity or minds so diseased that they didn't know the nature and quality of the crime they were committing, and even if they did know this, they didn't know that it was wrong.

The 1972 Model Penal Code more or less followed the McNaughten Rule and was accepted by a number of states. After Congress enacted the Comprehensive Crime Control Act in 1984, defendants were required to prove that their offense was caused by severe mental disease or defect that resulted in their inability to distinguish right from wrong or, if they were able to differentiate right from wrong, they couldn't act upon this knowledge because of their mental impairment. A plea of insanity was equivalent to pleading not guilty, but pleading diminished capacity was an admission of a less severe crime. Whatever the plea, diminished capacity related not only to their intentions and predispositions but also to their ability to talk and act voluntarily.

Often, unfortunately, the legal standards for criminal insanity and mental impairment do not comport with the psychiatric and psychological criteria indicating subjects' capacity to control their impulses. A diminished capacity defense argues that the defendants are incapable of *intending* to cause a death and at most had done so *recklessly*. This position, if successfully argued and proved, could reduce the charge from murder to manslaughter. Not surprisingly, much debate centers on whether or not a suspect has diminished capacity, including whether such diminishment extends to the due process clause of the Fourteenth Amendment—the competence of a defendant to stand trial.

When mental health experts diagnose criminal suspects as mentally incapacitated, one role of the linguist is to analyze the language evidence to determine whether it comports with the psychological or psychiatric findings. The common first step is to ensure that any written transcripts of spoken evidence, in most cases the transcripts of police interviews, are accurate. Transcripts are not evidence, but they are often used at trial to assist the jury, who lean heavily on them to keep the threads of evidence straight. Transcripts are also important because both prosecutors and defense attorneys can use them to refer to passages on the tapes. Using transcripts can save precious time during trials. Both the government and the defense may do the best they can to produce accurate transcripts, but the results often contain errors, some of which can be crucially important. Linguists have far better training to produce accurate transcripts than do less well-trained transcribers. Not being advocates for either side, linguists also can and should be more objective than either the prosecution or defense.

When psychological analyses of suspects are produced, the linguist's task is to search the spoken and written evidence for linguistic features that relate to such psychological assessments and to determine not only whether the suspects confessed to the crime but also whether their language indicates that they did so voluntarily. Linguistic analysis differs from psychological assessment in that linguists rely on only the government's own language evidence, whereas psychologists usually test suspects in various ways, interview them, and relate their findings to norms developed in their field. Both the contributions of psychology and linguistics are important, but language evidence can also provide clues to voluntariness, even when psychological assessments are not available.

The linguistic contributions to three cases involving mentally incapacitated suspects are described here. Psychological assessments were made for the severely handicapped Jerry Townsend and for the less severely handicapped Benjamin Hauswirth, but not for the mildly handicapped Larry Gentry. It is unclear why the defense lawyers did not request a psychological assessment of Gentry.

THE STATE OF FLORIDA V. JERRY TOWNSEND

In 1973 the Miami police discovered the bodies of several female prostitutes who had been brutally killed during a period of many months. Since the local police were unable to identify any viable suspects, they turned their attention to homeless drifters. One of these was Jerry Townsend, an uneducated, mentally impaired man with no permanent address. When they called him in for questioning, Townsend clearly admitted that he had committed some of the murders. Although a more detailed description of this case can be found in my book *Language Crimes* (1993, 175–85), here I focus only on the voluntariness of the statements he made during his interviews with Miami detectives.

With Townsend's confession in hand, it appeared that the police had finally cleared their files of several unresolved murder cases.

But Townsend's public defender wisely decided to have his client psychologically tested just before the police began what turned out to be four days of interviews with him. A Miami psychologist spent many hours with Townsend, giving him various intelligence tests, including the Bender–Gestalt, Rorschach, and other diagnostic instruments, all of which led him to conclude that Townsend functioned at a very low level and exhibited possible brain damage. Tests of his reading ability showed that Townsend could read at the second grade level, and other indicators demonstrated that he fell well within the range of mental retardation. Later, that psychologist's reviews of the recordings made during Townsend's four days of police interviews led him to report that Townsend gave no indication of faking while he tried very hard to make a good impression on the police, as he functioned at the level of a seven- or eight-year-old child. Two additional clinical psychologists verified the first psychologist's findings, adding that Townsend was not competent to understand the rational and factual proceedings that were about to be brought against him. They also pointed out that Townsend's intellectual capacities were so limited that investigators could not accept as accurate any of his references of even the most elementary nature about times, places, names, or details.

As might be expected, the prosecutor then called on his own psychologist, who agreed that Townsend's IQ score was "51 or so" but nevertheless claimed that Townsend functioned at the level of a nineteen-year-old. In a battle of the experts at a court hearing, the judge ruled that since the prosecutor's expert did not hold a doctorate degree, he was not an expert and could not be offered as an expert witness at trial. Even so, as odd as this might sound, the judge eventually permitted this same prosecution psychologist to testify about his findings at Townsend's trial, although not in the capacity of an expert witness. This became a great advantage to the prosecutor, because since the psychologist did not testify as an expert witness, Townsend's defense lawyers were therefore not permitted to cross-examine him.

The prosecution then called two additional psychologists who held doctoral degrees and were therefore more qualified as experts than the first one. They reported that any efforts to determine grade-level equivalence findings were absurd, although they agreed that Townsend had considerable difficulty in his ability to identify events in sequence and had little or no concept of chronological time. Nevertheless, both of the new prosecution psychologists concluded that Townsend had adequate mental ability to consult with his attorney because he had a rational understanding of what was going on. Their testimony at the preliminary hearing was just what the prosecutor needed to take the case to trial. When the trial took place, perhaps predictably, the prosecutor called on only the first psychologist to testify, but not as an expert witness, thus removing the possibility of cross-examination by the defense. Despite the various psychologists' interpretations of Townsend's functional age level, they all agreed that he was retarded.

My linguistic task was to examine the police interviews with Townsend to determine the voluntariness of his confessions and, where possible, to support the defense psychologist's analysis. Townsend's four days of police interviews took place between September 6 and 10, 1979, during which time the police questioned Townsend at the various sites where the bodies had been found. Townsend readily agreed that he murdered some of the prostitutes, but the question was whether he admitted this voluntarily.

Townsend's questioning by the police could be easy to describe as disgracefully unfair. For one thing, only parts of the interviews with him were tape-recorded. Frequently the recorder was turned off and then came back on again later, usually without any indication on tape about why the tape was turned off and on. Nor did the tapes or government transcripts of these conversations give any indication about when the clearly audible off and on signature clicks took place. Jurors relying on the transcript found it easy to believe the recorded speech was continuous rather than interrupted. Many times Townsend could be heard running two topically different utterances together as though they represented his continuous conversation. In one example of this the government's transcript reads, "Uh-huh, that's walk down about one block, come up through there," while on the tape one can hear, "Un-huh, that's [tape turned off, then back on] walk down about one block, come up through there." A dog could be heard barking continuously up to and including Townsend's words, "uh-huh, that's," but no barking could be heard during the rest of his sentence.

Other examples of the way the police reconstructed Townsend's alleged responses were evident when he started to answer a question and the tape clicked off in midsentence, followed by Townsend then talking about a totally different topic when the tape came back on. On other occasions one can hear Townsend answering questions that the police did not record on the tape. And whenever Townsend would get a fact wrong, such as the color of a victim's blouse or the method of her strangulation, the tape would click off and then back on, after which his voice could then be heard correcting his previous answers. All of this led to serious questions about the voluntariness of his statements.

Linguistic analysis may not be appropriate as a means of determining the mental competence of a suspect, but when the speaker uses expressions such as "commit suicide on her" to indicate "kill her," this at least raises questions about what to kill somebody meant in Thompson's incapacitated mind:

DETECTIVE: Jerry, did you kill these girls up there in Fort Lauderdale?

TOWNSEND: No, I didn't commit suicide on 'em but, you know, I just put 'em where they can't be of a use no more.

Townsend could not independently produce a consistent and viable answer to most of the officers' many questions relating to the times, places, or names of persons. Throughout the four days that the police drove Townsend around to various victim sites, the interviewers could be heard spoon-feeding crucial information to Townsend about the victims, but even when he was scripted with accurate information, his answers were still often inconsistent. On the second day of interviewing, for example, Townsend said he didn't know the name of a victim, but on the next day he called her Darlene. On the third day of his interviewing he called the same girl by a still different name. On one day he said he choked two women at a baseball park but three minutes later he said he choked them at very different locations. At one time he described a victim as a black girl in a white car. The tape clicked off and when it came back on again, he reported that it was a white girl in a black car. There were many other examples of this evidence of unfair interviewing practice, all of which supported the defense psychologist's claim that Townsend lacked mental competence to understand what was happening to him.

Important questions were whether Townsend was lying, was simply producing information that the police fed to him, or was lacking the mental ability to keep his stories straight. If he was lying, he was clearly the worst liar on earth, for there were large amounts of inconsistency in his statements until the tape clicked off, after which he then supplied the responses that suited the facts of the crime. This made his voluntariness highly suspicious. His answers often could be directly related to the way the interviewers' asked their questions and to Townsend's mental incapacity to volunteer what actually happened. There is also the lingering suspicion that the police may have spliced together the tape recordings to make Townsend look guilty. However awkwardly, he seemed to admit to five of the unsolved murder cases, but as he did so the police needed to make his accounts match the facts that they already knew. This was relatively easy for the police, because Townsend's cooperative and naïve mental condition made it a simple task.

Aftermath

Despite all of these problems, the jury convicted Jerry Townsend of first-degree murder of the five female prostitutes and gave him a death sentence. He spent twenty-five two years on Florida's death row until 1998, when the mother of one of the victims convinced the police to review Townsend's case file about her daughter's death. Subsequently they found a DNA sample on the victim's shorts that excluded Townsend and implicated another man. They then took a DNA sample from that other man, who was already in prison serving a life sentence. After they found that it matched the DNA on the victim's shorts, the man confessed to all of the murders. With this evidence, prosecutors had to concede that there was substantial doubt about the truthfulness of Townsend's confessions. Subsequently a judge dismissed Townsend's conviction, saying: "Given the deficiency of the state's evidence, a lack of trust in its evidence, including the obtained confessions, and in some cases what may very well be Mr. Townsend's outright innocence, it is abundantly clear that he is the victim of an enormous tragedy." Townsend was immediately released after being wrongfully imprisoned for twenty-two years.

Townsend's legal guardian then filed a civil rights suit against the City of Miami and several police officers, claiming that Townsend's rights were violated by his coerced confessions, malicious prosecution, altered interview tapes, and the withholding of exculpatory evidence. In May 2008 the City of Miami agreed to settle the case for 2.2 million dollars.

Despite the efforts of the police interviewers to make it appear that he voluntarily admitted to committing the five murders, analysis of the language in these interviews demonstrated that the government's own evidence was so flawed that it actually contained nothing that could prove Townsend's intentionality, premeditation, willfulness, heat of passion, malice, and, most relevant to this chapter, voluntariness of his admissions. In fact, the district attorney finally had to conclude that Townsend didn't even commit the murders.

THE STATE OF MICHIGAN V. BENJAMIN HAUSWIRTH

A New Baltimore, Michigan solicitation to murder case began in 2008, when Benjamin Hauswirth became very upset with his live-in girlfriend's parents, because he believed (with apparent justification) that they were succeeding in breaking up his relationship with their daughter. The problem began after she had given birth to a baby girl that had subsequently suffered a serious head injury. Calling it a shaken baby case, the parents blamed the injury on Hauswirth and brought a child custody lawsuit against him. At about this time, one of Hauswirth's friends reported to the police that Hauswirth told him he wanted to buy a gun to shoot his girlfriend's family and eventually came to realize that he couldn't do this himself. The friend inferred that Hauswirth was now looking for someone else to kill the parents for him and so he reported this to the police. The local police began undercover work almost immediately by having his friend record a telephone call to Hauswirth, telling him that he had found someone who could "help you with your problem." Neither party in that call specified what "your problem" referred to.

Hauswirth agreed to meet the caller along with that "someone" at a McDonald's restaurant. The meeting lasted one hour and a half. Unbeknownst to Hauswirth, that "someone" actually was an undercover detective posing as a hit man. After considerable hesitation and coaxing, Hauswirth finally promised to give the hit man $350 for the murders, but since he could round up only $60, the hit man agreed to take it as a down payment, possibly qualifying as one of the cheapest murder-for-hire cases on record. Hauswirth was arrested immediately and eventually was tried for soliciting murder.

Before the trial took place, an impressive amount of evidence was made available about Hauswirth's low mental capacity. Psychologists agreed that his IQ was very low and that he functioned at about the fifth grade level, but nevertheless the state's Michigan Center for Forensic Psychiatry found him competent to stand trial. Hauswirth's friends and family told the judge that soliciting murder was far removed from Hauswirth's character. The judge was impressed with the confidence this support provided for Hauswirth, even telling him in court, "They believe that is not the real you." This might suggest that the "real you" was someone other than the young man who solicited murder. But perhaps the most convincing support for Hauswirth's mental incapacity was found in the way he talked and functioned during the tape-recorded undercover sting operation at the restaurant, which provided the major evidence in his case. And since his mental incapacitation appeared to influence or even govern his statements, the issue of his voluntariness was ripe for debate.

There were ninety-seven topics introduced in the hour and a half tape-recorded conversation at the restaurant. The detective introduced ninety-one (92 percent) of them, a clear indication that he controlled the entire solicitation to murder speech event. Although the problem phase of the speech event was only vaguely determined, it was the policeman who initiated the offer to carry out a hit, after which he engineered Hauswirth's ultimate agreement to it. Eliciting Hauswirth's agreement, however, was not easy for him. During the first thirty minutes of their conversation, the detective made twenty-five efforts to get Hauswirth to say what he wanted to happen to various members of his girlfriend's family, receiving only the noncommittal "I don't know" or sequential responses that stopped short of murder such as:

- I want them gone.
- Just taken out.
- Just get rid of.
- Just something.
- Just take him out.
- Probably hit him in the head, not hurt him.
- Just like out cold.
- Take him out.
- Make sure he doesn't move.

More than once Hauswirth asked the detective how *he* would like to have it done, supporting the psychologist's report about his compliance and susceptibility to suggestions.

In the recorded phone call that initiated this meeting, the policeman offered vaguely "to help you with your problem," not specifying what either that problem or that help might be. Clearly, Hauswirth wanted his unstated "problem" to go away, to be gotten rid of, and gone. Without serious, persistent prodding by the officer, Hauswirth was unable, either from lack of language ability or from lack of cognitive skills, to decide *how* he wanted his still vaguely defined problem to be "helped."

Probably because the detective realized that Hauswirth's responses were not specific commitments for a hit, he finally resorted to introducing the topic of killing the three people himself. He did this by abandoning the "problem" topic and introducing the topic of how much Hauswirth would pay for a killing that Hauswirth hadn't even mentioned or asked for. The detective inferred what Hauswirth wanted: "You're asking me to kill three people; give me $100 up front and we will start." Hauswirth appeared to have bought into this suggestion when he asked, "Can I pay in sections? How much do you want up front? All I have is $60." Since Hauswirth wasn't even predisposed enough to bring that $60 with him, the detective sent him home to get it. Hauswirth complied and went home to try to find $350. After he returned, he reported, "All I have is seventy," to which the officer replied, "Give me the seventy now, it shows you're serious; worst case I got gas money if you tell me no." This statement is important, for his "if you tell me no" demonstrates that in the detective's mind the quid pro quo agreement had not yet been accomplished. Hauswirth then asked, "Could we hold off until I get the money?" which also verified that they had not yet reached an agreement. But the officer quickly agreed to take the $70 as "a deposit." When Hauswirth counted out what he managed to find at home, he discovered that it was actually only $60, saying, "I'm sorry."

At forty-two minutes into the conversation the detective finally elicited Hauswirth's clear quid pro quo for the hit:

DETECTIVE: Okay, you gave me sixty bucks and the sixty is to kill them, right?
HAUSWIRTH: Yes.

Having finally gotten the positive response he was after, the detective then quickly introduced the topic of the method to be used to murder the three people, offering his own suggestions twenty-four times. When the officer finally asked Hauswirth how he wanted the killings to take place, Hauswirth confusingly replied, "Shot up like quick," "not bloody all over," "painless," "probably at their house," and "not necessarily right away." His self-contradictory responses indicated that murder was clearly a new idea for Hauswirth to try to embrace, and it supported the psychologist's diagnosis about his cognitive incapacitation.

Throughout this latter part of their conversation, most of Hauswirth's answers were off topic, explaining that the baby's injury was not his fault because he was asleep and didn't even know what had happened. It was here, near the end of their discussion, that Hauswirth finally identified his own agenda and the nature of his problem. He rambled on about the upcoming custody hearing and his inability to make child support payments. It was at this point that he introduced his only eight topics in their entire conversation, all of them explanations about why he was so upset: "Everything is closing in," "They're back in court for a custody hearing this week," and "My girlfriend wants my son back." But the officer ignored these problems that Hauswirth had finally identified and abruptly shifted the topic back to their arrangement: "If I guarantee by Wednesday, are you willing to throw in another fifty bucks?" to which Hauswirth agreed but again quickly returned to his own agenda: "I lost my job. I'm on unemployment. I was paying her $20 out of it before and it went up to $100. She went to court saying I wasn't paying her. Now she's suing for child support. She's coming after me."

These responses were clear evidence of Hauswirth's view of the problem phase of this speech event, which contrasted sharply with the detective's earlier construction of the problem as Hauswirth's desire to have the people killed. The conversation then quickly ended as the detective restated that he was going to kill the people. He then arrested Hauswirth for soliciting murder.

Hauswirth's attorney requested a hearing to suppress the evidence, claiming that Hauswirth's mental state, based on both psychological testing and the linguistic support of his malleability in the face of the strong pressure made by the officer. Robert Leonard provided our combined linguistic analysis in his testimony at the hearing, but it did not deter the court from judging Hauswirth competent enough to stand trial. Even though the judge permitted no consideration of Hauswirth's mental incapacity, he clearly recognized that something was wrong, because he ruled that Hauswirth could see an outside psychologist up to three days per week. To some it would seem that if Hauswirth was mentally incapacitated after the hearing, it would be equally possible that he had some problems before the hearing.

The language evidence demonstrated that after considerable pressure, Hauswirth clearly agreed to the officer's suggestion that he kill the people. There was no way for the defense to claim that this agreement was ambiguous, so the defense attorney asked that the case be dismissed because of entrapment, based on the totality of the circumstances and especially on the impropriety of the methods used by the undercover policeman who created and facilitated the solicitation to commit murder. The defense attorney also stressed that Hauswirth had an obviously limited mental capacity as a factor that should be considered in determining whether he acted voluntarily during the reprehensible and aggressive conduct of the police officer.

The defense lawyer also presented evidence regarding the psychological testing that demonstrated Hauswirth's cognitive learning disabilities causing him to be easily influenced and confused about how to present and resolve his problems. The linguistic analysis that Leonard and I produced clearly supported the psychologist's findings. We pointed out how Hauswirth's language showed that he was initially undecided about what to do and very passive and compliant to the aggressive agenda of the undercover detective posing as a hit man.

Based on the language used in this conversation, it was clear to us that despite Hauswirth's initial uncertainty about what to do, the officer not only provided the opportunity but also coerced Hauswirth into agreeing to the killings. In terms of the structure of this speech event of soliciting murder, it was only after reaching the agreement stage that Hauswirth finally identified the problem that led to his obviously reluctant decision. Our report supported the psychologist's assessment that Hauswirth was uncertain and unable to make decisions on his own, that his language suggested paranoia about others who were unfairly doing bad things to him, that he was polite and forgetful (he couldn't remember the addresses or even the names of the streets), and that the overall language evidence showed his lack of cognitive ability.

We also pointed out that the officer exhibited all the power and control in this conversation, enabling him to direct it wherever he apparently wanted it to go while allowing for little or no objection, especially from an intellectually challenged and compliant listener like Hauswirth, whose lack of power was demonstrated in his sixteen requests for directives from the officer, including "What do you want me to do?" "What do you want me to say exactly?" "Do you want me to make payments?" "Could we hold off?" and "Is this what you want me to do?" His ten responses of "I don't know" throughout the conversation were equally uncharacteristic of a man who was clear and decided about finding a hit man to kill someone.

As in good scientific research, a good linguistic analysis begins with hypotheses to be tested against the evidence. In this case, there are three:

1. Hauswirth wished the three people were dead but found it difficult to ask the officer to do it. He clearly would like them gone, but having them murdered was a different question.

2. Hauswirth was too cognitively and linguistically handicapped to initiate the words that the officer wanted to hear, but he indeed wanted to solicit murder. His pronunciation and grammar were roughly acceptable, but he gave much evidence of failing to make logical connections, produce logical time sequences, respond to the point of questions, and indicate or understand causality.
3. Hauswirth believed he had been unjustly harmed by the three people but did not really know what he wanted to do, which is why several times he asked the officer what he should do. He was unable to state what he wanted during the first twenty-five minutes of probing by the officer. He gave indications that he was confused by the purpose of their meeting. He was unclear about what he wanted the officer to do, and he was frequently unresponsive or off-topic when he responded to the officer's questions. His own agenda came only near the end of their talk when he elaborated about his problems with the family, not his interest in killing them.

Based on the language used in this conversation, hypothesis three was the most reasonable. In these undercover conversations, Benjamin Hauswirth was indeed an easy mark for the undercover detective.

Aftermath

The judge dismissed the psychologist's testimony concerning Hauswirth's intellectual level, based on his interpretation of the objective test of entrapment, saying: "Since Michigan follows the objective test in analyzing entrapment, Defendant's intellectual level is not a factor to be considered in determining whether he was entrapped." Here the judge appeared to equate Hauswirth's predisposition to commit a crime (the subjective test of entrapment) with his previous and continuing mental state. Such an equation thereby eliminated the relationship of Hauswirth's agreed upon cognitive deficits from the objective test of entrapment, which considers whether the undercover detective was overreaching when his actions rose to the level of reprehensible conduct.

The judge ruled that the tactics used by the police did not rise to the level of reprehensible conduct (the objective test of entrapment). He ruled that Hauswirth clearly understood what the meeting was about and "informed the detective of his problem," and "had the intent" to want them dead, even though "it took some time" for the detective to get him to say this. In short, the ruling was that the detective merely provided the opportunity for Hauswirth to commit a crime of soliciting murder. The judge did not consider the issue of payment for the hit, in this case sixty dollars, since he relied on the statute defining *solicitation*: "offer to give, promise to give, or give *any* money, services, or anything of value." Hauswirth clearly paid sixty dollars for the proposed hit, which in the court's mind, made him guilty, regardless of whether or not there were psychological and linguistic factors that would mitigate the situation. In short, the detective was not accused of coercive conduct even though the person with whom he was speaking admittedly lacked the mental capacity that might enable him to fully understand their conversational exchanges. Despite the linguistic testimony that Hauswirth was a passive actor in which the detective controlled their conversation and himself produced the offer of the hit, the judge rejected the entrapment defense. The judge also ruled that Hauswirth clearly understood what the meeting was about and informed the detective of his problem. Hauswirth's expressions, "these three people is who I want gone" and "taken out" played an important role in the judge's ruling. At trial Hauswirth was convicted of soliciting murder.

THE STATE OF ALASKA V. LARRY GENTRY

In October 1985 an Alaska Airline senior pilot named Robert Pfeil was shot and killed in Anchorage by someone thought to be driving a 1974 Lincoln Continental automobile owned by Larry Gentry. The police did not accuse Gentry of being the driver or shooter, but since his car was identified at the crime scene, he was charged with aiding and abetting murder. Making matters more difficult for Gentry, the man who was eventually accused of being the shooter, John Bright, had been Gentry's housemate until he recently moved out just after Gentry got married a few months before the crime occurred. Bright was mechanically inclined, had often worked on the old Lincoln, and had wired it so that no ignition key was needed. The question for the police was whether Gentry knew that his car was used in the shooting because if he did know, he aided and abetted the murder.

Unlike the cases of Townsend and Hauswirth, neither the defense nor the prosecution sought psychological assessments of Gentry, although both sides admitted at a pretrial hearing that he had an IQ of about 80 and limited comprehension abilities. One linguistic task here was to analyze the way Gentry used language during his interviews and hearings. Another task was to determine whether the language of the police and prosecutor confused Gentry to the extent that they didn't fully understand Gentry's responses or that they distorted them in their restatements and summaries. Voluntariness was also an issue, since the police interpreted some of Gentry's statements as though he had made them voluntarily when they actually appeared to be the products of questionable interview tactics.

Gentry's sister, an Anchorage police officer, had noticed that while Gentry and his new bride were honeymooning in Hawaii, someone had been shooting a gun in the area of his home. She feared that his former housemate, John Bright, was up to no good and was using his car without Gentry's knowledge. She warned Gentry that he should get rid of it. Shortly after this, Gentry junked the Lincoln, unaware that the police now believed it was used in the recent murder of Robert Pfeil. Further suspicion fell on Gentry because he worked as a bartender at a saloon run by Gilbert (Junior) Pauole, who was thought to be associated with an organized crime boss in Hawaii who had sent him to Anchorage to run saloons and send skimmed profits back to him. At one time, Gentry had overheard a conversation between Pauole and Bright about doing "a job," but Gentry claimed that he didn't know what that job was. Meanwhile, Gentry followed his sister's advice and had his old Lincoln turned into scrap.

About two weeks after Pfeil's murder, the police brought in a young man who had been bragging at a pool hall that he had something to do with the case. He confessed that he was the driver that and made a deal with the police for immunity in exchange for wearing a transmitter to confront a man named Betts, who had supplied the gun to John Bright, the shooter. After the police called in Betts, he agreed to wear a wire to confront John Bright. Bright was out of town and no longer lived with Gentry, so Betts approached Gentry about a debt of $700 that he claimed Bright still owed him. The tape of this meeting did not help the police, for it indicated only that Gentry didn't know what Betts was talking about.

After his meeting with Betts, Gentry, taking the advice of his sister once again, voluntarily went to the police and filed a complaint of harassment against Betts, claiming that he feared for his life. He had even received some threat letters from Betts, justifying his fears. Gentry had no idea that Betts was a decoy sent by the police to try to learn whether Gentry was involved in the murder. The police were surprised that Gentry came to them with this complaint about Betts, but they let him go, also informing him that it looked very odd that he had his car scrapped at that particular time.

Four days later, Gentry again came to the police station voluntarily and admitted that he had not been totally forthright during his first visit to them. He now admitted that he knew some things about what had happened and he now feared for his life even more. He implicated his boss, Junior Pauole, as the person behind the shooting and added that Pauole had threatened to kill him if he told anyone. The key words are emphasized below in Gentry's interview by the police:

GENTRY: I can't even remember how it all started now. It just started over some drugs and shit. **I think maybe** Junior [Pauole] had something to do with it. It's the reason we wind up gettin' ripped off. Junior gave me an ounce of coke to sell...he came up to John [Bright] one day and asked him if he wanted to **do somethin' for him** and John said, "sure." Junior looked at me and said, "Do you want to hear about it?" I said, "No I don't," so I left.

POLICE: So Junior fronted you this ounce of coke?

GENTRY: Right, and it got stolen. John [Bright] made a deal with him. John said he was gonna pay Junior off for his job he was gonna get paid for. I said, "Well great, then we ain't got nothin' to worry about." So that there was taken care of there and that was the last we heard about that.

POLICEMAN: Did you **know** what job he was referring to?

GENTRY: No I **did not.**

POLICEMAN: Did he tell you it was gonna be for Junior?

GENTRY: No he did not. **I found out later. I figured** it was for Junior. I **figured it out** myself. I done been told if I opened my mouth or anything I'd get killed...John [Bright] **told me** that night he shot **the guy** and shit and then he started hollerin'. He figured Junior wasn't gonna pay.

During this interview, Gentry voluntarily confessed that he had been buying and selling small quantities of cocaine and that he had destroyed his twelve-year-old Lincoln Continental, which was now considered evidence in the murder case. Gentry said that Bright told him he shot someone (identified only as "the guy") in a job that was supposed to replace the money lost when the drugs were stolen. Gentry's use of "I think maybe," "do something," and "did not know" are far from representations of his knowledge about the killing before it happened. Nor did Gentry admit to knowing who was killed. He said that afterward he "figured it out" that the hit was done for Pauole and that Bright told him only that he had shot "the guy," without identifying who "the guy" was. This is a classic example of Garner's (1995) distinction between knowledge (*awareness of* a fact) and notice (awareness *about* a fact). The prosecution was apparently unaware of this distinction.

At the end of this meeting the police then asked Gentry to cooperate with them by wearing a body mike during any future conversations he might have with Bright or Pauole. Gentry compliantly agreed. Alaska state law requires a hearing in front of a judge before a citizen can be authorized to wear a body mike to tape other people. This meant that Gentry had to participate in that hearing. It is very important to know that before Gentry appeared in the courtroom, the prosecutor told the court that Gentry had "confessed to his involvement in the matter," without specifying what his involvement was or what he had confessed to.

The first witness at this hearing was the police officer who had talked with Gentry earlier. He testified that Gentry had said that he *knew* that Pauole had hired Bright to do "the job" of shooting someone and that Gentry had reported to this policeman that Bright asked Gentry to borrow his shotgun, and that Gentry also told this officer that Bright would be using the Lincoln. The taped recording of that earlier meeting does not substantiate any of these statements the police officer made at this hearing. He had either inferred these things, had a terrible memory, or was taking a fictional shortcut to ensure a conviction.

The judge was apparently impressed with the officer's (inaccurate) testimony and asked him, "I wonder if you could just comment on the voluntariness of his confession to you." The clarity of Gentry's voluntary confession about his buying and selling cocaine and his voluntary admission about destroying his old Lincoln were now hopelessly confused with the officer's garbled report about the voluntariness of Gentry's purported knowledge about the murder, which did not occur in the tape recording of the officer's meeting with Gentry.

Since the sole purpose of this hearing was to get the judge to authorize Gentry to wear a body mike, Gentry was not represented by a lawyer. There was no need for one, because he had not been charged with any crimes, even the drug dealing he had admitted to. In fact, Gentry was not permitted to be in the courtroom to hear the prosecutor tell the judge that he "confessed to his involvement in the matter." Therefore, nobody was present to challenge or refute the officer's skewed, creative, and inaccurate testimony. Both the judge and the prosecutor now heard this information for the first time and they likely assumed that the officer's report of Gentry's "confession to his involvement in the matter" referred to Gentry's actual involvement in the murder. In fact, the judge himself, not being properly informed, referred to it as Gentry's "confession about his involvement in the shooting."

When Gentry finally was called into the hearing room, he believed that his agreement to wear the body mike indicated that he was on the side of the police in their effort to get solid evidence on the shooter. What Gentry actually said was expanded far beyond what Bright had told him—that he shot an unidentified person he referred to only as "the guy."

Gentry had every reason to expect to have to pay the consequence for his crime of drug dealing and maybe even for destroying his old Lincoln, but he had no way to know that the prosecutor would be grooming him to be charged as a conspirator in a murder case. During his questioning by the prosecutor, Gentry had not been advised of his Miranda rights (he had not yet been accused of a crime) and he had no idea what was about to happen. He understood that he should be cooperative and tell the truth as he knew it. He did the best he could without help of counsel, but in the end he was indicted for conspiracy to murder and brought to trial.

The same prosecutor questioned him at his trial. In *Language Crimes* (1993) I discuss this case in detail, but here I will focus only on the issue of voluntariness of what was inferred to be his confession, first reminding you that Gentry had already volunteered to come to the police in the first place, had voluntarily admitted his own drug offense, and had volunteered to wear a body mike to get the needed evidence on Pauole and Bright.

The wily prosecutor must have sensed that Gentry had less than average intelligence, because he played vocabulary games with him. One example of this is their exchange about what it means to *know* something.

Black's Law Dictionary (2004) defines the noun *knowledge* as "having or showing awareness or understanding; being well-informed, deliberate, conscious." Garner's *Dictionary of Modern Legal Usage* (1995) defines *knowledge* as the required awareness of a fact or condition, contrasting with "notice," which merely requires a reason to know *about* a fact or condition. In the following exchange between the prosecutor and Gentry, it is clear that Gentry did not display complete awareness or understanding. He was not well informed or deliberate. He showed that he may have had notice *about* a fact or condition but not knowledge of it. Again the key terms are emphasized:

PROSECUTOR: But you **knew** it was some kind of shooting, but nothing more specific than that?

GENTRY: I **wasn't too sure** on it even being a shooting. **I wasn't sure, but I kind of knew and I kind of didn't know.**

PROSECUTOR: You **kind of suspected** though?

GENTRY: Yeah, **I suspected**, 'cause it was bits and pieces I was hearing, picking up, you know, and started getting a hold of.

PROSECUTOR: Now by then you **knew** that it involved a shooting, but you didn't know who the guy was?

GENTRY: Yeah, it went on so long **I just figured** it wasn't gonna happen. You know, **it was just a bunch of bullshit**.

PROSECUTOR: Was it **clear in your mind** that this was the money that Pauole had promised to pay John for **this shooting**?

GENTRY: I was **pretty sure** of it, yes.

PROSECUTOR: Before **the shooting**, right?

GENTRY: By the time **it** was going to happen,**yeah, I knew about it**. I'd done **figured it out**.

PROSECUTOR: So you **knew it** was going to happen?

GENTRY: Yes. I **knew about it**. I'd done **figured it out**.

PROSECUTOR: Your car was to be used?

GENTRY: No, I **did not know** he was going to use that car.

PROSECUTOR: Isn't it true that in your mind **you realized** that you were assisting John to do this shooting?

GENTRY: I was still trying to ignore it. I didn't want to believe it and I knew it was a nightmare I couldn't get out of.

PROSECUTOR: But you **know** what you did.

GENTRY: That's the **way it looks**, yeah. It **looks like** I assisted in it and I didn't want to.

This exchange is one of those trains passing in the night experiences in which unclear referencing and different schemas by both parties leads to simultaneous conversation about two different things. The important issue is what it tells us about what Gentry knew *about* the murder of Pfeil, after Gentry had admitted that he knew that Bright was going to shoot someone as repayment to Pauole for the drugs that were stolen under Gentry's watch.

Indefinite referencing

In the above exchange the prosecutor used the indefinite pronoun "it," which could refer to either Bright's admission that he shot "the guy" or the specific shooting of Pfeil. Gentry's responses were "not too sure," "kind of knew," "kind of didn't know," "suspected," "just figured it out," and even thought it might be "a bunch of bullshit." In contrast, the prosecutor apparently believed that Gentry was talking specifically about the murder of Pfeil, even though this referent had not been identified clearly by either participant. When the prosecutor asked Gentry if he knew that Bright was going to use "that car," his topic, the killing of Pfeil, suddenly must have become clear to Gentry. The car was irrelevant to Gentry's topic of Bright's boast about shooting the unidentified "guy." Gentry was more worried about it being used in the Pfeil murder, and now that the prosecutor had made this topic clear, Gentry denied it strongly.

The semantics of "to know"

The prosecutor's focus was on what Gentry knew about the Pfeil murder. He was apparently talking about this murder when he used the expressions *knew, clear in your mind, realized,* and *knowingly.* Gentry, with his mind fixed on the topic of Bright's statements about shooting "someone" and shooting "the guy," answered with the expressions "wasn't too sure," "kind of knew and kind of didn't know," "suspected," "started getting a hold of," "figured," "pretty sure," "done figured it out," "did not know," "trying to ignore," "didn't want to believe," and "trying to believe." When the prosecutor finally brought up the topic of whether the car was used, Gentry understood him to refer to the Pfeil killing and meekly offered "that's the way it looks," "it looks like," and "I didn't want to," none of which can be considered admissions that he **knew** that his car was used when someone murdered Pfeil, which was the only basis for possible charges against him.

In order to know something, a person must believe it to be true, have good reason to believe it to be true, and have a substantial probability that it is true. Gentry never got to the point of believing anything he referred to was true. He expressed no good reason to believe it was true that his car was used in the Pfeil murder. Likewise he found no substantial probability that this was true, but he admitted that it could "look like" it was, but he didn't want to assist in Pfeil's death. This is a far cry from a voluntary admission of his involvement in the murder.

Contrasting schemas

Five times during his trial testimony, Gentry's language revealed that his schema was fear of retribution from Bright and Pauole. To one such expression the prosecutor's own schema of Gentry's guilt led him to interpret this as Gentry's fear of testifying in the courtroom. The prosecutor simply ignored Gentry's other four statements about how he feared Pauole. Gentry's other schema was that he was cooperating with law enforcement, which the prosecutor sidestepped completely. In contrast, the prosecutor's main schema was that Gentry was deeply involved in the murder. He tried to get Gentry to admit under oath that he had previously confessed his guilt in his earlier statement to the police. The tape of this earlier meeting shows clearly that Gentry did not admit this. When schemas and agendas are not shared, miscommunication is a likely result, which is exactly what happened here.

Intelligence and style of communicating

Gentry was not nearly as mentally incapacitated as Townsend or even Hauswirth. But with an incomplete high school education, a low IQ, a strong tendency to comply, and a penchant for cooperativeness, Gentry was an easy target for the police and the prosecutor. His language indicated that he was far from an articulate speaker. His ability to narrate suffered from some of the same problems that mentally incapacitated speakers have, such as keeping time references straight. The prosecutor, a very articulate speaker, could not get Gentry to place events accurately in the three simple time frames that he established: (1) what happened before the shooting; (2) what happened the day of the shooting; and (3) what happened after the shooting. Gentry confused them consistently, making his answers difficult for anyone to understand.

A competent speaker with sufficient mental capacity would have been better able to handle the prosecutor's simple time frame questions. Gentry could not. For example, in answer to the prosecutor's time frame question concerning the use of the Lincoln before the shooting, Gentry answered that Bright told him about "a guy driving the car." Perhaps surprised at what he considered the present tense of the verb, the prosecutor requested clarification, "He was going to drive the car?" Gentry replied, "This was after the shooting."

On other occasions Gentry clearly didn't understand the questions and sometimes gave conflicting answers. For example, when asked if the police made any promises to him, Gentry first answered "no," then later pointed out that they promised him protection. Then came the following exchange:

PROSECUTOR: You're talking about conversations that happened about two weeks before the shooting?

GENTRY: Yeah.

PROSECUTOR: Am I right?

GENTRY: No. The payment deal happened after the shooting.

One important issue was whether the prosecutor had a coercive influence on Gentry's responses or perhaps even misled him to say something he didn't intend to say. More likely it was a case of the prosecutor using conventional courtroom language that made the testimony of an unintelligent and less than competent speaker appear to be voluntary admissions of guilt.

The speech events of police interviews and trial testimony can provide serious problems for anyone, but when suspects or defendants have great difficulty telling their side of the story to adversarial opponents who are far more skilled in their craft, the odds are stacked against the less than competent suspects. *Black's Law Dictionary* (2004) defines "justice" as the fair and proper administration of laws. In an effort to ensure such fairness, laws now protect suspects who are mentally incapacitated, inebriated when interviewed, and juveniles. Yet no such laws exist for those who are simply ignorant, linguistically unsophisticated, and unable to defend themselves against the more linguistically competent police and prosecutors. Larry Gentry was an easy mark.

Aftermath

I testified to the above at Gentry's trial, but to no avail because the jury convicted him of first-degree murder. His attorneys appealed his conviction, claiming that because Gentry talked to the police voluntarily and was then coerced by them as well as by the prosecutor, any inculpatory statements he had made to state authorities violated the due process clause of the Fourteenth Amendment. His attorneys also claimed that Gentry was not in custody during his interview (the information that the police provided came from Gentry's hearing testimony). The appellate court denied all of these claims, adding that even though Gentry said that he feared for his life from the threats made to him, he made these statements voluntarily and that there was no coercion on the part of the police. Apparently the prosecutor's misstatements about what Gentry had earlier told the police was were not even considered. The appellate court denied all of Gentry's claims and affirmed the district court's decision.

After the trial, a long and convoluted legal process demonstrated that Gilbert Pauole was indeed the mastermind behind Pfeil's murder. Pauole then struck a deal with the prosecutor and testified against Neil Mackay, who was accused of paying Pauole $10,000 to subcontract with John Bright to kill Pfeil, which was "the job" that Gentry either did or did not understand, depending on how the prosecution interpreted it when Gentry talked about it. The story is even more convoluted, because Mackay was Pfeil's father-in-law. Pfeil's wife had been killed in a car bomb explosion several years earlier and her father, Neil Mackay, believed that Pfeil had engineered his daughter's murder in order to inherit her considerable assets. Larry Gentry turned out to be only a very minor player in this whole sad saga.

8

VOLUNTARINESS OF SUSPECTS IMPAIRED BY ALCOHOL OR DRUGS

Although intoxication from alcohol or drugs is not a legal defense to a crime, some defense lawyers use this impairment as a way to raise doubts about their clients' intentions while they committed their crimes. More commonly, however, suspects' impairment from alcohol or drugs relates to their voluntariness during police interviews during a period when their mental capacities are besotted. Such occasions can raise serious questions about the validity of the process law enforcement uses during such interviews. In jurisdictions where diminished capacity defenses are permitted in murder cases, lawyers sometimes argue diminished capacity to identify a lesser crime, usually manslaughter, which, if successful, can avoid the death penalty.

The debate about whether intoxication should or should not be an excuse for committing a crime has raged for centuries. Aristotle thought inebriation made the crime even worse. Some states permit mens rea defenses while others do not. In federal jurisdictions, drug and alcohol intoxication, also called "diminished capacity" (the meaning of which seems to be closely related to "diminished responsibility") can be the basis for a downward departure in sentencing. The debate about what to call this continued in California in 1980 when voters replaced "diminished capacity" with "diminished actuality," which seems to have moved the meaning a bit closer to intentionality, and the semantic psychological battle over degrees and definitions of intentionality continues.

The following three murder case examples provide different perspectives on the diminished capacity defense. In the first case, the facts and language of the defendant indicate that the police interviewed her while she was still under the debilitating effects of a night of excessive alcoholic indulgence. The second case describes a long unresolved murder case in which an accused but still not indicted suspect swore that he was intoxicated on the night his wife was murdered and had no memory of anything that happened. The case went dormant, but a few years later the police reopened it and hauled in the husband of the murdered wife for additional questioning. The third case involves the tape-recorded interrogation of a man who was under the influence of marijuana and depressants at the time the police read him his Miranda rights, which led to a strong debate about whether or not he voluntarily waived them.

THE STATE OF NEVADA V. SHELLI DEWEY

In September 2004, Shelli Dewey was tried and convicted of second-degree murder with a deadly weapon for allegedly stabbing her husband Steven to death in the parking lot of an Elko Nevada honky-tonk bar. She was given the maximum penalty for the crime—two consecutive life terms with the possibility of parole after twenty years. In January 2011 she was back in court for an evidentiary hearing on a writ of habeas corpus, claiming that she had ineffective counsel during the trial at which she was convicted.

The evidentiary hearing included the testimony of linguistics expert Robert Leonard. In preparation for the hearing Leonard and I analyzed the taped interviews conducted by the Elko detectives in 2004 in order to determine whether or not the exchanges between Dewey and the police provided any clues to either her innocence or her guilt. The police and prosecutor claimed that Dewey voluntarily confessed to the murder in that tape-recorded interview, but Leonard and I could not find language evidence that could lead the police and prosecutor to even infer such a conclusion.

Shelli and Steven Dewey had two small children and could be described as a relatively uneducated working-class young couple. One serious problem in their life was that they partied far too much, sometimes staying up all night drinking at various bars in and around Elko. One night after they both drank heavily, Steven fell over drunkenly and broke the bar's jukebox, after which they were both ejected. It was in the bar's parking lot during the early morning hours that Dewey's problems with the law began. She became the first and only suspect in the case.

Exactly what happened in that semilighted parking lot was the subject of what took place during Shelli Dewey's subsequent trial as well as in the later evidentiary hearing petition for a retrial. The events immediately after Steven's death were critical, for when the Elko police appeared on the scene, they quickly decided that Shelli Dewey was their only suspect. None of the many other people in the bar that night, even those that had argued with Steven, were seriously questioned.

The police first took Shelli to a nearby hospital for a blood alcohol test, which registered.15, well over the level determining intoxication. They then quickly drove her from the hospital to the police station, where an Elko policeman read her the Miranda warning and interviewed her briefly. Two hours later a different policeman gave her a fresh Miranda warning and interviewed her in more detail. After these two interviews, the police were convinced that Shelli had voluntarily given them a valid confession.

Miranda waiver

In the first brief interview, Shelli refused to sign a waiver of her rights and on the tape she can be heard saying, "I want a la—," with the vowel of "la-" having the low back "aw" sound found in the vowel of the words "law" and "saw." As she was uttering that word, the interviewer interrupted and talked over her, slightly muffling the last sound of her "la—," asking her, "You don't want to talk to anybody?" The officer's question itself indicated that he understood that Dewey's "I want a la—" was her refusal to waive her rights. To this Dewey said, "No, cause you'll think I did it and I didn't do it." Her beginning this sentence with "no" follows the English negative concord rule specifying that her negative "no" agreed with the negative in the officer's question. That is, when a question uses a negative form, an answer in a negative form indicates agreement with the officer's negative "don't want to." It is difficult to imagine how the police or prosecutor could consider this as a waiver of her rights. But somehow they did.

Another problem was that the second police interviewer apparently was unaware that Dewey had said, "I want a la—" to the first interviewer. When this new officer interviewed Dewey two hours later, he gave her a fresh Miranda warning along with a waiver form worded differently from the one given her by the first policeman. Her blood alcohol level was not remeasured at that time, but there was no reason to suspect that she had suddenly become sober. She told this officer, "I just want to go home, take my kids back to the desert first, then I'll come talk to you. I need to see the babies." Her offer to talk with them later supported her decision not to talk to the police at that time. Dewey later related that she was confused by the wording of the second Miranda but signed the form anyway, waiving her rights to counsel even though two hours earlier she said she wanted a law[yer] present and this time she said she'd talk to them later. She said she believed that by hastily signing "a paper" that she didn't (or couldn't) process, she could get to her children more quickly. As noted in chapters 2 and 6, there is considerable research on suspects' misunderstandings of the whole Miranda process.

To this point the investigation presented a number of issues. First, the Elko police force had overlooked some pieces of crime scene evidence and they, as well as the emergency workers, had trampled over potential evidence. Although many patrons of the bar were nearby and one of them had even argued with Steven, the police did not explore the possibility that anyone other than Shelli had stabbed Steven to death. Second, Shelli Dewey, their only suspect, was still intoxicated when the police interviewed her. Linguistic analysis helped support this, because her erratic and slurred speech during the interviews was consistent with the results of her blood alcohol test. Third, when first interviewed, Dewey did not waive her Miranda rights. Finally, where the linguistic analysis is even stronger, at no time during her two tape-recorded interrogations did Shelli Dewey confess to any crime and clearly not to the crime of stabbing her husband to death. In fact, she consistently denied this twenty-six times from the beginning of the two interviews to the end.

Motive

There is no question that Dewey had the opportunity to kill her husband, because she was with him at the bar where they had argued about whether it was time to go home, but any motivation for killing him because of this argument was never established. Nevertheless, the officer tried to convince her that her motive was anger. Dewey admitted that she was angry with Steven for his drunken behavior, especially when several times he shouted to everyone at the bar, "I am God." Not surprisingly, she told him that she wanted to go home. Over and over again she told the interviewing officer that she loved Steven. In fact, when police arrived, they found Dewey kneeling on the ground tenderly holding her dying husband in her arms. The motive of anger at her husband was not very convincing.

Means and method

The second police officer began his interview with Dewey by trying to establish her means and method for killing Steven. Even though it was clear that her husband had been stabbed to death with a knife, for some unknown reason the officer first asked her about a broken bottle:

Officer's accusations	Dewey's denials
You stabbed him with a broken beer bottle.	I didn't have a beer bottle.
You hit him on his chest.	I don't remember hitting him.
What did you hit him with?	I hit him with his knife?

Although Dewey's rising intonation in her last response indicated that she was requesting clarification about the implication of the officer's question, this was overlooked by both the government's transcriber, who did not include a question mark, and at trial by the prosecutor. The prosecution relied heavily on this erroneous transcription, claiming that it constituted Dewey's voluntary confession statement. In reality, Dewey was requesting clarification of a charge she didn't understand. Reliance on transcripts may have some value at trial but not when the transcript distorts the spoken language it is supposed to represent.

Hypotheticals

When the second interviewing officer realized that his effort to discover the motivation and means by which Dewey allegedly committed the crime was going nowhere, he decided to pursue another method. Earlier Dewey had mentioned that when the couple had argued in the past, it was common for her to pound her husband on his chest, illustrating this with the heels of her closed fists (key hypothetical words used by both parties are emphasized):

Officer's question	Dewey's answer
Where, in what part of his body **would** you hit him?	I **would have** hit him in the chest because that's what I always did when he was talking to me like that.

Here the officer asked a hypothetical question ("would you") and Dewey responded with a hypothetical answer ("I would have"), as speakers normally do. Because this is an imaginative hypothetical exchange that is not time related, it cannot be considered a voluntary admission that Dewey had hit her husband at the time he was killed. Although up to that time Dewey hadn't mentioned hitting her husband on the chest the night he died, the officer apparently saw this hypothetical time confusion as a way of exposing Dewey's method of killing her husband.

Ambiguous time reference

At this point, the officer tried to use Dewey's hypothetical answer above to connect it to reality, asking: "What did you do when you hit him **that time**?" The officer was not specific about what his "that time" referred to, but it prompted Dewey to recall that she had pounded her husband on his chest earlier that night, just after she left the bar to go to their truck: "I turned around and I thumped him and I turned around and walked back to the pickup and he said something and I turned around to ask him what and he fell to the ground. I don't remember what he said." Now the interviewer thought he heard what he was after: Dewey admitted pounding her husband on his chest shortly before he was killed, but she said nothing about having a knife in her hand when she thumped him.

The officer then focused on the knife that killed Steven. It was established that Steven had carried his hunting knife into the bar that night. Shelli was fuzzy as she hypothesized about this, saying, "He **must have** dropped it and I picked it up off the ground. I was trying to take everything back to the pickup. I **might have** put it in the truck when I went back to call 911." This was, of course, her hypothetical speculation about something that was the best that her alcohol-muddled mind could produce. The officer then asked her to describe the knife. She answered with less than certainty: "I think it's black. I think it had a sheath." The officer then asked if she ever had the knife in her hand that night, to which she replied, "**I guess, I don't know. It's a possibility. If I did,** it was a complete accident. **I'm assuming** he followed me outside. I would never have done that [picked up the knife] unless it got bumped and fell on the ground. **I believe** it's in the truck now."

In the conversation above, both the officer and Dewey produced confused references. Dewey returned to her earlier topic about how she usually thumped Steven on the chest when they argued, while the officer's references were to her hitting her husband with the knife. As in the Davis case described in chapter 5, the two speakers were stuck on simultaneously different topics.

Aftermath

It is clear that intoxication is not an excuse for committing a crime, but when the police interview intoxicated suspects, voluntariness of their responses can certainly be questioned. The evidence from Dewey's two police interviews was very weak in terms of establishing her intentionality and predisposition, leaving the prosecutor to rely only on what he believed or inferred that she had volunteered.

In her 2005 conviction for her husband's second-degree murder with a deadly weapon, Dewey's lawyer did not request any linguistic analysis. She was sentenced to two consecutive life terms with the possibility of parole after twenty years. In 2007 her attorney's appeal of her conviction was denied. The appellate judges declared that she made no request whatsoever for an attorney: "We conclude that her confession was voluntary and the district court did not err in admitting the confession into evidence."

In January 2011 Dewey hired a new lawyer, who petitioned for a new trial based on the ineffective counsel in her previous trial. Before this hearing, Dewey's attorney asked Robert Leonard and me to linguistically analyze the police interviews. Leonard testified at the hearing, but at the time of this writing the court's response for a request for a new trial was still pending. The unresolved issues from Dewey's original trial include her failure to waive her Miranda rights, her consistent denials of guilt, the failure of the police to obtain the confession they inferred they had, the muddled and confusing interview techniques of the police, their failure to pursue any other leads and, of course, the fact that Dewey was intoxicated during the interviews, all of which speak loudly to issues of voluntariness.

THE STATE OF FLORIDA V. ROBERT ALBEN

Robert Alben (name changed at the request of his lawyer) was one of the many natives of New York City who moved to Florida's sunny climate in the early 1970s. One morning in January 1978 Alben, then in his mid-fifties, woke up and discovered his wife brutally beaten and unconscious on their living room floor. He called for an ambulance that took her directly to the hospital, and when the police arrived they interviewed Alben in the hospital waiting room. His wife did not survive the vicious attack by a blunt instrument, and Alben became one of several suspects that the police interviewed. In such cases, it is common for law enforcement officers to suspect the victim's close relatives, especially spouses. But with no useful physical evidence and little to go on from Alben's interview with the police, the case went cold until twelve years later in 1990, when it was reopened with the police now viewing Alben as their only suspect and threatening to indict him for capital murder.

The only evidence against Alben was this hospital interview back in 1978. But when the police reopened the investigation they reviewed that earlier interview and now believed that it actually showed that Alben had confessed to the murder, even though twelve years earlier a different prosecutor had come to a very different conclusion. The police now thought Alben had been lying about his memory loss during that first interview and brought him in for a second one.

Alben's defense attorney, with whom I had consulted on several other cases, asked me to review that 1978 police interview, and I agreed. If my analysis proved to be helpful, the lawyer planned to use it to try to quash the planned indictment. There were three questions to resolve: (1) was Alben lying during his 1978 interview; (2) did he confess to the murder; and if so (3) did he confess voluntarily. I dealt with the first two questions in my book *The Language of Confession, Interrogation, and Deception* (Sage 1998). Here I focus on the issue of voluntariness.

The 1978 questioning was a rather effective tape-recorded police interview speech event. The officer first read Alben his Miranda rights and had him sign that he understood them. He began by asking Alben to tell everything he remembered, interrupting only with "who, when, and where" questions. His major problem was that Alben said he couldn't recall anything that was germane to solving the murder. He remembered going to dinner with his wife and a mutual female friend, during which time he had "five or six vodka" drinks and complained about feeling ill.

From that point on, his memory was irregular and inconsistent. He remembered getting into the car after they left the restaurant but not whether he was in the front or back seat. He recalled arguing with his wife about whether she should drive him home. In spite of his objections, he reported that she drove to the dog racing track, where his wife and friend were eager to win some money. But Alben lost all memory at that point and recalled nothing more until waking up at home in his bed the next morning. There were no inconsistencies in his accounts of what he did remember, which I charted in my earlier book. I direct attention now to his voluntariness throughout the interview. For one thing, he volunteered things that would *not* be in the best interest of a murder suspect, such as:

- he argued with his wife at the restaurant about a waitress who seemed to his wife to be overly friendly with him;
- he argued with his wife about going to the racetrack after dinner;
- their twenty-nine-year marriage relationship had become strained;
- he had a drinking problem that causes him to pass out;
- he had a temper;
- he slapped his wife across the face the previous week after she complained (falsely) to her mother that he had "beaten her";
- his wife had been driving him crazy for months;

- he carried a hammer in the trunk of his car along with other tools; and
- he had some unreported income from laundry machines he had placed in other properties that he owns.

Such voluntariness is very unusual in a person suspected of murder because these admissions could only work against him rather than for him. Guilty suspects tend to omit, downplay, or deny such matters, but Alben brought them up himself. In addition, several times he pleaded with the police interviewer to please tell him whether or not he did it:

> Talk to me. Tell me something, please. I have nothing else to say to you. Talk to me. I'm pleading with you now. I'm looking at you. Please be honest with me. You have my fingerprints. If I did the goddamn thing, for God sakes tell me. You've got to be honest with me. I want to know. I blame myself because I don't know what happened, don't you understand?

Unlike the Dewey case, the issue was not Alben's intoxication during the interview. Instead it was the effects that his intoxication had at the time of his wife's death on the efforts of the police to establish what actually happened and who committed the crime. Also unlike the Dewey case in which the suspect's voluntariness could be challenged by her intoxication during her interviews, the Alben case reversed the issue. Here the police did not infringe on the principle of voluntariness; it was Alben who was voluntary to the extreme.

In my report for Alben's defense attorney, I included the above analysis of the interview, which supported his own approach to the case. He subsequently gave my report to the prosecutor, who apparently gave it serious consideration.

Aftermath

In an effective bit of intelligence analysis, the prosecutor examined the evidence available at that time along with my written report and decided to not charge Alben with murder after all. If Alben really committed the crime, the evidence was just not there. This is one of the times when the prosecutor's intelligence analysis was right.

THE STATE OF OHIO V. CHARLES LORRAINE

Many criminal cases provide linguists with large amounts of language evidence, but sometimes the amount is very small and highly focused. Charles Lorraine's case was one of the latter types, where my only assignment was to analyze the government's videotape recording as the police administered the Miranda warning to the suspect. Only after my task was finished did I learn that the defense claimed that Lorraine was under the influence of drugs during the videotaped Miranda warning part of the police interview, so his purported incapacitation was not the focus of my analysis. I place Loraine's case in this chapter because my only task was to discover Lorraine's voluntariness during his Mirandizing.

In the summer of 1986 eighteen-year-old Charles Lorraine was interviewed by the Warren Ohio police about the recent murders of an elderly couple in that city. Although I was not instructed to find any linguistic evidence of Lorraine's mental state, the public defender later told me that Lorraine had a very low IQ and that he was under the influence of four marijuana joints and a large dose of Nortriptyline (a tricyclic antidepressant) at the time of his confession. I couldn't assess the effect of the drugs and medications on his speech because I was given no taped language evidence of the later period during the interview when Lorraine confessed to the crime, and I was given no substantiated information that he was "shooting up on drugs" at the time the murders were committed.

The police had shut off the videotape recorder shortly after Lorraine asked them to do so. Therefore, the government's charges of murder were built on what the interviewing officers reported about what Lorraine had said to them after he was Mirandized. This was a case in which the charge of murder was based on Lorraine's ultimate confession, but there was questionable evidence about whether he had voluntarily waived his rights before the substantive part of his interview began.

The public defender believed that his client had not voluntarily waived his rights before the police shut off the tape, and therefore none of his following very inculpatory statements should have been allowed. For this reason he filed for a suppression hearing for which I was asked to analyze the taped passage of the Miranda warning and testify about my findings. This task consisted largely of a phonetic and semantic analysis of the videotaped Miranda procedure, for which the police had prepared their own transcript. It read as follows, with the disputed passage emphasized and the turns of talk numbered for later reference:

1. Police: It ain't gonna go away, Chuck, it's gonna stay there. It's going to be here today, tomorrow, the next day.
2. Lorraine: Can't you shut the tape off?
3. Police: We need it on, Charles. For your benefit as well as ours.
4. Lorraine: I, I don't wanna talk.
5. Police: You don't want to talk? If I turn the tape off, will you tell us?
6. Lorraine: I, **I'd wanna talk.** Turn the tape off.
7. Police: Okay, okay.

8. Lorraine: And the T.V.
9. Police: Alright.
10. Officer operating the video recorder: You want it off or on?
11. Unknown speaker: _____(**one syllable**, as if the word was cut off).[Video turned off]

Both the police and prosecutor believed that after Lorraine clearly had said, "I don't want to talk" in turn 4, he then indicated that he meant only that he didn't want to talk with the video recorder running. They supported this interpretation by citing Lorraine's following "I'd wanna talk" in turn 6, which he uttered in response to the police asking in turn 5, "If I turn the tape off will you tell us?" The public defender, however, could not tell whether in turn 6 Lorraine had actually said, "I'd wanna talk" or something else. He called me to help him clarify this.

Back in 1986, when the Warren police department prepared its transcripts, they did not have the best available listening equipment. In contrast, I used state-of-the-art equipment that was regarded as much better than theirs, which in this case was my Bang and Olufsen Beocord 8004, which had many features superior to the standard equipment. The Warren police also followed the then standard procedure of having departmental secretaries produce their transcripts and then had them reviewed and corrected by the police officers who participated in those recordings. The opportunity for the police to interpret certain critical passages to their own advantage is common in such cases, for law enforcement begins with a schema of guilt, making it easy for them to hear what they anticipate hearing or perhaps even what they want to hear. Psychologist call this "the confirmation bias" while physicians call it "a diagnosis trap" in which the diagnosis becomes the controlling schema even if it turns out to be wrong.

My review of the same passage cited by the police above yielded the following numbered turns of talk, with corrections and disputed passages emphasized:

1. Police: It ain't gonna go away, Chuck. It's gonna stay there. It's going to be here today, tomorrow, the next day.
2. Lorraine: Can't you shut the tape off?
3. Police: We need it on, Charles. For your benefit as well as ours.
4. Lorraine: I, I **don wanna** talk.
5. Police: You don't want to talk? If we turn the tape off will you tell us?
6. Lorraine: **Look,** I,**I duh wanna** talk. (Shakes his head negatively) Turn the tape off.
7. Police: Okay, okay.
8. Lorraine: And the T.V.
9. Police: Alright.
10. Officer operating the video recorder: You want it off or on?
11. Unknown person: **(two syllables) or on**?[Video turned off]

My analysis demonstrated that Lorraine had made three critical negative statements. In utterance 2, he said, "Can't you shut the tape off." This utterance was undisputed. He clearly indicated that he did not want to talk to them.

In utterance 4, Lorraine said, "I, I don wanna talk." The police transcript accurately reported his elided "wanna" but missed the common consonant cluster reduction of "n't" to "n" in the negative verb "don."

Contrasting with the government's transcript showing Lorraine's agreement to talk, in utterance 6 the tape recording is clear that Lorraine said, "Look, I duh wanna talk." This indicated that he had not changed his mind from his utterance 4, when he clearly said he did not want to talk to the police. In his utterance 6 there are four linguistic aspects indicating that Lorraine repeated that he did not want to talk: his use of nonverbal information, his semantic use of "look" as a negative discourse marker, his use of phonetic reduction in contracted forms, and his sentence intonation.

Nonverbal information

I pointed out above that Lorraine shook his head "no" while uttering what he said during utterance 6. I was surprised that the police did not attend to the visual evidence of his response, but perhaps I should not have been, for I have found that in such cases the police tend to listen only for what is said, not how it is said. This was also illustrated in the Davis case (chapter 5). Nonverbal information can't be ignored, for it can play a critical role in determining a speaker's intended meaning.

The semantics of "look" as a discourse marker

The police transcript completely omitted the first word, "look," in Lorraine's utterance 6, which he spoke quickly and with heightened emotion, and which was clearly audible on the tape. Lorraine's sentence beginning with the discourse marker "look" was significant at this juncture, for it signaled a change in the direction of the conversation and highlighted Lorraine's frustration and disagreement with what the police had said immediately preceding it. When in turn 5 the police officer asked, "You don't want to talk?" he requested clarification of something that Lorraine had just made very clear in his turn 4 utterance. After the officer requested clarification about what turn 4 meant, Lorraine's "look" expressed his frustration about the officer's request for clarification about two things: whether Lorraine really wanted the tape turned off and whether his "I don't wanna talk" in turn 4 really meant something he had already made perfectly clear. Lorraine, by beginning his utterance with "look," signaled his frustration with what the officer had just said. This use of "look" as a sentence-beginning discourse marker is a common response in everyday exchanges such as this:

HUSBAND: Let's have beef stew for dinner tonight.
WIFE: Look, I told you that we don't have any beef.

The semantics of "look" in Lorraine's utterance 6 carries exactly the same discourse meaning—frustrated disagreement with what the officer had just said.

Phonetic reduction of contracted negatives

Emotionally charged speech is often spoken rapidly, and Lorraine spoke rapidly in turn 6 when he said, "Look, I, I duh wanna talk." Phonetic reductions occur often in rapid speech. When people produce negatively contracted verbs, as in "I don't wanna," they often reduce the "n't" to "n," dropping the "t" as in "I don wanna," which was the proper transcription of Lorraine's utterance 4. An even further consonant cluster reduction can also replace the remaining nasal consonant "n" (don) with a nasalized vowel, yielding "I duh wanna." Native speakers of English are accustomed to hearing phonetic reductions in negative contracted forms such as these, especially in rapid speech, and they usually have no trouble understanding them in the same way that they would understand the full forms. However, when listeners hold a schema of the speaker's guilt, it is possible for them to misunderstand this normal rapid speech phonetic reduction as a positive statement with no nasalized vowel that conveys the negativization. Most native English speakers themselves use these phonetic reductions and recognize them in other speakers. In this case, the transcriber and the prosecutor failed to do so.

Sentence intonation

Intonation is the combined pitch level and stress patterns of spoken language. Spoken pitch ranges from high to low, while stress ranges from loud to soft. In English, high pitch tends to accompany loud stress. Describing this linguistic feature to juries can be difficult, but one way to communicate this is to display the text on lines of three different heights: a high line for high intonation, a mid line for middle intonation, and a low line for low intonation. Lorraine's actual statement is then represented in this way:

Illustration 1:

```
high      Look            wanna          ____
mid                I,I duh _______            talk
low____________________________________
```

This intonation pattern is consistent with a speaker's objection or negative reaction to something the other person has just said and is inconsistent with that speaker's agreement or passivity.

If Lorraine had given his positive agreement, the intonation pattern would be the following:

Illustration 2:

```
high                        talk
mid______Look I, I wanna______
low____________________________
```

Here the high intonation and stress of the last word, "talk," would convey that Lorraine was agreeing to talk.

The tape recording showed that Lorraine's intonation was that noted in illustration 1 above, but not in illustration 2. It conveyed an objection to what the police officer had just said and provided another signal could not be interpreted as Lorraine's agreement to talk.

Syllabic structure

Careful listening to Lorraine's statement in his utterance 6 indicates that in addition to the syllable represented by "look," he produced another full syllable, represented here as "duh." To check this further I slowed down the tape speed in order to hear syllabication more clearly. This procedure verified that there were two more syllables in Lorraine's statement that the government's transcript had omitted. To illustrate this, I used the following representation to the court:

The government's transcript showed five syllables:

Syllables:	I	I'd	wan	na	talk
	1	2	3	4	5

The government argued that Lorraine's second "I" here was actually "I'd" (a single syllable meaning "I would"). One reason to reject this is that such an interpretation is unmotivated by the context of his preceding utterance 4 in which he clearly indicated that he did not want to talk. Perhaps more important evidence that the government's transcript was in error is shown by the fact that this utterance actually contained seven syllables, not the five represented by the government's transcript:

	Look	I	I	duh	wan	na	talk
Syllables	1	2	3	4	5	6	7

In addition to the syllable represented by "look," the fourth syllable was Lorraine's phonetically reduced negativization that was overlooked by the prosecution.

In summary, based on a linguistic analysis in which Lorraine's use of nonverbal head shaking, his negative discourse marker "look," his phonetic reduction of "n't" in the contraction "don't," his intonation that conveyed the meaning of objection to what the police had said earlier, and his production of seven syllables rather that the five that the government reported, the tape of the government's own language evidence made it clear that Lorraine's utterance in turn 6 did not convey his agreement to waive his Miranda rights.

Aftermath

My efforts to help the public defender quash the Miranda warning did not succeed. Subsequently, in November 1986 Lorraine was convicted of four counts of aggravated murder and two counts of aggravated burglary. He was given a death sentence. I was not informed about Lorraine's drug-induced status, so this played no role in my analysis. I was also not informed about Lorraine's mental status and could not help the psychologist's assessment that he had a low IQ and was less than mentally sound. Despite being mentally incapacitated and interviewed while under the influence of narcotics, the fact remains that he was able to convey his objection to talking with the police, even though they didn't seem to understand it.

In the month following the hearing, his lawyers filed a petition claiming that his conviction violated the Eighth Amendment's prohibition against the execution of mentally retarded persons on the basis of cruel and unusual punishment. The appellate court found that dismissal was not appropriate because Lorraine had not met the burden of demonstrating factual issues about whether or not he was retarded, but that court did permit the defense to hold an evidentiary hearing with experts who could evaluate whether or not Lorraine was mentally incapacitated. A legal battle ensued about whether Lorraine's previous records of mental retardation could apply to his current mental status rather than basing the defense claim on Lorraine's current mental status at the time of the trial. The Atkins standards were applied, meaning that determination of mental ability had to be made at the time of the murder and could not be based on any previous assessments of his mental state.

The appellate court agreed with the defense that any previous records of Lorraine's mental status should have been considered, because mental retardation is developmental before the age of eighteen. Although such evidence was not presented at the mitigation hearing, it could have been. After twenty-five years on death row, Lorraine's execution by lethal injection was scheduled for January 2012. It was delayed, however, when a federal judge scolded the state for failing to document the drugs to be used and the medical chart of the inmate, calling the state's procedure a "self-inflected wound." It is possible that this wounding actually began at the time of the Miranda warning.

9

VOLUNTARINESS OF JUVENILE SUSPECTS

Juvenile courts were created over a hundred years ago, based on the idea that the crimes of children should be judged by different standards than the crimes of adults. The idea at that time was that the courts should provide treatment for children who commit crimes rather than merely punishing them the same way the courts punished adults.

The state of Illinois devised a separated juvenile court system in 1899 and other states soon followed this lead. This took juveniles out of adult courts and focused on their rehabilitation, reasoning that they were less responsible for their actions and more likely to benefit from treatment. The U.S. Supreme Court addressed this concern in 1967 (In re Gault 387 U.S. 1), granting juveniles the right to legal counsel and the privilege against self-incrimination in court proceedings. Judges were to focus on the individual history of child criminals and devise individual treatment programs for them that would address the cause of their errant behavior. One judge at the beginning of the twentieth century is reported to have said that our laws against crime are as inapplicable to children as they would be to idiots.

This evolving legal and public attitude toward child crimes took a hit in the late twentieth century, however, when youth gang crimes increased significantly and ensuing public outrage about this put considerable pressure on the courts to require more severe penalties for juvenile murderers.

The older practices of punishing children who commit crimes are still evident today, however, when more and more offenders younger than eighteen are tried as adults and, until a Supreme Court decision in June of 2012 stopped this, thirty-nine states allowed fourteen-year-olds to be sentenced to life in prison without parole. In recent years some changes appear to be evident. For example, in 2005 the Supreme Court abolished executions of juvenile offenders. Although in 2010 the court ruled that it is unconstitutional to impose life sentences on juveniles for crimes that do *not* involve homicide, that penalty still remained for juvenile murderers until 2012. At the time of this writing, American prisons still hold 2,500 adults who committed murder before they were eighteen years old, a majority of whom were sentenced to life imprisonment without parole.

Courts are to look at the totality of the circumstances in such cases as they try to determine whether or not a juvenile's statement was made freely and voluntarily without coercion or inducements and whether parents or guardians were present at the time juveniles were interviewed. Today's courts also are to consider the juvenile's age, education, intelligence, whether their Miranda rights were given properly, and their previous criminal history.

Psychologists now recognize that from ages eleven to twenty many children's lives are filled with stress that can easily lead to despondency. A well-developed body of psychological and neurological research has now distinguished the developmental characteristics of juveniles from those of adults, including the capacity to reason, based on brain development and growth in the prefrontal cortex, where informed decisions are made. Other research shows that juveniles are still developing an adult sense of time and orientation to the future, have changing but unstable emotions relating to risk and gain, and are more easily susceptible to pressure than are adults.

Understanding Miranda rights is problematic for even intelligent adults, but this task is exacerbated in children who are raised to be obedient to authority figures such as the police, making them highly susceptible to coercion. All of these factors raise the question of voluntariness of a juvenile's statements to the police and courts. Grisso (1981) was the first to articulate the implications of juveniles' false beliefs about the Miranda warning, especially their right to have an attorney present to protect them against self-incrimination. Grisso also found that the juvenile offenders had the false belief that if they shared any inculpatory information with their lawyers, those lawyers were required to communicate it to the judge. He also found that many juveniles believed that even if they asserted their Miranda rights, this could be revoked by the police (21.1 percent) and by judges (55.3 percent).

As a result of this and other research, the American Psychological Association has endorsed the policy reflected in the United Nations Convention on the Rights of the Child that rejects life imprisonment without possibility of parole for offenses committed by individuals under eighteen years of age. The National Association of Social Workers opposes any legislation or prosecutorial discretion that permits children to be charged and punished under adult standards.

This growing body of scientific knowledge supports the claim that statements obtained by the police during interviews with juveniles should receive special scrutiny for psychological influence or coercion. Of particular interest is whether juveniles understand their Miranda rights that are difficult enough for mature adults to comprehend. It is particularly important that law enforcement audio- or videotape record their entire interviews with juvenile suspects, because doing so provides more information for judges to rely on when they determine issues of the voluntariness of waivers.

The two cases of juveniles prosecuted for murder discussed here differ in terms of the locus of voluntariness. The case of Michael Carter involved the comparison of his tape-recorded spoken language with his signed written confession, while the case of Kevin Rogers focused on his language during a police interview, which was based only on the interviewer's interpretation of what Rogers said because the police made no tape recording of the interview. In these cases, linguistic analyses of both boys' purported voluntariness was used at trial by the defense attorneys.

THE STATE OF LOUISIANA V. MICHAEL CARTER

In some murder cases, the police obtain both a written confession and an electronic recording of the interview leading up to the confession to use as evidence at trial. Even though both types of evidence may be present, police, prosecutors, and juries tend to find written confessions more convincing than the suspect's spoken words (Inbau, Reid, and Buckley 1986, 176). A comparison of these two types of evidence was tested in the Baton Rouge, Louisiana murder investigation of seventeen-year-old Michael Carter, one of three juveniles known to have participated in events that culminated in the killing of a police officer. To obtain immunity, one of these participants subsequently identified Michael as the shooter, after which he was indicted for first-degree murder.

The turning point in the investigation came when the prosecution's partially tape-recorded police interview with Michael and a written confession statement signed by Michael were turned over to the defense. His attorney quickly filed a motion to suppress, saying that Michael's confession was not voluntarily given and that it was the product of unconstitutionally coercive tactics used by Baton Rouge detectives. The defense attorney then called me to see whether a linguistic analysis of the spoken and written evidence might help the defense case. If my analysis proved helpful, she planned to use it in a hearing to suppress the evidence that took place in March of 1989.

The victim was a white motorcycle officer who was shot and killed while patrolling in a predominantly white Baton Rouge neighborhood. Three young, black inner-city boys were caught and accused. They admitted to being in that neighborhood for the purpose of robbing houses. They all came on bicycles and Michael's role was to hide the bikes in nearby bushes and to serve as the lookout in case somebody might notice them. By chance, a motorcycle officer was patrolling in that area when he happened upon them. All four boys began to run away, at which time one of them shot and killed the officer. When all were interviewed, one of them fingered Michael as the shooter, which was sufficient evidence for the police to interrogate him.

Since the tape recording of this police interview speech event stopped before the questioning ended, we can't determine the entirety of what Michael told the officers. But we can know that some conversation went on before they started taping, because the tape began with a reference to something said earlier but not recorded on tape:

> OFFICER: Better tell the truth, Michael.
>
> CARTER: Didn't do it.
>
> OFFICER: Come on, Michael. They came over and got you with your bicycle and ya'll left. You and Lobo and Kermit left.

The forty-one-minute tape recording that followed clicked off at a very crucial part, as will be discussed. The police also made a transcript of this tape and then had Michael sign a confession statement.

When asked at a hearing to suppress the evidence, the interviewing detective testified that he wrote down exactly what Michael said in the written confession statement. He added that the handwriting was his own, but the signature at the bottom was Michael's.

The first analytical step, as always, was to correct the nineteen-page transcript of this interrogation. I was able to retrieve the passages the government's transcript called "inaudible," and I also corrected many totally erroneous transcriptions, some of which made a significant difference. Not surprisingly, these errors favored the prosecution's case. Throughout the interview, Michael was crying, sobbing, stammering, and hyperventilating, which undoubtedly made it difficult for the transcriber to determine exactly what he was saying. But other transcript errors were not justifiable, such as the errors in transcribing the names, places, and times that Michael mentioned. After forty-one minutes, the police terminated the interview because Michael's continuing discomfort led him to begin to vomit. After the recording stopped, the police inferred that Michael had voluntarily confessed not only to planning to rob some houses but also to killing the policeman, although on the tape he had not even come close to confessing to the latter.

Michael reported that as the three boys ran away, the one who had a gun tossed it to Michael, who, while running, had reflexively caught it momentarily before throwing it into a nearby creek. The police claimed to have his fingerprints from the water-soaked pistol and told him that they knew that the shooter was left handed. Michael was indeed left handed.

The interview speech event

This police interview speech event followed none of the sequential steps of a preferred and competent police interview described in Chapter 2. The police didn't ask Michael to tell his own story at all but instead moved directly into the accusation phase, the charges in which Michael denied over and over again. The sequence of these accusations is noted by page numbers of the nineteen-page transcript:

P. 2	CARTER:	I didn't shoot nobody though.
	OFFICER:	Yes you did, Michael.
P. 3	ARTER:	I didn't shoot nobody though.
	OFFICER:	Michael, tell us the truth.
P.7	OFFICER:	Michael, the gun did not go off when you threw it.
P. 9	OFFICER:	It did not go off when you threw it. It can't happen.
P.10	OFFICER:	He was shot by a left-handed man. You're left handed.
P. 10	OFFICER:	What made you shoot him, Michael?
P. 11	CARTER:	I ain't know what happened.
	OFFICER:	No, no, Michael. You know what happened. You know exactly what happened.
P. 12	OFFICER:	Okay, he was on the ground. The gun was in your hand and what did you do then?
	CARTER:	Ran.
	OFFICER:	No, no, Michael. You shot him twice.
P. 12	OFFICER:	Michael, why did you feel it necessary to shoot him the second time?
P. 13	OFFICER:	So before you ran, you fired again.
P. 15	OFFICER:	You get blood on your clothes?
P. 19	CARTER:	I didn't see him go down.
	OFFICER:	No. You seen him go down.

Although Michael volunteered that he and his friends had planned to break into some houses, they never got that far. They had the intention and predisposition to break in and rob, but since it never happened, their plans likely might not lead to a conviction on that charge. In contrast, ten times Michael sobbingly denied shooting the patrolman and never came close to admitting doing it or having such an intention or predisposition.

Voluntariness

The issue of voluntariness often rests on whether or not the interviewers led or coached their suspects by suggesting answers that they would like to get from them. Michael was the last boy interviewed and some information was already available from the other two boys. The tape-recorded interview in this case contained evidence of this, including the following (again by page numbers of the transcript):

p. 10 And he saw you with the gun and you felt you had to do something.

p.11 You didn't really mean to shoot, did you?

p. 11 He caught you by surprise, didn't he?

p. 12 Okay, he was on the ground; the gun was in your hand. You had the gun in your hand, right, Michael?

p. 12 Michael, why did you feel it necessary to shoot him the second time?

p. 13 So before you ran, you fired again, right?

p. 13 What kind of fenders did it [motorcycle] have, silver?

p. 15 Which of you was wearing a white jumpsuit? It was Kermit, wasn't it?

p. 16 You asked him if the officer was dead.

p. 18 When you had the gun in your left hand, he went down to the ground, didn't he?

p. 19 You fired the gun, the policeman was shot, and he went to the ground, right?

The written confession

So far at least, the police could only infer from this language evidence that Michael was the shooter but, as Inbau et al. (1986, 176) point out, a written confession would be more persuasive to a jury than a garbled and hard-to-hear tape. So no matter how much Michael denied the murder on tape, the police may have thought that their case could be made more solid with a signed confession. The entire handwritten confession statement reads as follows:

> Tuesday, June 21st, myself, my cousin Lobo (Freddie Mills) and Kermit Parker left me and Lobo's house on bicycles and went over to the neighborhood off Wooddale. We put the bicycles by some bushes and went on foot. Kermit and Lobo were going to try to break in some houses and I was supposed to watch out for them. As we were on the street looking at houses to break in a cop came up on a motorcycle and started checking us. He made us lay face down and put our hands out. Kermit had a pistol in his pants. It was a nice size gun with brown handles and a round thing you put the bullets in.
>
> As the cop went to use his CB radio Kermit passed me the gun and told me to get rid of it. But the cop turned around and I had the gun still in my hand. We both froze for a moment. The gun I had went off and the next thing I knew the motorcycle cop was down. Just before that he had told me "Hold it!" He had his gun out but pointed town toward the ground kind of out to his side. When my gun went off he went down and he kind of started bucking and shaking. His body made a quick jerk.

At the top of the statement were the initials "M.C." At the bottom were the time, date, witnesses, and Michael Carter's signature.

To this point, my analysis of the tape had shown that Michael didn't confess to the murder and that the interviewer had pushed the voluntariness limits of what the police were permitted to do. My testimony about this might be useful at a trial, but the purpose of this hearing before a judge was different. It was to suppress the entire confession statement before it even got to a trial, where the judge might decide to let a jury decide whether or not the written confession was voluntary and whether it comported with the spoken evidence. Suppressing the evidence called for an even deeper analysis of the language used. To avoid a jury trial, it was necessary to show the possibility that the written confession was not an accurate account of what Michael purportedly volunteered. The defense needed to ward off the question of whether it was possible that even though Michael did not admit the murder during the tape-recorded part of the interview, he might have changed his mind and admitted it afterward. This was probably what the police would claim.

Central to the defense effort was the fact that the officer had testified earlier that he wrote down what Michael said "exactly" as he said it. He claimed to be only an amanuensis. This suggested the idea of comparing the officer's language with Michael's to see how the two might be the same or different. But such a comparison would require an adequate sample of Michael's normal speech outside of the police interview. Even the interview didn't provide an adequate sample of his speech, because throughout it he spoke very little and was emotionally distraught and physically ill. We needed a suitable exemplar of his habitual and normal speech to compare with the language represented in the written confession statement that he signed.

In this type of case it's normally best for linguistic expert witnesses to analyze only the language evidence and avoid talking with suspects and defendants. Distancing from the suspect preserves both the impression and reality of professional objectivity. But since it would be useful to know how Michael normally talked and since I had never met Michael or heard him speak, I asked the defense attorney to go to the jail and tape-record a conversation with him. I didn't care what the topic was, but preferably it would have nothing to do with the case, because I was afraid that topic might generate the language register of agitated, emotional utterances that Michael used during the police interview rather than the calmer more articulate language register found in his written confession statement. Following conventional sociolinguistic field methods, I suggested that the lawyer get Michael to talk about his favorite TV shows and see where this took them. Training a lawyer to be a linguistic fieldworker can be difficult, but this defense attorney did a fairly good job. She got Michael to talk about martial arts movies and professional wrestling, which provided ten minutes of natural speech with very little of the lawyer and a whole lot of Michael on her taped speech sample. This was what I needed, for it provided a good picture of his natural speech register to use as a touchstone for determining whether the register he allegedly used in the written confession actually was in his own words, as the officer had testified.

Vocabulary comparison

Some of the words the interviewing officer used during his interview with Michael appeared in Michael's written confession even though Michael did not use them in the police interview or in the interview with his lawyer. For example, the officer described the gun as having a "round thing where you put the bullets in." Michael didn't use these words in the police interview tape, but in the transcript they appear exactly as the officer had said them. The written confession also added details that Michael did not provide during the interview. Attempting to identify the street, Michael said, "I don't know where it is over there," while his written confession identified the street by its name: "and went over to the neighborhood off *Wooddale*." Michael's spoken description of what happened when the patrolman arrived was "I froze for a while." In the written statement he is alleged to have referred to both himself and the officer when he said, "We *both* froze for a moment."

The written confession also reordered the sequence of events that Michael mentioned on tape. At one point on the tape Michael said that while the three boys were running away, Kermit tossed the gun to him and Michael threw it into a creek. Here he voluntarily admitted to "having" the gun very briefly. The written confession, however, has Michael saying, "But the cop turned around and I had the gun *still* in my hand... The gun I had went off and the next thing I knew the motorcycle cop was down." No support for this time sequence can be found in the oral interview.

The written statement also upgraded Michael's inner-city vocabulary from the words he used in the interview. In the previous paragraph I noted that although Michael said he froze "*for a while*," his written statement has him saying "for *a moment*." In the interview it was the officer who said, "You and Lobo and Kermit left, right, Michael?" To this Michael answered, "yes," but Michael's alleged words in the written confession were "*Myself*, my cousin Lobo, Freddie Mills, and Kermit Parker left me and Lobo's house." In his interview Michael said the patrolman "told all of us to *lay down* on our stomachs and *have* our hands up." In his written statement this is represented as "He made us *lie face down* and *put* our hands up." Michael had not mastered the "lie–lay" distinction, and the reflexive pronoun "myself" and the expression "face down" were also not evident in Michael's vocabulary. The reflexive pronoun "myself" used here as the subject of a sentence is a hypercorrection that is common in middle-class speech but not common in the speech of inner-city, poorly educated youths.

If I were to establish that the written confession was not in Michael's own language, as the detective testified that it was, it would also be helpful to demonstrate whose language it actually was. To help with this, the defense lawyer located several of the officer's past deposition and trial testimony transcripts in other cases, and when I compared his language in them with Michael's written confession, I found some interesting similarities. For example, I discovered that the detective also used the reflexive pronoun "myself" as the subject in many of his sentences, and he also commonly used the time expression "for a moment" instead of "for a while." He used "lie face down" several times as well.

Syntax

It is possible, of course, that Michael may have mentioned Wooddale Avenue or other vocabulary items noted above during parts of the interview that were not recorded. Therefore, it seemed necessary to probe more deeply to find more than vocabulary comparisons. Syntax seemed to be the obvious place to discover this. I have learned that when describing syntax in legal contexts such as hearings or trials, it's often better to use traditional syntax explanations to make understanding as simple as possible. Therefore, I decided to use the terms that might be understood easily in court for comparing Michael's characteristic sentence structure during the police interview with his sentence structure in the written statement:

Sentence type	*Interview*	*Written statement*
Simple	81 percent	32 percent
Compound	8 percent	48 percent
Complex	11 percent	20 percent

If Michael had actually dictated the sentences in his written confession statement, he somehow had reduced his habitual use of mostly simple sentences from 80 percent to 32 percent and had increased his use of more compound and complex sentences from 19 percent to 68 percent, something that would seem rather unlikely. One particularly long sentence in the written statement was "As we were on the street looking at houses to break in, a cop came up on a motorcycle and started checking us." This complex sentence was nothing like anything Michael said in the police interview or in the tape recording made by his attorney.

The question then became where did these compound and complex sentences come from? I used some of the transcripts of the officer's testimony in other cases to form a comparison of the syntax he used during his interview with Michael:

Sentence type	*In Carter interview*	*In other testimony*
Simple	38 percent	43 percent
Compound	27 percent	26 percent
Complex	35 percent	31 percent

The officer's sentence structure was very consistent in his interview with Michael and in his testimony in the other cases. I also noted his frequent use of the reflexive pronoun "myself" in his testimony in other cases. The following are only some of the many examples of his characteristic use of "myself":

- The police officers involved including myself, were. . .
- At various times myself, Detective A, and Detective B. . .
- Several people including myself. . .
- Myself and Detective B . . .

When a comparative analysis of this type is used, single language features are weak evidence of certainty, but when a combination of such features is present, the analysis can be very useful. The bottom line is that it was unlikely that the officer was merely the amanuensis that he claimed to be here. It is more likely that he created the written statement himself rather than writing down the words and sentences spoken by Michael, who even during his sick and emotionally charged mental state managed to vehemently deny that he shot the officer but compliantly signed the statement anyway.

Voluntariness was an important issue in this case. If the police gave Carter a Miranda warning, it was not on the tape of their interview with him. Therefore we can't tell whether he voluntarily waived his rights to having an attorney present, but there was certainly no attorney there to assist him. Although it was evident that Carter was predisposed to help his friends rob some houses and had the intention of doing so, this crime never actually happened and he was not indicted for it. There was also no language evidence on the tape that indicated Carter was predisposed or had the intention to kill the patrolman. In fact, ten times Carter denied that he shot the patrolman. There was considerable language evidence on the tape that the interviewer attempted to influence Carter's answers by feeding him inculpatory information. The interviewer's schema of Carter's guilt was obvious from the very start of this police interrogation speech event, never allowing Carter to tell his side of the story. And, of course, the voluntariness of his answers was highly suspect.

Aftermath

With the supporting testimony of both a psychiatrist and my linguistic analysis, the defense lawyer argued that his signed statement was not voluntarily produced and that it was the product of unconstitutionally coercive tactics by the police detectives on a fragile and mentally challenged young man. At the time of the hearing to suppress the evidence, Michael Carter had spent 434 days in jail awaiting trial. He was freed almost immediately after this hearing ended, when the district attorney assessed the evidence then withdrew all charges, after which the judge said: "This is definitely in keeping with the charge they have as the legal representative of the people of this parish. The system works." If spending 434 days in jail means the system works, then the judge may be right.

As I was testifying during the hearing, I was amused at the reaction of the detective whose spoken English usage I was analyzing. I could see the shock on his face when I talked about the linguistic insecurity that led him to use the reflexive pronoun "myself" as the subject and object of his sentences. He apparently was learning about this hypercorrection for the first time as he shook his head in disbelief. Like most occupations and disciplines, participants learn to think and talk like the other practitioners in their fields. Law enforcement officers are no different from physicians, lawyers, and linguists in this. We all learn to talk and write the way our fields approve. The detective in this case wasn't aware of how he used his own language, but what he was not aware of became a good clue that left its traces about who actually worded Michaels's confession statement and supported the argument that the shooter wasn't Michael. Most important, it was also clear that Michael's behavior in this interview supported my contention that he did not sign the confession statement voluntarily.

THE STATE OF TEXAS V. KEVIN ROGERS

On the evening of May 5, 1994 someone broke into the Houston, Texas home of an elderly lady then raped her and stabbed her to death. When the attack began, she was talking on the telephone with a friend. Her friend heard her scream, "Leave me alone" and then after hearing no more, she called 911 for emergency help, after which a patrolman in a nearby squad car arrived and found Miss Lilly Lockhart's naked body in a pool of blood. Her friend also telephoned Miss Lilly's brother, who arrived while the police officer was still there.

Since the patrolman had no communication device with him, he went next door to use a neighbor's telephone to call his superior at the police station. The patrolman also explained that he went next door because he didn't want to disturb any fingerprints that might remain on Miss Lilly's phone. It is important to know that while he was calling the station from the neighbor's phone, various people in the neighbor's house, including an eighth-grade boy named Shelton, could easily hear the details of the crime that the patrolman reported. On the following day, Shelton told his classmates in school, including his friend Kevin, many of the details he overheard the patrolman say.

The police discovered very little physical evidence. A knife with no fingerprints on it was still in Miss Lilly's chest and there was no blood on her clothing strewn around on the floor. The police quickly deduced that the murder was the work of amateurs and began to fingerprint the boys in the neighborhood, including Kevin, but for unknown reasons not including his classmate and neighbor Shelton, who lived next door. They then compared the few fingerprints they found at the scene with those of the neighborhood boys and discovered that only Kevin's fingerprints matched. In fact, his fingerprints were all over Miss Lilly's house. This made Kevin their only suspect.

Kevin was fifteen years old and severely impaired intellectually. He was in the eighth grade at a school where his teachers admitted that they promoted children to the next grade whether or not they functioned at grade level. Kevin had been socially promoted this way for several years now and, according to his teachers, he functioned like a second grader. They added that he was always pleasant, compliant, and cooperative, and never gave them any trouble. Kevin's neighbors reported the same opinion of him.

On the day following the murder, one of the detectives pulled Kevin out of school and interviewed him for seven consecutive hours. First he read Kevin his Miranda rights, including the words, "consult with," "waive my right to a lawyer," and "knowingly make the following statement." Then the policeman asked Kevin if he understood his rights, and Kevin said he did.

The police interview speech event

The interview was not electronically recorded, but the police reported that Kevin told them he knew Miss Lilly well and he often did odd jobs for her, sometimes even doing some housecleaning for her. He also told them that he visited her home regularly to play with her dog. But nothing could dissuade the police from believing that Kevin's fingerprints indicated that they had found the killer. In fact, that evening the investigating detective appeared on a television news program and commented that his interview with Kevin indicated that he was a "serial killer."

One might expect that the Houston police would have made an audiotape or video recording of their seven-hour interview with Kevin. They didn't. But failing that, one might expect that they had audio- or videotaped at least that small portion of the seven hours at the end when Kevin confessed to the murder. They didn't. But failing even that, one might expect that at least a stenographic record might have been made. There was none. But failing that, one might expect the detective to have taken some notes that would support his findings. He reported that there were no notes. Unfortunately, none of these common expectations in police procedure were fulfilled in Kevin's case. Other than Kevin's fingerprints, which could easily be discounted because he spent so much time in Miss Lilly's home, the following signed confession statement was all that the police offered as evidence. I reproduce it here with the same numbered statements, spacing, punctuation, layout, and all-capitalized type, exactly the way it was used at trial.

JUVENILE CONFESSION

Taken at 8300 Mykawa Rd. May 6, 1994.

1. I DO NOT WANT TO CONSULT WITH A LAWYER BEFORE IMAKE THIS STATEMENT, AND I DO NOT WANT TO REMAIN SILENT, AND I NOW FREELY AND VOLUNTARILY WAIVE MY RIGHT TO A LAWYER AND TO REMAIN SILENT AND I KNOWINGLY MAKE THE FOLLOWING VOLUNTARY STATEMENT.
2. I LIVE AT 3220 BINZ AND THAT'S ABOUT FIVE OR SIX HOUSES FROM MS. LOCKHART'S HOUSE.
3. I HAVE KNOWN MS. LOCKHART FOR ABOUT 2 YEARS.
4. SOMETIME I CALL HER MISS LILLY.
5. MY MOTHER HAS KNOWN HER FOR A LONG TIME.
6. MY MOM KNEW MS. LOCKHART'S MOM.
7. MS. LOCKHARD DIDN'T HARDLY LIKE ME BUT SHE WOULD LET ME COME TO HER HOUSE AND PLAY WITH HER LITTLE DOG, BERTRAM.
8. I THINK IT WAS LAST YEAR WHEN I WAS SHOOTING BIRDS IN THE TREES IN THE BACK YARD BEHIND

MS. LOCKHART'S YARD AT NALOW'S HOUSE WAS WHEN SHE TOOK MY PELLET GUN FROM ME.

9. I BEEN ASKING MS. LOCKHART TO GIVE ME BACK MY PELLET GUN.
10. MS. LOCKHART ALWAYS SAID NO.
11. MONDAY, THE DAY MS. LOCKHART GOT KILLED, I WENT TO SCHOOL.
12. WHEN I GOT OUT OF SCHOOL, I WENT HOME AND CLEANED UP MY HOUSE.
13. AFTER I CLEANED UP THE HOUSE, I WENT TO MS. LOCK-HART'S HOUSE.
14. I WENT INSIDE THE BACK PORCH AND PLAYED WITH THE PUPPY.
15. THE PUPPY RAN INSIDE THE HOUSE, AND I RAN INSIDE THE HOUSE BEHIND THE PUPPY.
16. THE PUPPY RAN UPSTAIRS, AND I RAN UPSTAIRS BEHIND THE PUPPY.
17. I HEARD THE TV ON IN MS. LOCKHART'S BEDROOM.
18. I LOOKED IN THE BEDROOM JUST TO SEE WHAT IT LOOKED LIKE.
19. THE PUPPY RAN IN THE OTHER ROOM WITH THE TWO BEDS.
20. THE ROOM IS TO THE RIGHT AT THE TOP OF THE STAIRS, THEN I WENT TO THE BACK ROOM.
21. I OPENED THE WINDOW ABOUT (KEVIN RAISED HIS HANDS ABOUT 18 INCHES, SHOWING ME HOW HIGH HE OPENED THE WINDOW). I WAS GOING TO COME BACK TO GET MY PELLET GUN.

22. THEN I PICKED UP THE DOG AND I WENT BACK DOWN THE STAIRS.
23. MS. LOCKHART WAS IN THE KITCHEN, SHE GAVE ME A GLASS OF KOOL-AID. BUT I DON'T REMEMBER WHAT KIND OF KOOL-AID IT WAS.
24. I DRINK THE KOOL-AID.
25. AS I WAS LEAVING THROUGH THE BACK DOOR, I SAW THE KNIFE THAT I USED TO STAB MS. LOCKHART WITH LAYING ON THE TABLE IN THE LIVING ROOM BY THE DOOR.
26. THEN I WENT TO MY FRIEND JOHN'S HOUSE DOWN THE STREET.
27. WHEN I LEFT JOHN'S HOUSE, I WENT TO TEXAS SOUTHERN UNIVERSITY AND I PLAYED BASKETBALL.
28. THENICAMEBACKTOMS.LOCKHART'SHOUSE.
29. I WALKED UP TO THE SIDE OF HER HOUSE, AND I SAW THE DOG PLAYING IN THE BACK PORCH.
30. I OPENED THE SCREEN DOOR, AND I WENT INSIDE THE HOUSE.
31. THE DOG WENT INSIDE THE HOUSE.
32. I CRAWLED INTO THE LIVING ROOM WHERE MS. LOCKHART WAS SITTING ON A CHAIR TALKING ON THE PHONE WITH HER BACK TO THE DOOR.
33. I THINK SHE HAD ON SOME BLUE SILK PANTS.
34. I SAW THE KNIFE STILL LAYING ON THE TABLE IN THE LIVING ROOM, AND I PICKED UP THE KNIFE AND SHE HEARD ME AND TURNED AROUND.
35. SHE SAID SOMETHING.

36. I FORGOT WHAT SHE SAID.
37. I PUSHED HER TO THE FLOOR.
38. I TOOK THE KNIFE AND STABBED HER ABOUT THREE TIMES I THINK.
39. I STABBED HER IN THE CHEST.
40. I STABBED HER IN THE NECK.
41. I SAW HER BLOUSE OPENED BECAUSE IT CAME WHEN SHE WAS FIGHTING WITH ME.
42. I PULLED HER PANTS OFF OF HER.
43. I LAYED ON TOP OF HER FOR A FEW MINUTES, BUT I DIDN'T PUT MY PENIS IN HER.
44. I HAD MY PANTS OPENED WITH MY PENIS OUT, BUT I DIDN'T PUT IT IN HER.
45. I GOT UP AND LEFT THE KNIFE IN HER CHEST.
46. I SEEN SOME MONEY ON THE TABLE, AND THEN I TOOK THE MONEY UP.
47. I SAW MY PELLET GUN LAYING ON THE FLOOR BY THE COUCH. I FORGOT TO PICK UP THE PELLET GUN.
48. I WENT OUT THE SAME WAY I CAME IN THROUGH THE BACK DOOR.
49. I RAN HOME.
50. I AM SORRY FOR WHAT I DID.
51. I WISH THAT IT DIDN'T HAPPEN.

Since the interview was not tape-recorded, there was no way to determine how the police obtained this signed confession or the extent to which Kevin's statements were made voluntarily. We also can't know whether Kevin's answers were in the sequence reported here and, equally important, we don't know what questions yielded Kevin's responses. The issue of his voluntariness, therefore, could not be discovered from the meager evidence of this statement. After signing the confession, the fifteen-year-old Kevin Rogers was indicted for murder and charged as an adult.

Comparative language

I was immediately reminded of the earlier, Michael Carter case in which the major evidence was a similar signed confession. In the Carter case, however, at least a portion of the interview was tape-recorded. But here, since there was no language evidence to compare it with Kevin's written confession and since I felt that it might be helpful to learn what his natural language was, I asked his lawyer to tape-record a conversation with Kevin.

The lawyer taped nearly two hours of talk and sent it to me. In my comparison of his language on this tape with the language of the confession statement, I found Kevin used no sentence embedding at all with his lawyer, while 8 percent of the sentences in his confession statement had embedded clauses. Kevin used the historical present tense ("I say I ain't kill her") for the past tense over 50 percent of the time to the lawyer, but there was only one such instance in his confession. Kevin's participles were typically nonstandard in his talk with the lawyers, but 100 percent Standard English in his confession. He used four double negatives to the lawyer but only one (the rather common "didn't hardly") in his confession. In short, it looked very much as though the language found in Kevin's confession may not have been his own.

This avenue of analysis ultimately went nowhere, however, because when the defense lawyer asked the detective about how he came to write down what Kevin said in the confession statement, the detective declared that the confession was *not* a verbatim record in Kevin's own words. Instead, the detective said that he sat at a word processor while he asked Kevin questions. As Kevin answered, the detective recorded Kevin's answers as he phrased it, "in approximations that were not necessarily in Kevin's own words." This process, called "verballing," was commonly used by police departments in Australia in the 1980s and eventually was exposed and heavily criticized by the 1989 Australian Fitzgerald inquiry, which found verballing to be commonly used by police officers, some of whom were otherwise considered to be honest (Eades 2008, 71). According to Komter, a similar verballing technique had been in use in the Netherlands as well (2002, 173–175).

Whether or not the police used the verballing technique honestly in Kevin's case, the practice clearly distorts the Miranda warning that says, "Anything you say can be held against you." Wigmore defines a confession as "an acknowledgement *in express words* by the accused in a criminal case of the truth of the main fact charged or some essential part of it" (1970, 308). The verballing technique of producing a confession wanders far off the path of the "express words" of the suspect, and the issue of voluntariness can be questioned when the words that suspects are alleged to have said were not what they actually said. Even worse in Kevin's case, because of the lack of electronically recorded language evidence, we can't really know what Kevin actually said.

The basis of Kevin's knowledge

Since the lack of any recorded evidence made it apparently impossible to impeach the detective for his verballing technique in eliciting Kevin's confession statement, I turned my attention to other possible ways that Kevin could have acquired the details that he reported. The analogy of etymology seemed appropriate, since we had a corpus of information of various sources from which I could determine the source of Kevin's knowledge in a procedure similar to the way language historians trace the origins of language sounds, vocabulary, and semantics, based on various known and recorded stages of changes. In a murder event, the origins of knowledge have three possible sources: (1) immediate firsthand knowledge from specific things that only the killer would know; (2) general world knowledge that anyone could know; and (3) secondhand knowledge that comes from other people and sources, such as the media and friends.

The reported evidence revealed that Kevin certainly had firsthand knowledge about Miss Lilly and her house, based on the fact that he had been there often, played with her dog, sometimes saw her talking on the telephone, and noticed things in her home, such as where she kept her kitchen utensils, including her knives. To the extent that other people who knew Miss Lilly also could have this knowledge, it could also be considered general world knowledge.

Kevin also had secondhand knowledge of the murder. The confession statement failsed to indicate that Kevin's friend Sheldon had heard many of the details of the murder from the patrolman who had used the phone in his house. It was known that Sheldon had broadcasted what he heard widely at school. This knowledge included Miss Lilly's blouse being found opened, that she was stabbed in her neck and chest, and that money had been stolen. Sheldon passed this information along to his classmates, including Kevin, on the day after her body was found. A second source of secondhand information came from the TV news reports saying that Miss Lilly was on the telephone when she was attacked. The third source of secondhand information came from the police, who told Kevin directly or inadvertently that Miss Lilly had been raped and that she was wearing a blue blouse, although Kevin got this wrong in his confession statement when he told the police that she was wearing blue pants.

The police apparently interpreted Kevin's firsthand knowledge and secondhand knowledge as his specific knowledge about the murder, things that only the killer would know. If the police had tape-recorded their seven-hour interview with Kevin, these issues concerning his sources of his knowledge could have been checked and verified, whether they worked for Kevin or against him. Without such a recording, there is no way to know.

Voluntariness

Although the defense lawyer's two-hour-long tape-recorded interview with Kevin could not be admitted as evidence, it threw some light on a number of voluntariness issues. In the defense lawyer's tape of this interview, Kevin reported the following about the time the police read him his Miranda rights:

LAWYER: She (the magistrate) told you all that? *[about his rights]*

KEVIN: Yeah.

LAWYER: Did you tell her that you understood all of that?

KEVIN: Yeah.

LAWYER: Did you really understand all that she was telling you?

KEVIN: No.

LAWYER: Then why did you say you understood it?

KEVIN: I don't know.

LAWYER: Have you ever been involved in anything where your rights were read to you before?

KEVIN: Yes.

LAWYER: What situation was that?

KEVIN: I don't know.

LAWYER: I mean have you ever been involved in anything where somebody read you your rights, saying you have the right to remain silent before that time?

KEVIN: No.

LAWYER: Did you understand what they were saying?

KEVIN: No, I was just listening to them. I know the right to remain silence, and I ain't say nothing and I ain't understand the others. I ain't know what they was talking about then. I knew the right to remain silence.

LAWYER: How come you didn't request an attorney?

KEVIN: I ain't know.

This passage speaks strongly about Kevin's lack of voluntariness when he was given his Miranda rights. Also, his lack of intellectual competence is illustrated in this exchange, during which he contradicted himself twice (that he understood his rights and that he had been asked about his rights on other occasions). He said he didn't know what his right to an attorney meant, but as this interview made very clear, Kevin said he asked for his mother to be present several times.

LAWYER: Did you ask to see your mama?

KEVIN: I ask him there and I ask him is my mama gonna be up at juvenile to pick me up. They say she might gonna to be there to pick me up.

LAWYER: What did he say then?

KEVIN: No. Wait till we go to juvenile.

LAWYER: And what did you say when he said, "No, wait?"

KEVIN: I start cryin' and they start askin' me question. And that's when you know then I made confession.

LAWYER: What made you give the confession?

KEVIN: They say I might be able to go home.

Even though information from this interview with his lawyer was precluded from his trial, the voluntariness of his confession was clearly in doubt. Later, at his trial, he testified that he asked to see her five or six times but the detectives denied that Kevin had ever asked for his mother. They maintained that they had followed standard procedure at all times. Kevin may not have understood what it meant to have a right to an attorney, but he certainly knew that he wanted his mama present.

Motive

Kevin's motive for killing Miss Lilly wasn't easy for the police to determine, but when in statement 8 he mentioned that she had taken his pellet gun away from him, they apparently believed they found what they were searching for. The problem with this theory was that whoever killed Miss Lilly had left that gun exactly where she kept it. Although the police heralded Kevin's motive as wanting to get his gun back, they didn't pursue it with Kevin when they interviewed him. It is likely that if they had done so, this would have only emphasized that Kevin's failure to retrieve the gun supported his mental incapacity of not being able to remember why he killed her.

The gun issue was clouded further by the difference between a BB gun and a pellet gun. In his confession statement, Kevin purportedly said he saw a pellet gun. In his interview with his defense lawyer, however, Kevin reported that at some time before the murder, he had replaced the BB gun that Miss Lilly took away from him with a new pellet gun. In the confession statement, Kevin allegedly said that it was a pellet gun that she took away from him (in statement 8) and that he forgot to take it (in statement 47). One can only wonder further about Kevin's voluntariness during this unrecorded interview.

Method

Since the detectives apparently were satisfied that Kevin's motive was to get his pellet gun back from Miss Lilly, they next turned their attention to the method he used to kill her. They knew that Miss Lilly died from a knife wound in her chest. From the defense lawyer's two hours of recorded conversation with Kevin, it was clear that his consistent language style was to respond to questions rather than to introduce topics himself. So it is very likely that the police had to bring up this topic of method by themselves. Although the confession statement reveals none of the officer's questions, Kevin described a knife in four separate statements: 25, 34, 38, and 42. It seems obvious that the officer must have asked multiple questions about the knife, such as "When did you see the knife?" "Where did you see it?" and "What did you do with it?" Without taped evidence, we can't know what Kevin actually answered.

In Kevin's interview with his lawyer he produced information about the knife that was very different from that which appears in his confession statement:

KEVIN: I just told them that I saw a knife like on the table like... when I walked through the kitchen.

LAWYER: But you're saying that you denied that you killed her. How come you told them that you saw the knife and you grabbed the knife?

KEVIN: I say I ain't grabbed the knife.

LAWYER: But in the confession you said you grabbed the knife and you walked toward her and she turned around. Tell me, why did you tell the officers about that?

KEVIN: I just said it.

LAWYER: You've been denying it all this time. What made you decide to say that you grabbed the knife and walked toward her?

KEVIN: 'Cause they say I **had** to use a knife 'cause that what they found in her chest.

LAWYER: And when they said you had to use a knife, what did you say?

KEVIN: That when I say I grabbed the knife.

LAWYER: Go on.

KEVIN: Then they say, "You stab?" Then I say, "No." Then they say, "Why you grab the knife?" Then he start cursing and say, "You lying." Then I say, "Yeah." They say I had to use the knife.

LAWYER: How did you tell them there was a knife on the table if you weren't there?

KEVIN: That was, Shelton just, I was just listening to what Shelton was talking about.

LAWYER: When you talked about the knife, were you still reporting what Shelton told you?

KEVIN: Uh-huh. I was tellin' 'em about what Shelton told me. Then they say she got killed with a knife. Then I just told 'em that I saw a knife on the table. Then they said that.

LAWYER: So they told you that she got killed with a knife?

KEVIN: Uh-huh. I was just sayin' 'cause I was ready to go home.

LAWYER: Why didn't you say that you didn't kill her?

KEVIN: I say I ain't do it.

LAWYER: What made you jump from what Shelton was telling you to you did it?

KEVIN: 'Cause I ain't know until Shelton told me. 'Cause that when they said I had to use a knife. That I grabbed it. Then I said she just got stabbed. But I didn't say I stabbed her. I say she got stabbed.

LAWYER: Then did you say where she was stabbed?

KEVIN: In the chest and throat.

LAWYER: How did you know where she got stabbed?

KEVIN: From when Shelton told me.

LAWYER: Who else told you where she was stabbed?
KEVIN: It was on TV once. It say a stabbing of Miss Lockhart.

Again we see that Kevin had secondhand knowledge about the method of the use of a knife in the murder that came from his friend and neighbor Shelton. Kevin's use of the passive voice in "she just got stabbed" is a clue that he did not stab Miss Lilly himself, although this distinction was unused at trial and possibly even unnoticed by the police. Based on this conversation, we can easily conclude that the police interviewer deduced Kevin's admission of "grabbing" the knife based on his statement that he had seen a knife in Miss Lilly's kitchen at some unidentified time, possibly in the past, for it is common for kitchens to have knives in them. Here the detective promoted Kevin's secondhand knowledge gained from his friend Shelton into Kevin's firsthand, specific method of killing Miss Lilly. Without verifiable evidence of what was actually asked and answered in the police interview or in Kevin's confession statement, we cannot know how voluntary Kevin's confession was. But when we compare it with what Kevin said to his own attorney, we can certainly have doubts about the voluntariness here.

Kevin's speech act of apologizing

As far as the prosecution was concerned, Kevin's apologies in statements 50 and 51 were icing on the cake. What they reported Kevin to have said was "I'm sorry for what I did" and "I wish that it didn't happen." As apologies, these are infelicitous and unconvincing. For the speech act of apologizing to be felicitous, it must be understood by both the apologizer and the listener that they are talking about the same things. It may be true that Kevin had told the detective, under what is likely to be the type of pressure he depicted in his interview with his own attorney, that he stabbed and killed Miss

Lilly with a knife. So when the detective wrote down, "I am sorry for what I did," he probably thought this statement meant that Kevin was sorry that he murdered Miss Lilly. If so, it's possible either that the detective was only inferring this or, as Kevin reported in his interview with his own lawyer, that the officer had coerced it from Kevin. In any case, the required characteristics of a felicitous apology are (1) it must be for an offense committed by the apologizer, and (2) it must be specific about the specified offense for which the apology is made (Searle 1978).

Kevin's purported apology, "I'm sorry for what I did," is far from specific about what offense he "did." Both parties must understand, not merely infer, what the apology was for. Clarity about Kevin's meaning in this apology came when his attorney discussed it with Kevin during his two-hour taped interview:

LAWYER: You said you were sorry that it happened?
KEVIN: Uh-huh.
LAWYER: That you shouldn't have done it?
KEVIN: No, I ain't say that.
LAWYER: What did you say?
KEVIN: I said *I'm sorry for what happened.* Then they say, "Did you stab?" Then I say, "No." Then they say, "Why you grab the knife?" Then he say start cursing and say, "You lyin." Then I say, "Yeah." Then that's when he say, "You sorry for what happened." I say, "Yes."

Even though I appear to keep riding the same old horse, I have to point out once again that a tape recording of the entire police interview could have clarified a number of things, including the voluntariness of a confession made by a frightened fifteen-year-old cooperative, compliant, and cognitively slow or impaired boy, whose teachers reported that he functioned like a second-grade student and never gave them any trouble. Even if the detective accurately reported Kevin's vague "I'm sorry for what I did," it is unclear which events in the past he was sorry about. His allegedly quoted words were not specific, and nowhere in the confession statement did Kevin indicate that he was sorry for murdering Miss Lilly. These words can be considered as an expression either of Kevin's regret about Miss Lilly's death or, as Ainsworth points out, "submission and willingness to engage in a prescribed ritual" (2009, 200), rather than a felicitous apology about causing the offense.

Aftermath

Kevin's family had no money, and since his Houston lawyer took the case pro bono, I decided to do the same. I worked with him by telephone from my home in Washington, DC, reporting my analysis and preparing my testimony. I've learned since that time that I should never let the lawyer I'm working with make the offer of proof for my testimony without my first checking it carefully myself. He meant well, but there are few attorneys who can absorb the details of linguistic analysis well enough to write an offer of proof without first having it checked by the expert who will actually testify. I can only believe that he must have gotten some important things wrong. He was a good man, but apparently not on top of what was necessary to present to the judge. At any rate, the judge disallowed my testimony.

The lawyer was still hopeful that if and when the judge met me, he'd change his mind and let me testify, so naively I flew to Houston at my own expense and waited outside the courtroom until the lawyer told me to come in. He had just explained to the judge that I had flown there in spite of his decision to not let me testify. The judge was surprised that I had come and asked me why I did so. I answered that I felt that my testimony would be important and that I wanted to give it. He was sympathetic, but he stood by his earlier decision. He asked me, however, to come to his chambers and talk with him when the trial took its next break. I asked the attorney whether I should do this, because I feared that it might be improper procedure. The lawyer said to go ahead, so I did.

When I entered his chambers, the judge asked me many questions about linguistics and what this field might have to say about cases like this one. I told him as much as I could in the short period of time allowed, after which he thanked me for caring enough to come there and commented that linguistic analysis sounded like it might be helpful in cases like this. But he held firm about denying my testimony. Apparently he felt that it was too late to change his ruling.

Meanwhile, Kevin was convicted of murder and sentenced to life in prison, in my opinion a victim of a terrible tragedy that could have been prevented.

10

VOLUNTARINESS OF EMOTIONALLY DISTRAUGHT SUSPECTS

As noted in chapter 2, even though some suspects exhibit extreme degrees of emotional stress during police interrogations, the statutes do not consider their emotional state relevant to their voluntariness. In this chapter I do not refer to suspects who are mentally incapacitated, intoxicated, or juveniles, all of whom might be emotionally distraught, but rather to other adult suspects in murder cases whose high emotional stress is not taken into consideration by statutes, precedents, or legal arguments. One could make the case that it's justifiable to ignore the effects of heightened emotions because virtually all murder suspects are under some degree of emotional stress and it is not currently possible to measure accurately the varying degrees of emotional stress that might be relevant during police interviews or testimony. Nevertheless, in *Schneckloth v. Bustamonte* (412 U.S. 216 (1973)), the court said: "In determining whether a defendant's will was overborne in a particular case, the Court must assesses the totality of all the surrounding circumstances—both the characteristics of the accused and the details of the interrogation." Directly relating to this, law professor and legal critic Eric A. Posner said: "The role of the emotions is much neglected in legal theory. This should be puzzling because emotions play an important role in many areas of the law" (1977, 1,977). Later, citing psychological research, Posner added, "Abilities may also change in the grip of an emotion... A grief-stricken person may experience a decline in abilities; everything becomes more difficult to do. Evidence of physiological changes—hormonal changes, increase in the heart rate, and so forth—supports the view that abilities change during emotional states" (2001, 1,892).

Even the FBI has come to recognize the dangers of misinterpreting the emotional reactions of suspects. In *The FBI Law Enforcement Bulletin* (August 2012, 8–9), retired FBI agent Joe Navarro writes:

> When the interviewer becomes suspicious of a statement or begins to accuse a suspect, a negative emotional response usually results—the kind most people feel when someone blames them for something. When stimulated this way, the interviewee's emotional state and nonverbal behavior become altered, masking true sentiments. This affects the innocent as well as the guilty... It is better to be curious than accusatory. Once interviewers cross the line, the suspect's behaviors result from emotions, not guilt.

Emotional stress must surely contain linguistic factors that are relevant to the characteristics and details of investigations, because language and emotions are two concurrent, parallel, and functional language systems in which one system has an impact on the other. Because a speaker's emotionally charged language does not clearly display its full meaning, listeners easily can become confused by it. That is, it's difficult for listeners to determine what speakers are happy or sad about, to say nothing of how they would feel when interviewed by police after they learned that a loved one has just been murdered.

Posner has written convincingly about the relationship of law and emotions, arguing that even though emotions play an important role in many areas of the law, that role is much neglected in legal theory (2000). Posner says the law's lack of attention to emotions grows out of its dominant strains of normative legal theory such as economic analysis, moral–philosophical analysis, and constitutional analysis, none of which are well suited for analyzing emotions. Law's focus has been on cognition rather than emotion, on judgment about probabilities, on what Posner calls "anchoring devices" when evaluating behavior, and on information immediately at hand. Although murder law says that a person who kills someone in a calm and unemotional state deserves stronger punishment than one who kills in a state of raging anger, it says nothing about the role of a suspect's emotional state during police interviews, hearings, or trials, and it says very little about the effect of emotions on jurors.

It is fair to say that speakers are fully responsible for their actions, but in some cases the context of their emotions affects their linguistic performance to the extent that it produces unexpected consequences. Interestingly, murder law does recognize that while the emotion ofhatred does not excuse murder, the emotion offear might mitigate culpability. It's easy for the courts to understand that during an emotional state of fear, persons can strike out against those who challenge or threaten to harm them, but it is apparently more difficult for the courts to understand that while experiencing the emotion of grief, persons' alertness seriously declines to the extent that their statements are less than trustworthy representations of facts. Some psychologists argue that emotions are constraints on cognition; others argue that emotions are cognitive choices about a state of affairs. Even though the psychology of emotions is still developing, the idea that emotions are cognitive choices seems to confuse moral action with the emotional motivation for that action.

In murder cases, despite this veneer of avoiding information provided by emotions, the degree, timing, and acceptable role of emotions occur inconsistently in rather obvious ways. For example, although expert witnesses are properly charged with presenting their analyses of the evidence without a hint of emotion, it would be ludicrous to claim that defense lawyers and prosecutors in murder cases avoid playing on the emotions of juries. In fact, in their proper role as advocates in trials, they do this from their opening statements through their closing summations as well as in the ways they conduct their cross-examinations of witnesses. And at capital murder sentencing hearings, a major tactic of victim impact statements is to create sympathy and pity for the victim and the victim's family as a counterbalance to any sympathy jurors might have developed for the defendant during the trial. Curiously, although lawyers appeal to the emotions of jurors throughout the trial, after it's over the judges commonly instruct jurors to be calm and dispassionate as they deliberate and not to let any emotions such as anger, pity, disgust, or sympathy influence them in their decisions.

Although murder statutes apparently are not yet ready to consider the effects of suspects who make statements while in a high emotional state, there is no good reason that the language evidence of such emotional states can't be pointed out to juries, because linguistic evidence of emotions is one of the component parts of linguistic expert witness analysis and testimony. Linguistic analysis can show how emotions are revealed in both nonverbal communication and actual language use. In short, not being experts in linguistics, the police, the courts, and juries have the opportunity to ignore the role of emotional language, judge it inaccurately, or assess it improperly.

There is a common stereotype of emotions specifying that certain types of emotional behavior are required (or at least expected) under specific circumstances. A murder case in the state of Oklahoma provides an example of this when the suspect's perceived lack of emotion after he came home and found his wife murdered created in the minds of the police that he was hiding his own guilt. This interpretation of his emotional state caused him serious damage at trial. His purported stoic demeanor during his 911 call for help and his lack of expected emotion during the time he was sitting at his house while the local police were doing their initial investigation were major factors that led the police to believe that he was the killer.

In a second murder case, a woman who had discovered her boyfriend's body became the major suspect when she passively succumbed to the emotional suggestions of the police interviewer, who appeared to be trying to hypnotize her into believing that she was present at the time of the murder and that she was the one who killed her lover. Both cases illustrate important ways that emotions were interpreted by the police and prosecutors as they attempted to deal with the suspects' intentions, predisposition, and especially their voluntariness.

THE STATE OF OKLAHOMA V. STEPHEN ALLEN

In Bartlesville, Oklahoma on the evening of June 11, 1990, Stephen Allen, an accountant at the local Phillips Petroleum Company, took his two-year-old son for a soft drink treat and then stopped off at his church, where he had a small task to finish as church treasurer. When they arrived home at about 9:30 p.m., Allen noticed that his front door was standing wide open. Concerned about this, he told his young son to wait in the car while he entered the house. There he found his wife beaten dead on the kitchen floor. After he called 911, the police arrived and inspected the area in and around the house. During this time several different detectives interviewed Allen, quickly concluding that he was their number one suspect. They were especially bothered by what they perceived to be Allen's stoical reactions to the tragedy as well as by his calm responses to their questions. An important issue in this investigation concerned Allen's voluntariness during his subsequent interviews.

The police interviewed Allen the first time at about 12:30 a.m. at his pastor's home. He told the investigating officers that as he pulled into his driveway, he caught a brief glimpse of someone on his patio. He agreed to let the police search his home and cars, after which two different investigators interviewed him again at about 3:00 a.m. on the same night.

The evidence

The search of his home revealed a small bloodstained tack hammer tucked under a piece of carpet in the attic. The police were led to it by the bloodstains they found on the pull-down attic stairway. They didn't have to mention this to Allen, because he had himself already volunteered this information to a different officer, telling him that as he was trying to revive his wife on the kitchen floor, he got her blood on his hands. At that point he saw the tack hammer on the kitchen table and in a fit of frustration slammed it on the counter. Suddenly realizing that his fingerprints on the tack hammer would make him look suspicious, he stupidly and emotionally hid it in the attic. From the time Allen entered the house, he kept trying to revive his wife, and about twenty minutes had elapsed before he called 911. The police didn't buy his story and accused him of murder.

Since the officers apparently believed that this tack hammer evidence would not be enough, they looked for more. Their first clue came from Allen's 911 call for help. The 911 operator told them that Allen's language seemed very strange, reporting that he was not as emotionally aroused as most 911 callers were. She, as well as the responding officers at the scene later testified that they were concerned about how emotionally calm and detached Allen seemed to be. From Allen's pastor, the police learned that Allen had at one time engaged in a brief affair with another woman. In their minds, all of these things fit together to make Allen their only suspect.

Other evidence included the recording of his 911 call and the partially tape-recorded 12:30 a.m. interview with Allen at his pastor's home, most of which was their discussion with the pastor and his wife until the tape stopped abruptly after twenty-five minutes. The police also tape-recorded a second interview with Allen at 3:00 a.m., but they claimed that they lost the tape before the defense could hear it. Somehow, however, they had managed to make a transcript of it before they lost it, and this unverifiable transcript also became part of the evidence. The officers who talked with Allen at the scene gave depositions about what he told them, as did his neighbors and the 911 operator, who also were interviewed by the police. This, plus the bloodstained tack hammer, was all of the useful evidence gathered and used.

Concerning Allen's report of seeing a man on the patio, the investigators believed they found some inconsistencies in Allen's story about this, but they made no effort to investigate the possibility of such an intruder.

Heightened emotional stress

Like most transcripts that include only audible words, the government's transcript of the 911 tape did not include supersegmental indicators (language pitch, height, pauses) that are common indicators of emotional stress. In most of this six-minute call, the operator asked Allen to wait on the line while she contacted the appropriate services. When Allen did get the opportunity to speak, however, his speech displayed relatively high pitched emotion and heavy breathing that the operator failed to report and that the transcript didn't show. The following is the way the operator described this to the police:

> Considering the incidence, the circumstances, he was very much in control... The subject was very calm. Usually they will be so hysterical that they don't even realize that they maybe have not given me an address. They'll just scream that you send the police or whatever, and hang up on you.

Later at trial, the prosecutor asked her to describe her impression, to which her one-word answer was "calm."

During the trial I asked the jury to listen to the 911 tape to determine whether her testimony was accurate. I called their attention to the parts where Allen indeed exhibited a degree of heightened emotion as he pleaded in a high pitch, "Help me please," "Hurry," "Please hurry," "There's blood all over the place." Twice he pleaded, "I need an ambulance." It may not have been the hysterical screaming that the operator was used to, but it was as close as an unemotional person like Allen typically gets to heightened emotion. The operator could not have known that Allen was by nature a low-keyed, stolid and methodical person who did what he was told in his occupation as an accountant. She couldn't have known that his lower keyed intonation and rationality during his pleas for help were equivalent to shouting and screaming in the style of the typical emotional callers that 911 operators are more accustomed to hearing.

The police also interviewed a neighbor who reported that he had walked over to Allen's house while the police were there. He reported that at the crime scene he tried to talk with Allen five or six times, asking him, "What's going on?" He also told the police that Allen was "in shock," and he complained that Allen wouldn't talk with him. He said that at one point Allen grabbed his arm and asked him to call his pastor, adding that Allen looked "dumbfounded" and commenting, "Maybe if I saw what he saw maybe I wouldn't talk to anybody... but the fact that he said nothing to me strikes me as odd." Later, when the police interviewed this neighbor a second time, he changed his story, now saying: "There was no hysteria in him walking in and finding his wife like this... I couldn't have been that cool if I'd walked in and found my wife butchered." At trial the prosecutor cited only the neighbor's more damaging second statement and ignored his earlier somewhat contradictory observations. The neighbor's second statement nicely provided verification of the 911 operator's opinion about Allen's apparent lack of emotions.

Allen's presumed inconsistency

There was no reason for the police to pursue any perceived inconsistencies in Allen's statements, unless they believed these alleged inconsistencies demonstrated that he was lying about the whole matter. Following Posner's observations (1997, 9,977) a person in the high emotional state of finding his wife murdered would likely be rattled and it is not usual for such persons to give inconsistent information. The police first focused on Allen's statements concerning the intruder on the patio, considering them inconsistent and therefore unbelievable lies. By comparing the statements of the police with the taped evidence, it was a straightforward matter for me to show that it was actually the police who were inconsistent, not Allen. I contrasted their claims with the taped evidence that Allen volunteered on this topic, as follows:

Allen's statement in his 911 call:

I saw somebody running through my backyard.

I pulled in and they'd gone.

He saw me, turned, and went to the other direction.

Allen's statement in his first police interview at 12:30:

My lights caught somebody on the patio.
I don't know what door he came out of.
He was on the patio.
He turned in the opposite direction.

Allen's statement in his second police interview at 3:00 a.m.:

I turned into the driveway and my lights panned.
I got a glimpse of someone.
They turned.
I had a sweeping glance.

Since Allen volunteered this to three different interviewers, the way he said it varied slightly, but the substance was the same. Actually, the mistaken idea that Allen was inconsistent had its origins in the 911 operator's initial report to the police. While Allen was still on this six-minute 911 call and after he told the operator that he saw somebody running through his backyard, the operator could be heard telling her supervisor, "He advised that somebody had ran out the *back door.*" To be sure, this information contradicted Allen's statement, but the contradiction was a product of the operator's own making, for Allen did not say this on the tape. The officer who interviewed Allen at 12:30 adopted the 911 operator's creative "back door" invention and asked Allen about it. Allen then told the officer that he didn't know what door the intruder came out of. The police considered this inconsistent with what he had said to the 911 operator, but it was actually inconsistent only with her erroneous version of what he actually said to her. When the operator testified at trial, the defense attorney forced her to admit that she had erroneously passed along what Allen told her, and she also admitted that she was the one who introduced the words "back door." Even when Allen volunteered information, it was twisted by law enforcement officers. In this case, apparently it was the 911 operator who was under extreme emotional stress.

The police reports preserved the idea that Allen's story was inconsistent. They perpetuated the 911 operator's mistake and ignored the inconsistencies between the neighbor's first and second interviews about Allen's purported lack of emotional distress but also the inconsistency of the investigating officers' reports. In one police report the investigator said that when he went into the living room, he saw that the door was open but that the screen door was locked. Later at trial he testified that he didn't check the screen door and didn't know if any other officers had checked it, admitting that he didn't actually do this but had relied on them to do this. Another officer variously testified at different times that Allen told him in an untaped conversation that the intruder "went out that door," "was standing at the corner of the house," "was standing in the family room," "stood in the doorway," "ran down the patio," and "ran around the corner." Still other officers reported that Allen said only that the intruder was "standing there." Such confusion points to the strong possibility that this small-town police force was unaccustomed to investigating murder cases, and apparently the officers were befuddled enough to experience their own levels of emotional distress.

These are only a few of the many alleged inconsistencies introduced by the police. I detail more of them in my book *The Language of Confession, Interrogation, and Deception* (1998). It's curious how many different perceptions could exist when these police officers were present to hear what Allen actually said. Once again I have to point out that it would have been a lot better if the police had tape-recorded everything. But they didn't.

I include this case in this chapter because it illustrates the problem the government has with situations in which the participants, including the police, were under heightened emotional stress. They expected Allen to have more and stronger emotional outbursts, even though it was his nature to avoid heightened emotions because he was a stolid, unemotional man. The 911 operator expected him to act like all of her other highly emotional callers. Allen volunteered that his sudden realization that he might be accused as the killer irrationally prompted him to hide the tack hammer that he used to whack the kitchen counter during a time of great frustration and grief. In contrast, the police violated the expectation that they would remain emotionally calm and collected during the time when the pressure of this highly emotional situation was apparently unfamiliar to them. Here the stereotypes were reversed and the role of heightened emotion in many aspects of this case was completely overlooked.

Aftermath

My trial testimony clearly was not sufficient. The jury convicted Stephen Allen of first-degree murder and the judge sentenced him to life in prison without parole. Allen's lawyers then appealed the decision, based on improper questioning by the police, the judge's refusal to grant a change of venue, the judge's admission into evidence of testimony about Allen's brief affair that had ended six months prior to the murder, and the failure of the police to follow up on the figure that Allen said he saw as he pulled into his driveway. The court denied this appeal and Allen remains in prison.

THE COMMONWEALTH OF VIRGINIA V. BEVERLY MONROE

In this case, the interviewer's cultivation of the suspect's emotions provided a different example of misdirected and misunderstood voluntariness. In 1992 Beverly Monroe was tried for the murder of her boyfriend, Roger Zygmundt de la Burde, a sixty-year-old divorced man who grew up in Poland during the Nazi occupation. Burde received a PhD from Krakow University, where he majored in chemistry, then moved to Virginia and had worked as a chemist at the Phillip Morris Tobacco Company since 1960. He also claimed to be a count, telling people that he was a descendent of a rich French aristocrat who settled in Krakow after the Napoleonic Wars. Some twenty-five years before his death, Burde had purchased a 220-acre horse farm that was once owned by the brother of General Robert E. Lee. It was in this house, called Windsor Farm, that he was either murdered or committed suicide.

Monroe was also a research scientist at a Phillip Morris. Burde and Beverly Monroe had developed a strong romantic relationship but were not living together. They had discussed marriage recently, but they still had some issues to work out, especially because Burde very recently had managed to get a different woman pregnant.

Monroe was an obvious suspect because she had dined with Burde at his home the evening he died from a single gunshot wound to his head. When Burde didn't answer his telephone the following morning, Monroe returned to Burde's home and found him dead on his couch. The local police interviewed her briefly on the day the body was discovered but they couldn't determine whether it was a case of suicide or murder. Three weeks later, a state police officer met with Monroe and asked her to take a polygraph test. She agreed to do this. After they finished, he told her that she had failed two questions: whether she was present at the time Burde died and whether she was the one who shot him. They talked briefly after the polygraph test, and he told her he would get back to her about this.

Intention and predisposition of motive

The officer admitted that initially his office was undecided about whether Burde had committed suicide or had been murdered. If he had been murdered, there was no better suspect than Monroe, since she was with Burde the evening he died. The officer believed that Monroe's motive to kill her boyfriend was her anger because he had impregnated another woman at about the very time he had proposed marriage to Monroe. As far as law enforcement was concerned, this established Monroe's intention and predisposition to commit the murder, if indeed she did commit it. Now the officer turned his attention to trying to get a voluntary confession from Monroe.

The speech events

After the brief face-to-face tape-recorded polygraph meeting, the officer made two badly recorded telephone calls to Monroe on two consecutive days, both of which began in the form of speech events of a friendly call rather than as interrogation speech events. In the first call, the officer was kind and sympathetic and even suggested that Burde may have committed suicide while Monroe was still at his home, and somehow she had emotionally blocked this from her memory. In *The Language of Confession, Interrogation, and Deception* (1993), I detailed the officer's technique of adopting the friendly and sympathetic role of a therapist rather than that of a police investigator. It's difficult to know for sure how Monroe considered these conversations, but at the end of the second call, she thanked the officer for his insights and ideas, suggesting that she thought of them as friendly or possibly even as therapeutic speech events. My main focus in this chapter, however, is on what the language evidence revealed about Monroe's voluntariness.

The tape evidence versus transcripts

The first thing to say about the two telephone interviews in this case is that the recordings were very difficult to hear. Monroe's audibility in her part of the conversations was so weak that the judge ultimately refused to allow both the prosecution and the defense to provide transcripts for the jury to follow at trial. Before his decision, however, the prosecution had already prepared transcripts and had turned them over to the defense during the discovery process. Some of the officer's language on the transcript was accurately transcribed and some of it appeared to be pure guesswork, but most of Monroe's statements were simply marked "inaudible" in the government's transcription of these conversations.

As usual, I spent hours listening to the tapes and correcting the government's incorrect and incomplete transcripts. A curious side effect of this was that I was not told about the judge's decision to exclude all transcripts until after I took the witness stand and began to discuss the errors I found in the prosecution's versions, with the goal of contrasting them with the transcripts that I had prepared for the defense. But as I began to testify, the judge stopped me and harshly admonished me for even mentioning transcripts in the presence of the jury. He had made his ruling to not allow transcripts during the period that I was waiting in the secured witness room and therefore had no way to know about it. This surprising decision seriously handicapped my ensuing testimony, but the defense attorney and I soldiered on as best we could. From that point on, I had to refer to the tape recordings only, while awkwardly finding and playing the crucial passages as I went along. Even though I had made timing marks on the transcripts, this was very time consuming, because it was time consuming took a considerable amount of effort to locate and play those passages of the tapes. Therefore, my testimony took much longer than it would have if transcripts had been permitted.

I later learned that the prosecution's main witness, the officer who made the recordings, had testified only about his personal interpretation of what he believed those tapes contained, without pointing out or playing specific passages of the tapes. His focus was particularly on what he claimed to remember about what Monroe said to him. It was clear that his schema was that Monroe was the killer.

Voluntariness in the police interview speech events

After the officer finished giving Monroe the polygraph test, he said he would come back in a few minutes with some questions for her. When the brief tape recording came on, Monroe was speaking in mid-sentence, talking about her father. It wasn't possible to know what conversation had taken place before the officer turned the tape on, but from their conversational topic it was relatively clear that they had been talking about something that related to Monroe's father's suicide some years past. On this tape Monroe claimed that she couldn't recall most of what happened the night of Burde's death, but she did say that Burde had kept a gun in his house and she remembered having seen it there often.

The following day, the officer telephoned Monroe and appeared to be trying to put Monroe in a kind of hypnotic state in which she would admit that she was actually present when Burde died from a gunshot wound to his head. If the officer could get her to admit that she was there, he could then move on to whether or not Monroe killed Burde. The officer took the approach of trying to refresh her memory while he scripted her about various things that purportedly happened:

> OFFICER: You remember seeing the gun, and then you remember that you were back home. You had this unconscious feeling that something was wrong. You couldn't remember

what. You made some calls and were surprised when he didn't answer the phone... All night long, all you wanted to do was go to him and be with him and see that he was found. It just ate at you all night long... It's something eatin' you right now, Beverly. You're gonna sleep better if you remember this.

MONROE: I'm gonna try. I'd like to be able to.

OFFICER: Tell me again. Just look through me right now. You hear the noise, you're asleep or you're in a sleepy state. You're on the couch. You remember him jumping and standing and seeing a gun. You remember standing over him and seeing the gun. And you remember leavin' him asleep on the couch, but you know now that he didn't walk you to the door. That's not true. That's what he always did before but you know that he really didn't walk you to the door because you left him asleep on the couch... and you remember lookin' down and seein' that gun. And you just couldn't face it. You couldn't face tellin' people and sayin', "I was there when this thing happened." It was just too much for you at that moment. And it was just overwhelming.

MONROE: That's a hard thing to understand.

OFFICER: No, no it's not. It's hard to admit, sure, but it's not hard to understand.

The officer continued to plant seeds in Monroe's mind that she actually witnessed the shooting, for his next step would be to try to get her to admit that she murdered her boyfriend. In both telephone conversations, Monroe spoke very softly, making her words very hard to understand. This forced the prosecutor to rely on the officer's testimony that during this period Monroe had actually admitted being present when Burde died, although nothing on the tape substantiated this. The officer's planting of seeds and, worse yet, suggesting facts, are far from the voluntariness of what Monroe said she actually recalled.

In the two telephone call interviews, the officer introduced five topics: (1) you left him dead, (2) you're not telling the truth, (3) you saw the gun, (4) you left his house later than you said you did, and (5) you were there when it happened. He introduced the first four topics in his first call, saving the accusation for the second call. An accurate, jury-ready transcript would have shown that Monroe's responses to these five topics did not implicate her in the shooting. Selected samples of these five topics along with her responses follow.

Topic 1: You left him dead

OFFICER: You couldn't stand the thought of him being there all day... not knowing when somebody would find him.

MONROE: It wasn't a conscious move. It's just when I started to go to work, I had (unintelligible).

Apparently to assist Monroe's memory, the officer then switched from saying "you" and began using the first person singular pronoun, scripting her responses by trying to put words into her mouth rather than letting her volunteer:

OFFICER: You remember in your dreams all night long that this thing was eatin' at you. I left Roger there. The family is just not going to understand because I left him there. You had to get him found... you didn't want him to be left there for a day or two days. You know that. Did you?

MONROE: I don't remember saying anything like that.

OFFICER: In your unconscious you're still tryin' to believe it didn't happen.

MONROE: I'm tryin' not to believe—(unfinished sentence)

It is clear from Monroe's responses that she said she did not leave Burde dead in his home.

Topic 2: You're not telling the truth

Preserving his ongoing sympathetic attitude, when the officer switched his topic to Monroe's lying, he continued the conversational strategy of scripting her by using the first person pronoun, rather than letting her volunteer what she might say:

> OFFICER: I'm not tellin' the truth... What is it that I know that keeps me from tellin' the truth? My mind says one thing but my heart's saying something else.
>
> MONROE: (unintelligible)
>
> OFFICER: I know it. And that's how it works.
>
> MONROE: I couldn't understand why those feeling were coming (unintelligible). That's the kind I had in the car. Sometimes (unintelligible) makes me jump. I just jump (unintelligible) I don't know exactly where it comes from.

Here Monroe admitted to having uneasy feelings when she left Burde that night and that she continued to be jumpy, which is not particularly surprising since she was under deep emotional stress because he impregnated another woman while at the same time discussing marriage with her. But since Monroe didn't know where these feelings came from, the officer escalated his accusation, now returning to the "you" pronoun and appealing to her emotion of guilt.

> OFFICER: You've known all along that there was something that made you feel guilty.
>
> MONROE: That's not true.

OFFICER: You know from talking what happened, don't you? Tell me yes.

MONROE: Yes, I guess so. I didn't really (unintelligible). I wish I could see it.

OFFICER: You do know this. You still havin' a hard time?

MONROE: Yeah, some things (interrupted)

OFFICER: You know what I've told you is true. You know it, don't you?

MONROE: I can't. I wish I could see it.

OFFICER: You can see it. You'll see it in your dreams and eventually you'll remember.

Rather than confessing her guilt about killing Burde, Monroe admitted only that she had undefined "feelings" about "some things" (also undefined) and was still having a hard time remembering what had happened that night. In spite of her emotional stress, she did not volunteer or admit guilt about Burde's murder. To the officer's "you know from talking what happened, don't you," she responded in her typical and consistently compliant manner, but her indecisive "I guess so" immediately following this showed that she was clearly unconvinced and after that her amplified negative statements were "I didn't really (unintelligible)," "I wish I could see it," and "I can't." None of Monroe's responses can be considered voluntary admissions of guilt.

This did not stop the officer, however, from *inferring* that she had admitted her guilt. In fact, at trial, he testified that she had indeed admitted it. In most murder cases when there are tape recordings, the jury can always clarify an interviewer's assumptions by comparing them with the recorded evidence. In this case, the prosecutor asked the jury to rely on the officer's version of what was said, and in disputes between law enforcement officers and defendants it is common for juries to believe the police.

Topic 3: You saw the gun

Initially Monroe said that she often had seen a gun at Burde's house. Since the gun was found near Burde's body, the officer's perceived task was to get her to say that she remembered seeing it that night:

OFFICER: You remember jumping and standing and seeing the gun.

MONROE: I'd like to be able to see it but—

.OFFICER: But you remember standing over him and seeing the gun... and you remember leavin' him asleep on the couch.

MONROE: I don't know how it got there. That's a hard thing to understand.

OFFICER: You'd have these flashes all night long, seein' that gun in his hand.

MONROE: I don't remember—

OFFICER: Don't rationalize it away. Don't do that.

MONROE: I won't. I won't—

OFFICER: You remember in your unconscious seein' the gun. You remember lookin' there. You remember hearin' the noise.

MONROE: I know I (unintelligible) (deep sigh)

OFFICER: And you couldn't find it. Or maybe you did.

MONROE: Huh-uh—

The officer interrupted Monroe's efforts to respond negatively to his topic six times during the exchange from which the above was excerpted. Her voice grew weaker and weaker, making it equally difficult for the judge and jury to hear what she actually said. Such interruptions are consistent with the officer's efforts to control the conversation to satisfy his perceived goal, but the evidence tape demonstrated that Monroe still didn't voluntarily admit any of these things.

Topic 4: You left Burde's house later than you said you did

When interviewers are unable to catch suspects in the major lie, they often try to elicit minor lies, because if they can establish that a suspect lied about minor things, the jury will likely think them guilty of lying about the major issues. Next, the officer tried to catch Monroe in a minor lie:

OFFICER: I know you didn't leave that early.
MONROE: But (unintelligible)
OFFICER: You left later than 9:20. Maybe an hour or so later.
MONROE: But how can you know that?

The first telephone interview ended with this exchange. To this point the officer had not been able to get Monroe to admit that she left Burde dead in his home, that she was being untruthful, that she actually saw the gun on the night of the murder, or that she lied about when she left Burde's house.

Topic 5: You were there when it happened

On the following day the same officer interviewed Monroe again by telephone. On this call Monroe's voice was equally muffled and hard to hear, while the officer's words were audible. The officer began by asserting that Monroe was present when "it happened":

OFFICER: You now realize that you were there.
MONROE: It doesn't come to my mind. I can't bring it to my vision.
OFFICER: Well look, we resolved one issue yesterday... that you were present. We got that out of the interview. That issue has been resolved.
MONROE: I don't understand that, and that's (unintelligible)—

OFFICER: Well you mean you don't feel like you can tell Corrina [Burde's daughter] the same way you told me?

MONROE: Have to think about it... but I have to tell her I feel responsible.

OFFICER: Beverly, you answered my questions yesterday.

MONROE: Did I? I don't know (unintelligible) my own yet.

OFFICER: Frankly, I don't think you were really conscious of what you did and said.

MONROE: I don't know (unintelligible) because I don't—(interrupted)

OFFICER: It's always on your mind.

MONROE: I really don't know.

OFFICER: Had you not been there, something would have been different or whatever... and that's why you have the tremendous guilt feelings.

MONROE: It seems I do have this feeling of responsibility... I was puttin' pressure on him.

OFFICER: I don't think you actually saw the gun go off.

MONROE: I couldn't have.

OFFICER: Then the routine mechanism takes over where you remember you need gas or you need to go to the grocery store... and little trivial things take over your consciousness.

MONROE: That'd help me shut it out then. I like your (unintelligible) opinion about this and your insights, what you thought of it, and I don't know if I'll get to that point or not... I don't understand what was happening.

OFFICER: I have all my questions answered as far as I'm concerned.

Even though Monroe was a cooperative and compliant subject under deep emotional stress about the death of her lover, at no point in the tape-recorded evidence can one find that she admitted to being present when Burde died or that she confessed to killing him. She voluntarily admitted being there the night of his death. She voluntarily admitted seeing a gun at his house, for having guns in the house is not unusual in the gun-friendly state of Virginia. She voluntarily admitted feeling some "responsibility" for putting pressure on Burde, but even this did not rise to the level of guilt for killing him. Even though the officer somehow was able to claim that their first interview established Monroe's presence when Burde died, there is no evidence for this claim in the tape-recorded evidence. In short, she didn't admit to being there at the time he died and she certainly didn't admit that she murdered him.

Undaunted by the taped evidence, the officer testified at trial that Monroe had voluntarily confessed to killing Burde. Even if Monroe actually had confessed, which she did not, any interpretation of her voluntariness would have to be dramatically stretched here. The officer interrupted her over and over again, particularly when it looked very much as though she was about to deny his accusations. Through his pseudopsychological counseling approach, the officer tried to coax her into a dream state. She was so cooperative and compliant that at the end she said she actually liked hearing the officer's "opinion" and "insights." Like it or not, there is nothing in the evidence on the tapes of their two interviews that comes close to being Monroe's admission that she murdered her boyfriend.

When someone dies quickly and tragically, it's not unusual for survivors to feel strong emotions of grief and befuddlement and even some sense of responsibility for their deaths. Still believing Burde had committed suicide, she volunteered that she felt some responsibility that may have caused him to commit suicide, but not responsibility for murdering him. The language evidence in this case did not demonstrate that Monroe had the intention or predisposition to murder her boyfriend. Even more strongly, despite the efforts of the officer, there was no language evidence here that she either voluntarily or involuntarily admitted to the murder. Apparently the language evidence of her emotionally distraught condition played no role in the prosecution of this case.

Aftermath

Perhaps the judge's ruling to not permit transcripts made my testimony less than convincing. I understand that the officer's testimony was crisp and authoritative. My own testimony was laboriously hampered by the surprise of my not being allowed to refer to transcripts of the tapes in an effort to help the jury understand what was really on them. Or perhaps I was simply not at my best that day. But for whatever reasons, my testimony at Monroe's trial was not sufficient to prevent the jury from convicting her of first-degree murder with a sentence of twenty-two years in prison.

But a full decade later, the U.S. District Court granted Monroe a writ of habeas corpus vacating her decade-old conviction on the grounds that the prosecutors had concealed evidence supporting her innocence. The federal court called this case a "monument to prosecutorial indiscretion and mishandling." The court also admonished the police for their work in the case, calling it deceitful and manipulative, which was what I had tried very hard to demonstrate in my trial testimony. For readers who would like to read more about this case, I recommend John Taylor's book *The Count and the Confession* (2002).

11

REASONABLE DOUBT IN MURDER CASES

In contrast with civil cases, where the standard of proof is the preponderance of evidence, murder cases have what is considered to be a stronger standard. The task for triers of the fact is to determine whether or not the prosecution has proven *beyond a reasonable doubt* that the defendant is guilty. Before jurors retire to deliberate in murder trials, judges give them instructions that include such things as how to pick a jury foreperson, how to press a buzzer when they reach their verdict, how to evaluate the evidence, and, most important, the "reasonable doubt" instruction.

DEFINITION OF REASONABLE DOUBT

Reasonable doubt, required by the due process clause of the Fifth Amendment to the U.S. Constitution, is sometimes defined as more than or beyond mere possible doubt, since virtually everything in human life can be accompanied by some possible or imagined doubt. Reasonable doubt represents the path to the jury's cognitive stage after they compare and consider all of the evidence. It is the point at which their minds tell them whether they have a strong enough conviction that the government's charges are true and accurate. The jury's verdict is expected to be based on reason and common sense rather than on sympathy or prejudice. *Reasonable doubt* relates to and grows out of the fundamental principle of all criminal trials—the presumption of a defendant's innocence until proven guilty.

In one important sense, linguists analyze the language of murder case evidence in the effort to help jurors determine whether or not reasonable doubt can become a consideration for triers of the fact to use when they deliberate. Linguistic expert witnesses, of course, do not address reasonable doubt directly in their analyses or testimony. Rather, they analyze the language evidence in the same way that they would analyze the data in any research project. It remains up to the jury alone to decide what that analysis concludes in relation to the specific case. Therefore, the focus of this chapter is only on how the linguistic analyses in the cases described here contributed or failed to contribute to the cases of the retaining lawyers. In some cases the lawyers chose to use this linguistic analysis and in other cases they did not use it, as Ellen Prince once phrased it, to help put "a value on the probability" (1990, 304).

So what can a jury understand by the judge's instruction about "reasonable doubt?" The definition in *Black's Law Dictionary* noted in chapter 2 may not be very helpful. David Mellinkoff, in his monumental *The Language of the Law* (1963), questioned whether vague expressions like this ever had a definite legal meaning, adding: "It is easy to forget that lack of precision is their only reason for existence" (301). In his usual and interesting style, Mellinkoff continued: "And when *reasonable* in one form or another is hitched onto another word, sound men grow giddy with excitement. It is assumed that the attachment can work a reformation, and that a word wild and amorphous can suddenly become tame and purposeful" (302). Mellinkoff even cited an English chief justice who once said, "I have never yet heard any court give a real definition of what is a *reasonable doubt,* and it would be much better if that expression was not used" (303).

The real problem is that nobody has come up with a better term. Regardless of the vagueness of its definition, judges use the expression to instruct juries largely because there seems to be no other way to convey what they want to say. Some legal terms seem to be that way. Recall, for example, what Justice Potter Stewart observed about obscenity, "I can't define it but I know it when I see it." *Reasonable doubt* is another one of those legal terms, like *intention, predisposition,* and *voluntariness,* that serve as prototypes for which it's necessary to try to find living examples about how to interpret from any language evidence that can attach a fleshly meaning to these vague terms.

SUMMARY OF REASONABLE DOUBT IN THESE FIFTEEN CASES

One can never be totally certain about how jurors actually consider and apply judges' instructions about reasonable doubt, but in this chapter I deal with the way *reasonable doubt* either was or could have been important in the cases where *intentionality, predisposition,* and *voluntariness* were central. I do not deal with the Unabomber case here, because my involvement was only to prepare a linguistic profile of a suspect who at that time was still unknown. I was not asked to be involved in his subsequent trial, but Ted Kaczynski's own words make it very clear that he had every intention to kill people, that he was predisposed to do so, and that nobody had coerced him. He wrote his threats voluntarily. At his trial, it was rather easy for the jury to have no reasonable doubts based on this evidence.

Likewise, I do not deal here with the Gary bomb threat case, because again my contribution was a linguistic profile for the FBI and also because no charges were ever brought against the sender of the threats. At any rate, the overt intentionality, predisposition, and voluntariness of the writer of the two threat messages sent to that women's medical clinic were very evident, even though the writer sent them to herself for a totally different reason.

REASONABLE DOUBT ABOUT INTENTIONALITY AND PREDISPOSITION

Although in the two cases where linguistic profiling was requested (Unabomber and Gary women's clinic) there could be no question about the intentionality and predisposition of the suspects, the three cases discussed in chapter 5 were very different. The path to reasonable doubt varies in cases in which the police carry out undercover investigations about potential solicitations to murder. In the case of T. Cullen Davis, linguistic analysis clearly opened the door for jurors to find reasonable doubt about the government's claim that he was soliciting murder. It can be verified that linguistic analysis was central to the jury's thinking, for when the defense lawyers interviewed the jury after the trial, the jurors confirmed that it was this linguistic analysis that convinced them. They cited my testimony demonstrating that Davis's language indicated that he believed he was in a speech event of a progress report on the employee's efforts to spy on his wife's activities, in contrast with the confidential informant's efforts to make this look like a speech event about finding a hit man to kill several people.

In the other two solicitation to murder cases, after first expressing some serious doubts, the targets eventually agreed to the hit. In these cases, it wasn't difficult for the jurors to find reasonable doubt about the defendants' evolving intentionality and predisposition to solicit murder. The linguistic issues in these cases were more focused on how these two men eventually reached their agreements to the hits as well as their voluntariness in doing so. Topic analyses demonstrated that the cooperating witnesses who recorded conversations with these two suspects defined the suspects' otherwise unspecified and vague problems for them, devised the methods by which the hits could be accomplished, provided the necessary means for carrying out the killing, and even gave strong evidence of coercing their targets to agree. Initially the suspects' intentions and predispositions were something other than murder and they arrived at their final decisions in a way that gave indications of being less than voluntarily. Analyses in these cases suggested an entrapment defense, which perhaps their attorneys might have advocated and pursued more effectively. As these cases turned out, either the juries must have been unimpressed with the linguistic analysis that I provided to the defense lawyers, or they my analyses may not have been used effectively. When linguists are not given the opportunity to present their analysis themselves, they can't be held responsible for how the lawyers use it or why they don't use it at all.

REASONABLE DOUBT ABOUT VOLUNTARINESS

Although intentionality and predisposition played important roles in the ten murder cases discussed in chapters 7 through 10, my central linguistic focus here was on voluntariness. I divided these ten cases into four chapters based on the physical and psychological status of the defendants, including diminished capacity (chapter 7), alcohol and drugs (chapter 8), juveniles (chapter 9), and what I referred to as suspects who were emotionally distraught (chapter 10). In all ten cases the linguist's tasks were to provide analysis of the language evidence that supported involuntariness in the suspects' interviews with the police and prosecution and, when possible, to support the findings of experts from the fields of psychology, psychiatry, medicine, and child development.

The language evidence in the case of Jerry Townsend overwhelmingly supported the reports and testimony of the psychologist and psychiatrist, who reported that Townsend was severely mentally incapacitated. Besides showing how Townsend's language supported the findings of these experts, linguistic analysis also pointed out many flaws in the police interviews with Townsend. There were so many of these, in fact, that it should have been possible for the jury to see that Townsend was manipulated, tricked, and coerced by the police, thereby countering the prosecution's claim that Townsend responded voluntarily. But since I was not called to testify, I had to leave my analysis in the hands of the defense attorneys, who may not have been able to use it effectively enough to prevent the jury from convicting him of murder and sentencing him to death. The jury was somehow unable to find reasonable doubt that Townsend committed the murders intentionally with predisposition and that his responses were involuntary. I can't say this with certainty since I was not asked to participate in the trial, but his lawyers may not have been able to make my findings clear. They also may not have helped the jury understand that the prosecution's own language evidence showed that Townsend did not voluntarily admit to the five murders.

The mental impairments of Benjamin Hauswirth were admittedly less severe than those of Townsend, but the psychologists called by his lawyers tried to show that Hauswirth was so mentally slow and incapacitated that the undercover policeman found it easy to convince him to agree to hire a hit man to kill his girlfriend's family. The analysis that Leonard and I provided to the defense lawyer supported the psychologists' position that the police manipulated Hauswirth away from his initial uncertainty, intention, and predisposition about how to resolve his problem into finally agreeing to the hit. Although entrapment appeared to be a possible way for the defense to deal with this case, the judge disallowed it and subsequently the jury convicted Hauswirth of voluntarily soliciting murder.

Larry Gentry's case was a convoluted one in which he found himself in the midst of a murder case for which he was a peripheral player at best. Linguistic analysis carried out in Gentry's case made it clear that the prosecutor was under a false impression about what Gentry had said to the police after he had gone to them voluntarily. That false impression continued throughout Gentry's subsequent hearings and testimony, in spite of my own attempts at trial to clarify his lack of intentionality and predisposition as well as his lack of a voluntary admission of guilt. Without a lawyer to protect him during the hearing that provided the evidence against him, Gentry's mental capacity appeared to be insufficient for him to know what was happening to him. But the jury was unable to find reasonable doubt about the government's position and they subsequently convicted him.

The three cases in the section on the voluntariness of suspects impaired by alcohol or drugs (chapter 8) provide illustrations of how the police interviewers failed to recognize and take these impairments into account. In the case of Shelli Dewey, the police tested the defendant for inebriation after she had spent a night of wild drinking. Even though her test results showed that she was inebriated, the police interviewed her two times and used the results of these interviews at trial. Leonard and I found that Dewey's language in these interviews demonstrated that she neither voluntarily waived her Miranda rights nor confessed to the murder. The police apparently inferred Dewey's intention and predisposition, for there was no evidence of this on the tape recordings of their interviews with her. Leonard and I also demonstrated that the interviewing strategies of the police were seriously overreaching and coercive. Despite Leonard's testimony about these matters in a hearing to suppress the evidence, the judge denied the motion and Dewey remained convicted of murder (although an appeal was in progress at the time of this writing).

The reopening of the cold case of Robert Alben never actually evolved into charges of murder because the prosecutor eventually decided not to indict him for murdering his wife. His intoxication from alcohol played an important role here, however, because Alben claimed that he had passed out from overconsumption of alcohol during the late evening that his wife was brutally killed and as a result had no memory about the night of the murder.

During the police interview speech event, Alben volunteered information that could be considered a motive for killing her (their recent arguments and even his striking her only a week earlier), and he even volunteered that the tools he habitually carried in his car included a hammer, which the police could consider his method of killing her. But he strongly denied having any knowledge about what happened the night of his wife's death, and in anguish he even pleaded with the police to tell him whether or not he did it. But he couldn't confess to anything because his memory of that alcoholic evening was totally missing. With nothing specific to go on, the prosecution dropped the case, perhaps because of their own reasonable doubts.

In the case of Charles Lorraine, I provided linguistic evidence about the suspect's lack of voluntariness when the detective tried to get him to waive his Miranda rights. Both the police and the prosecutor were unaware of the linguistic features involved in Lorraine's videotaped effort to say that he did not want to talk. Calling on linguistic knowledge about nonverbal communication, the role of "look" as a negative discourse marker, the phonetic reduction found in contracted negatives, sentence intonation, and syllabic structure,

I demonstrated that Lorraine did not voluntarily waive his rights. Despite this, my efforts were unsuccessful in convincing the court that there was reasonable doubt about the waiver of his rights.

In chapter 9, two cases described the trials of juvenile suspects. In the Michael Carter case, linguistic analysis demonstrated clearly that the police interviewers wrote Carter's confession in their own words, in contrast with their claim that they "wrote down exactly" what Carter had volunteered to them. They then got him to sign a confession while he was sobbing and vomiting uncontrollably. After the hearing to dismiss this evidence, it was relatively easy for the district attorney to find enough reasonable doubt and to withdraw charges before the case went to trial.

The police built their case against Kevin Rogers on questionable and unverifiable evidence. Even though there were no tape recordings or transcripts of what actually took place during the police interview speech event, linguistic analysis made it clear that this fifteen-year-old boy with severe learning ability neither understood his Miranda warning nor the questions the detectives asked him. The judge would not allow my testimony and the jury did not find the reasonable doubt that my analysis would have tried to demonstrate.

As I admitted earlier, there is no legal basis for considering the damaging effects on suspects who were emotionally distraught during the time they were interviewed by the police (chapter 10). Nevertheless I chose to discuss two such cases, because calling attention to this emotional condition could have provided some value for jurors to understand and consider, especially since the prosecution either ignored or misunderstood it.

Stephen Allen's purported stoical demeanor after he discovered his wife's body and during his 911 call led the police to consider him the murderer, even though he strongly denied it. Allen calmly volunteered information that the police interpreted as inculpatory. The police bungled the investigation in many ways, as they and other emergency workers tramped through the house and disturbed the evidence. The police even lost the tape recording of one of their interviews with Allen and the court surprisingly permitted them to use their unverifiable transcript in its place. In spite of my linguistic analysis of other language evidence that I presented at trial, the jury was unable to find reasonable doubt and subsequently convicted him of murder.

In the Beverly Monroe case the detective tried to put Monroe into some kind of trance in which she could then recall what happened the night that her boyfriend died. In the very difficult-to-hear tape recordings of these conversations, the detective's speech was relatively clear, but lack of audibility made Monroe's contributions much more difficult to make out. The judge refused to let the jury see any transcripts of the tapes, making it difficult but not impossible for me to enlighten the jury that what she said contradicted much of what the detective claimed. Even though at trial I presented what I thought to be a convincing linguistic analysis of their taped conversations showing that Monroe did not have the intention or predisposition to kill her boyfriend and that she voluntarily admitted some facts that were not especially in her favor, the jury was unable to find reasonable doubt about her guilt. It was a decade later, after several appeals, that the U.S. federal court reversed the jury's decision.

SUMMARY OF HOW AND WHERE THE LINGUISTIC TOOLS WERE USED IN THESE THIRTEEN CASES

In chapter 3 I briefly outlined the linguistic tools used in murder cases, including the speech event, schemas, topic and response analysis, speech acts, conversational strategies, and ambiguity resolution as revealed by syntax, semantics, and phonetics. Not all of the cases required the use of each of these linguistic tools, but initial recognition of the speech event in which the discourse appeared was important in virtually all of them. The following charts summarize the way linguistics was used in these thirteen cases. I do not include the two linguistic profile cases here because, as noted above, the linguistic task was very different in the Unabomber and Gary women's medical clinic investigations. As noted earlier, I included theose cases as model instances in which intentionality, predisposition, and voluntariness were evident and served as touchstone comparisons with the other cases in this book in which these legal terms were much less clear.

The following summarizes where the linguistic tools of speech events, schemas, agendas, speech acts, and conversational strategies, and the smaller language units of vocabulary, phonetics, and syntax were used.

Types of speech events

Conversations	*Interviews*	*Miranda warnings*
Davis		
Arshad		
Mockovac		
	Townsend	
Hauswirth		
	Gentry	
	Dewey	Dewey
	Alben	
		Lorraine
	Carter	

(Continued)

(CONTINUED)

Conversations	*Interviews*	*Miranda warnings*
	Rogers	Rogers
	Allen	
	Monroe	

Schemas of the targets

Not murder		*Eventual murder*	*Murder*
Davis			
Arshad	>	Arshad	
Mockovac	>	Mockovac	
			Townsend
Hauswirth	>	Hauswirth	
Gentry			
Dewey			
Alben			
Carter			
Rogers			
Allen			
Monroe			

Note: Lorraine's analysis was for his Miranda warning only.

The targets' agendas as revealed by their topics and responses

Different from police		*Same as police*	*No agenda*
Davis			
Arshad	>	Arshad	
Mockovac	>	Mockovac	
			Townsend
Hauswirth	>	Hauswirth	
Gentry			
Dewey			
Alben			
			Carter
			Rogers
Monroe			

Note: Lorraine's analysis was limited to the Miranda warning only

Significant speech acts used by the targets

Davis	requesting information, advising
Arshad	agreeing, denying
Mockovac	agreeing, denying
Townsend	agreeing
Hauswirth	requesting directives, agreeing, hypothesizing
Gentry	agreeing, hypothesizing
Dewey	agreeing, denying, hypothesizing, requesting clarification
Alben	denying, requesting information
Lorraine	requesting action
Carter	denying
Rogers	agreeing, denying, apologizing
Allen	denying, requesting information
Monroe	agreeing, denying

Conversational strategies used by the police to the targets

ambig to	*block target*	*interrupt target*	*speak for target*	*on/off switch*	*hit & run*	*ignore denial*	*restate target*	*script target*
Davis	Davis	Davis		Davis	Davis			
Arshad							Arshad	Arshad
Mock	Mock	Mock	Mock			Mock		
Town		Town						Town
Haus	Haus	Haus				Haus		
Gent	Gent				Gent	Gent		
Dewy	Dewy	Dewy				Dewy		
Lor		Lor				Lor		
Cart	Cart	Cart		Cart			Cart	
	Cart							
Rog			Rog			Rog		Rog
Allen		Allen		Allen		Allen	Allen	
Mon	Mon	Mon	Mon		Mon	Mon	Mon	Mon

Note: Police used no conversational strategies with Alben.

Target's vocabulary ambiguity unresolved by police

Davis: *good, alright, alibi, advance notice*

Arshad: *has to go, it, that, the deal, problem, in the picture, removed*

Mockovac: *gone, go away, remove, the thing we talked about, it, that*

Townsend: *commit suicide on* [and many others]

Hauswirth: *want gone, get rid of, just something, problem, take out*

Gentry: *I know, a job, I think, just something, figured out, suspected*

Dewey: *lawyer, I hit him, that time*

Lorraine: *look* (negative discourse marker)

Carter: *had the gun, a while, lay down*

Rogers: *know, sorry for what I did, I wish it didn't happen, pellet gun*

Monroe: *feelings about something, it*

Note: Alben produced no serious vocabulary ambiguities.

Phonetic issues unresolved by the police

Transcripts errors: Davis, Townsend, Gentry, Dewey, Lorraine, Allen, Monroe

Missed intonation: Davis, Hauswirth, Lorraine, Dewey

Missed syllables: Lorraine

Missed negative contraction reduction: Lorraine

Missed nonverbal information: Davis, Lorraine

Syntax used by targets but unnoticed by police

Carter: sentence types

Rogers: sentence types, passive voice, historical present tense

THE RESULTS OF LINGUISTIC ANALYSIS IN MURDER CASES

I freely admit that linguistic analysis did not lead jurors to overcome their reasonable doubts in all of these cases, but I should also point out that it is not possible to account for other evidence in the government's cases that may have gone beyond the language evidence available for linguistic analysis. Such evidence might well have caused jurors to convict without finding reasonable doubt in the prosecution's cases.

I testified at trials or hearings in seven of the thirteen relevant cases. In two of them, the suspects were acquitted (Davis) or dismissed (Carter) on the basis of reasonable doubt about the prosecution's cases. In one case, the jury could not find reasonable doubt and therefore convicted the defendant (Monroe), only to later find that its decision to convict was overturned. This offered some support for the usefulness of the earlier linguistic testimony. In one case (Gentry), the jury found no reasonable doubt and convicted the defendant on some but not all of the prosecution's charges. In three cases (Lorraine, Allen, and Rogers), the juries had no reasonable doubts about the defendants' guilt.

Leonard testified in two cases. In one of them the defendant (Dewey) was convicted, but at the time of this writing the case was being reviewed by the court, based largely on the outrageous police misconduct that Leonard described in his testimony. Leonard also testified in one case (Hauswirth), in which the defendant was found guilty but with reduced charges. Both of these cases point to some degree of success of his testimony.

In three of the remaining four cases, linguistic analysis was provided to the defense attorneys, but since they did not ask for linguistic testimony at trial it is not possible to evaluate how effectively the defense attorneys used these analyses or, for that matter, whether they even used them at all. In Alben's case, my report apparently had some influence on the district attorney's decision not to indict.

ISSUES OF INTENTIONALITY AND PREDISPOSITION

The following chart summarizes how the linguistic analysis of the evidence demonstrates the range of the mental states of intentionality and predisposition, indicating those clearly present, those eventually becoming present, those evidencing a different intention from that of the investigation, and those not present at all.

Suspect	*Clear intention to kill*	*Eventual intention to kill*	*Different intention than to kill*	*No evidence of intention to kill*
Unabomber	X			
Gary	X			
Davis			X	
Arshad		X		
Mockovac		X		
Townsend				X
Hauswirth		X		
Gentry				X
Dewey				X

(CONTINUED)

Suspect	*Clear intention to kill*	*Eventual intention to kill*	*Different intention than to kill*	*No evidence of intention to kill*
Alben				X
Carter			X	
Rogers			X	
Allen				X
Monroe				X

Note: Lorraine's case dealt only with the Miranda warning.

The intention and predisposition of the threat messages sent by the Unabomber and Gary bomb threat writer were very clear, even though the Gary bomber's threat turned out to be meaningless, because the sender's intention was legally benign.

The initial intentions and predispositions of Arshad, Mockovac, and Hauswirth were different from murder, but by the ends of their conversations with the undercover agents, the agents had managed to convince these three suspects to convert their initially less vicious intentions and predispositions into their final compliant agreements to have their targets killed.

Six of the eight suspects produced language evidence that offered no intentions or predispositions to commit murder (Thompson, Gentry, Dewey, Rogers, Allen, and Monroe), even though all six were convicted of possessing such intentions and predispositions. Monroe's case eventually was overturned and Dewey's case was under review at the time of this writing. My work in the case of

Lorraine dealt only with his intentionality and predisposition during his Miranda warning. It demonstrated that he had no intention or predisposition to talk with the police. The language used by Alben demonstrated that he gave the police no indication that he intended or was predisposed to kill his wife or, for that matter, that he committed the crime.

In the cases of Davis and Carter, linguistic analysis helped demonstrate that these suspects had different intentions and predispositions from those claimed by the prosecution. Davis's intention and predisposition were to have the cooperating witness spy on his wife's activities but not to have anyone killed. Carter's intention and predisposition were to rob houses, not to kill the policeman who caught him and his two companions as they attempted to flee.

THE ISSUE OF VOLUNTARINESS

The voluntariness during police interviews of suspects who have mental incapacities, who are impaired by the effects of alcohol or drugs, who are juveniles, or who are emotionally distraught during their interrogations can be difficult for the courts to identify. In the case of Alben, the prosecution apparently understood the effects of intoxication on the suspect's ability to recall the night in which his wife was murdered and appropriately dismissed him as a suspect. Linguistic analysis in the other nine cases demonstrated that these impairments likely were not appropriately considered by the police and prosecutors. They demonstrated the use of coercive and inconsiderate treatment by the police and prosecutors who interviewed these suspects.

AFTERWORD

Intentionality, predisposition, and voluntariness often walk arm in arm, ripe for juries to consider as they determine whether or not there is reasonable doubt about the evidence gathered by law enforcement and presented by prosecutors. The vague, normative statutes may not be able to define these terms specifically and clearly, but the window of language in which these terms are given flesh makes it possible for police, prosecutors, and triers of the fact to discover their meanings. Since juries have to deal with reasonable doubt, they need to know how to put flesh on these terms. These areas are precisely where linguistic analysis can help.

CASES CITED

Jacobellis v. Ohio. 387 U.S. 184, 197 (1964)
Miller v. California. 413 U.S. 15, 24-25 (1973)
Bram v. United States. 168 U.S. 532, 18 S.Ct. 183 (1897)
Brown v. Mississippi. 297 U.S. 278 (1936)
Ashcraft v. Tennessee. 322 U.S. 143, 64 S.Ct. 921 (1944)
Townsend v. Sain. 372 U.S. 293, 83 S.Ct. 745 (1963)
Miranda v. Arizona. 384 U.S. (1966)
Berghuis v. Thomkins. 130 S.Ct. 2250 (2010)
North Carolina v. Butler. 441 U.S. 369 (1979)
In re Gault 387 U.S. 1 (1967)
Schnekloth v. Bustamonte. 412 U.S. 216 (1973)
United States v. Franklin Delano Jeffries. II No. 11-5722
Davis v. United States. 512 U.S. 452 (1994)
Oregon v. Bradshaw. 462 U.S. 1039 (1983)

REFERENCES

Ainsworth, Janet. 2008. "You Have the Right to Remain Silent…but Only if You Ask It Just So." *International Journal of Speech, Language and Law* 15, no. 1: 1–15.

Ainsworth, Janet. 2009. "The Social Meaning of Apology." In *Criminal Law Conversations*, Paul Robinson, Stephen Garvey, and Kimberly Kessler Ferzan (eds.), 201–203. New York: Oxford U Press.

Austin, J.L. 1979. "Other Minds." In *Philosophical Papers,* J.O. Urmson and G.J.Warnock (eds.) New York: Oxford U Press.

Bartlett, Frederick. 1932. *Remembering.* Cambridge: Cambridge U Press.

Bauman, Richard and Joel Sherzer, eds. 1974. *Explorations in the Ethnography of Speaking.* New York: Cambridge U Press.

Berk-Seligson, Susan. 1990. *The Bilingual Courtroom*. Chicago: U Chicago Press.

Berk-Seligson, Susan. 2009. *Coerced Confessions: The Discourse of Bilingual Police Interrogations*. The Hague: Mouton de Gruyter.

Black's Law Dictionary. 2004. St. Paul, MN: Thomson West.

Campbell, John and Don DeNevi, eds. 2004. *Profilers*. New York: Prometheus Books.

Chaski, Carol. 2001. "Empirical Evaluations of Language Based Author Identification Techniques." *Forensic Linguistics* 8, no. 1: 1–65.

Chomsky, Noam. 1965. *Aspects of the Theory of Syntax*. Cambridge, MA: M.I.T Press.

Conley, John and William O'Barr. 1998. *Just Words: Law, Language and Power.* Chicago: U Chicago Press.

Duranti, Alessandro. 1997. *Linguistic Anthropology.* New York: Cambridge U Press.

Eades, Diana. 2008. *Courtroom Talk and Neocolonial Control.* Berlin: Mouton de Gruyter.

Garner, Bryan A. 1995. *A Dictionary of Modern Legal Usage*. New York: Oxford U Press.

Goodrich, Peter. 1987. *Legal Discourse: Studies in Linguistics, Rhetoric and Legal Analysis*. New York: St. Martin's Press.

Goodwin, Charles. 1996. "Professional Vision." *American Anthropologist* 96, no. 3: 606–633.

Grisso, Thomas. 1981. *Juveniles' Waiver of Rights: Legal and Psychological Competence*. New York: Plenum.

Gudjonsson, Gisli. 1992. *The Psychology of Interrogations, Confessions and Testimony*. New York: John Wiley.

Gumperz, John. 1990. *Language and Social Identity*. New York: Cambridge U Press.

Hansell, Mark and Cheryl Ajirotutu. 1992. "Negotiating Interpretations in Interethnic Settings." In *Language and Social Identity*, John Gumperz (ed.), 85–94. Cambridge: Cambridge U Press.

Husserl, Edmund. 1965. *Phenomenology and the Crisis of Philosophy*. New York: Harper & Row.

Hutton, Chris. 2009. *Language, Meaning and the Law*. Edinburgh: Edinburgh U Press.

Hymes, Dell. 1972. "Models of Interaction of Language and the Social Life." In *Directions in Sociolinguistics*, John Gumperz, Vera John, and Dell Hymes (eds.), 35–71. New York: Holt, Rinehart and Winston.

Inbau, Fred, John Reid, and Joseph Buckley. 1986. *Criminal Interrogation and Confessions*. Baltimore: Williams & Wilkins.

Komter, Martha L. 2002. "The Suspect's Own Words: The Treatment of Written Statements in Dutch Courtrooms." *Forensic Linguistics* 9, no. 2: 168–187.

Landau, Sidney. 2001. *Dictionaries: The Art and Craft of Lexicography*. New York: Cambridge U Press.

Leo, Richard. 2008. *Police Interrogation and American Justice*. Cambridge, MA: Harvard U Press.

Levinson, Stephen. 1893. *Pragmatics*. New York: Cambridge U Press.

McMenamin, Gerald. 1993. *Forensic Stylistics*. Amsterdam: Elsevier.

McMenamin, Gerald. 2002. *Forensic Linguistics: Advances in Forensic Stylistics*. Boca Raton, FL: CRC Press.

Mellinkoff, David. 1963. *The Language of the Law*. Boston: Little Brown.

Merriam-Webster's Collegiate Dictionary. 2003. Springfield, MA: Merriam-Webster, Inc.

Navarro, Joe. 2012. "Detecting Deception." *FBI Law Enforcement Bulletin* 81, no. 8: 7–11.

O'Barr, William. 1982. *Linguistic Evidence: Language, Power, and Strategy in the Courtroom*. New York: Academic Press.

Perkins, Rollin and Ronald Boyce. 1982. *Criminal Law*. Goleta, CA: Foundation Press.

Posner, Eric. 1978. "Law and the Emotions." *The Georgetown Law Journal* 89: 1977–2012.

Posner, Eric. 2001. "Law and the Emotions." *University of Chicago Law and Economics Working Paper* no. 103: n.p.

Prince, Ellen. 1990. "On the Use of Social Conversation as Evidence in a Court of Law." In *Language in the Judicial Process*, Judith Levi and Anne G. Walker. 279–289.New York: Plenum.

Rock, Frances. 2007. *Communicating Rights: The Language of Arrest and Detention*. Houndmills Bassingstoke: Macmillan Palgrave.

Rogers, Richard. 2008. "A Little Knowledge Is a Dangerous Thing: Emerging Miranda Research and Professional Roles for Psychologists." *American Psychologist* 63: 776–787.

Rogers, Richard. 2011. "Getting It Wrong about Miranda Rights: False Beliefs, Impaired Reasoning, and Professional Neglect." *American Psychologist* 66, no. 8: 728–736.

Rogers, Richard, J. Rogstad, N. Gillard, E. Drogan, H. Blackwood, and D. Shuman. 2010. "Everyone Knows Their Miranda Rights: Implicit Assumptions and Countervailing Evidence." *Psychology, Public Policy, and Law* 16: 300–318.

Runciman, Steven. 1958. *The Sicilian Vespers: A History of the Mediterranean World in the Later Thirteenth Century*. Cambridge, MA: Cambridge U Press.

Searle, John. 1969. *Speech Acts*. London: Cambridge U Press.

Searle, John. 1983. *Intentionality: An Essay in the Philosophy of Mind*. London: Cambridge U Press.

Shuy, Roger W. 1993. *Language Crimes*. Cambridge, MA: Blackwell.

Shuy, Roger W. 1998. *The Language of Confession, Interrogation, and Deception*. Thousand Oaks, CA: Sage.

Shuy, Roger W. 2005. *Creating Language Crimes*. New York: Oxford U Press.

Shuy, Roger W. 2010. *The Language of Defamation Cases*. New York: Oxford U Press.

Shuy, Roger W. 2011. *The Language of Perjury Cases*. New York: Oxford U Press.

Shuy, Roger W. 2013. *The Language of Bribery Cases*. New York: Oxford U Press.

Solan, Lawrence. 2009. "Blame, Praise, and the Structure of Legal Rules." *Brooklyn Law Review* 75, no. 2: 517–543.

Solan, Lawrence. 2010. *The Language of Statutes*. Chicago: U of Chicago Press.

Solan, Lawrence and Peter Tiersma. 2005. *Speaking of Crime: The Language of Criminal Justice*. Chicago: U Chicago Press.

Taylor, John. 2002. *The Count and the Confession*. New York: Random House.

Tiersma, Peter. 1986. "The Language of Offer and Acceptance: Speech Acts and the Question of Intent." *California Law Review* 74, no. 1: 189–232.

Turvey, Brent. 1999. *Criminal Profiling: An Introduction to Behavioral Evidence Analysis*. San Diego: Academic Press.

Tyler, Stephen. 1978. *The Said and the Unsaid: Mind, Meaning, and Culture*. New York: Academic Press.

Van Dijk, Teun. 1985. *Handbook of Discourse Analysis.* Vol. 1. New York: Academic Press.

Wigmore, John H. 1904. *Evidence in Trials at Common Law* (4th ed.). Boston: Little Brown.

Williams, Glanville. 1978. *Textbook of Criminal Law.* London: Stevens & Sons.

INDEX